**ALSO BY ELIZABETH WARREN**

*This Fight Is Our Fight:*
*The Battle to Save America's Middle Class*

*A Fighting Chance*

*All Your Worth: The Ultimate Lifetime Money Plan*
(coauthored with Amelia Warren Tyagi)

*The Two-Income Trap: Why Middle-Class Parents Are Going Broke*
(coauthored with Amelia Warren Tyagi)

*The Fragile Middle Class: Americans in Debt*
(coauthored with Teresa A. Sullivan and Jay Lawrence Westbrook)

*As We Forgive Our Debtors: Bankruptcy and Consumer Credit in America*
(coauthored with Teresa A. Sullivan and Jay Lawrence Westbrook)

# PERSIST

# PERSIST

## ELIZABETH WARREN

METROPOLITAN BOOKS

HENRY HOLT AND COMPANY    NEW YORK

Metropolitan Books
Henry Holt and Company
*Publishers since 1866*
120 Broadway
New York, New York 10271
www.henryholt.com

Metropolitan Books® and ⅿ® are registered trademarks of
Macmillan Publishing Group, LLC.

Distributed in Canada by Raincoast Book Distribution Limited

Library of Congress Control Number: 2021931052

ISBN: 9781250799241

Our books may be purchased in bulk for promotional, educational, or business use. Please
contact your local bookseller or the Macmillan Corporate and Premium Sales Department at
(800) 221-7945, extension 5442, or by e-mail at MacmillanSpecialMarkets@macmillan.com.

First Edition 2021

Designed by Kelly S. Too

Printed in the United States of America

1  3  5  7  9  10  8  6  4  2

For my brothers,
Don Reed, John, and David

# CONTENTS

# PERSIST

# You Don't Get What You Don't Fight For

At last: election night 2020.

The three of us—Bruce, Bailey, and me—were piled up on the couch. Husband Bruce on one side, golden retriever Bailey stretched out on the other, and me mushed in between with a blanket on my lap. We had a fresh supply of popcorn and plenty of beer. In memory of Sean Connery, who had just died, *Dr. No* was teed up on the television.

I was hopeful. But I'd been hopeful four years earlier, and we all saw what a dumpster fire election night 2016 had turned into. So tonight I munched popcorn and swigged beer with a mix of sky-high expectations and deep-down dread.

By the time the three of us had settled in to our eating-drinking-watching marathon and the movie's opening credits were starting to roll, some results were already trickling in.

Ping!

In came a text about the first presidential results. Actually, it wasn't a text sent specifically to me—it was a text sent to a group of Democratic senators.

The very early news looked good, and one member of our caucus couldn't wait to tell everyone about what was happening. The fact that exactly the same news was also on television/radio/internet/carrier pigeon and being shared with several hundred million people worldwide did not change the fact that senators were eager to tell each other what was going on.

Ping! Ping!

Responses to the original text poured in. Emojis. Exclamation points. LOL and OMG and even a WTF. Everyone was a little giddy, but hey, it had been a *very* long four years.

Ping! Ping!

And then more texts started coming in. Friends. Family. Former students. Folks who had been working for months in the trenches. "Have you heard?" "When will Katie's results come in?" "Can we flip North Carolina?" "What the hell is going on in Miami?"

Ping! Ping!

Bruce had to freeze the movie every few minutes so I could check the incoming messages. Not ideal, but I didn't have quite enough self-discipline to turn my phone off. After all, what if the world came to an end while I was watching James Bond battle the evil Dr. No?

Besides, the pinging brought some good info. I learned about the behind-the-scenes fights to prevent ballots in Michigan from getting tossed out. I got the scoop on which parts of Wisconsin had already been counted and which were still outstanding. A friend described the timelines for getting the remaining uncounted votes in Pennsylvania and Arizona. Another explained the dynamics of the two Senate races in Georgia. Even my granddaughters were in on the action—our Bitmojis were getting a real workout.

Election night was long, but Sean Connery was terrific and the popcorn tasty. And by a little after midnight, two things seemed to be true. First, Joe Biden, a good leader and fundamentally decent man, would replace Donald Trump as president of the United States. (Thank you, Lord!) Second, at least for the moment, control of the Senate was uncertain.

It was a happy—but not a backflips-happy—ending to a tense night.

About two in the morning, I sent my last text. Bruce had been reading news reports out loud, but he gave up, too. We both brushed our teeth and switched off our phones. Bailey had passed out hours ago and was now lying half under our bed and half out. I stepped over him and got under the covers.

But I couldn't sleep. Change was coming—and I was making a plan.

## LOSING HURTS

In 2012, I was new to politics. In 2020, I was new to losing.

I had given my campaign for president every ounce of my energy. I'd laid out my plans and fought as hard as I knew how. And I'd lost.

I dropped out of the race on March 5. The next morning, Bruce and I bundled Bailey into our car and headed for a walk around Fresh Pond, one of Cambridge's loveliest spots. I felt a little numb, not just because I'd lost but because for fourteen months almost every second of every day had been devoted to my campaign. Speeches. Team meetings. Airplanes. Town halls. Television interviews. Reading policy memos. Calling $3 donors. Writing plans. There was always something to do. Always.

And then—click—it was over. The curtain came down and my world instantly became quieter.

When Bruce and I got back from Fresh Pond, I noticed a message on the sidewalk in front of our house. In bright pink chalk, someone had written, "Thank you!" I smiled and went inside.

Our neighborhood is a bit of a jumble. Across the street is the oldest farmhouse in Cambridge—it was built in 1681. On either side of it are 1920s apartment houses. Down the block are rambling Victorians that have been cut into multiple units. The four houses on our side of the street date from the 1870s. The bumpy sidewalks are made of brick, so they don't provide a great canvas.

But later that morning someone left a box of chalk outside, and more messages appeared on the sidewalk throughout the day. "Dream Big Fight Hard." "Pinkie Promises Are Forever." "Our Queer Family Loves You." Children drew flowers and suns and ponies and rainbows.

Messages started overlapping and crawling up the driveway. Bouquets and notes piled up at our front door. Standing at our living-room window that afternoon, I teared up. So many people had been part of the campaign, so many people had worked so hard, and it always made me smile to know that millions of people had cheered me on from a distance. My race was over, yet I was feeling very loved. In fact, I thought I might just wallow in it for a while. I could nurse my wounds and think about all that might have been.

The next morning, I opened our kitchen door, which leads to a small porch on the side of our house. Out on the sidewalk next to the driveway was the biggest message yet. In two-foot-high letters, each letter heavily chalked in, was a single word:

PERSIST

I felt like I'd been hit with a bucket of cold water.

Yeah, I was bruised. Damn, I'd *lost*. But I had spent more than a year running for president because I cared passionately about making a lot of changes. And even though I'd dropped out, I still cared just as much about making those changes as I did when I was running.

I looked at the message on the sidewalk for a long time. As I did, I gave up any thought of wallowing. Then I said something to myself that millions of people have said to themselves after a painful loss: Suck it up and get back to work.

## WHEN THE WORLD CHANGES

There was still plenty to work on. The first wave of the COVID-19 pandemic was just beginning to hit our shores. The resulting economic pain would not be far behind.

Back in January, I had seen convincing evidence that we would soon be facing a dangerous pandemic. I'd issued a plan for immediately beginning to detect, treat, and contain COVID-19 outbreaks, and I followed it soon after with a second plan detailing the more advanced steps needed to address both the health and economic threats. Now, in early March, the coronavirus was taking off with a ferocity that was growing by the day. I gathered up those ideas from the campaign and began to push for an aggressive congressional response. I talked with then-candidate Joe Biden about the crisis several times, and he quickly embraced both a coherent public health response and a range of ideas for shoring up the finances of America's working families, including providing student loan relief and expanding Social Security.

The challenges were enormous. Our government needed to dramatically improve access to masks and testing materials. We needed to funnel money to hospitals and small businesses. We needed to support state, local, and tribal governments. With hundreds of billions of federal dollars starting to flow, we needed oversight to make sure money went where it was intended. I teamed up with Congresswoman Ayanna Pressley, a fellow member of the Massachusetts delegation, and we began thinking about how the government could determine whether communities of color were getting hit harder with COVID-19 and whether they were receiving the health care they needed. I also began working with Congresswoman Katherine Clark, another outstanding representative from Massachusetts, on how to keep day care centers open.

The need was expanding exponentially, but every attempt to mobilize Congress required a fight with Mitch McConnell and his Senate Republicans, who, typically, wanted to do nothing. Trump made everything worse by recommending quack cures and insisting that the virus would magically disappear any day. It was a big, stinky, dangerous mess.

So yes, there was plenty to do, but what kept echoing through my head was the financial crisis that had done terrible damage a little more than a decade earlier.

In 2008, I had been a professor at Harvard Law School, teaching my classes and minding my own business—at least most of the time.

I didn't like politics, and my only real dive into that world had ended badly. Back in the 1990s, credit card companies started pushing hard to get Congress to pass a really ugly bankruptcy bill. I had poured my heart into trying to stop it, and in the end I'd failed miserably. But in the early 2000s, I saw a new problem brewing, and it was so big I simply couldn't sit still.

For decades, banks and other financial institutions had been boosting their profits by tricking and trapping their customers. They'd used credit cards, payday loans, remittances, and overdraft penalties. Now they were making fortunes by misleading people about interest rates, fees, and other snares buried in home mortgage documents. Each year, these predators drove millions of hardworking people deep into debt. Black and Brown communities were prime targets, but the problem was spreading everywhere.

A number of federal laws were designed to rein in the bad actors, but responsibility for these laws was so spread out that no single agency felt any urgency about actually enforcing them. The Federal Reserve focused on monetary policy, not consumers. Banking regulators saw their mission as protecting *banks*, not regular people. Various federal agencies that should have gone after at least some of the predators chose to look away.

By 2007, the problem was getting so far out of control that I believed it might bring down our entire economy. If and when it did, tens of millions of families would get hammered. They would lose their homes, their jobs, their savings, their security. And none of this needed to happen.

So I had a plan: the government should create an agency with just one job—protect consumers. Using mostly existing laws, the agency could act as a watchdog to make sure that consumers weren't getting cheated by financial institutions. Banks would be prevented from loading up on risk, and families would be safer. To me, the idea seemed as sensible as a good pair of boots.

But a lot of people saw it very differently. For more than a year, I taught my classes in Cambridge and then got on a plane to Washington, where I would knock on the doors of powerful people and try to warn them about the looming financial crisis. I'd talk about the idea of a consumer agency to members of Congress and staffers and heads of agencies, and mostly they would ignore me or pretend to listen and then do nothing. I vividly remember sitting in a congressman's office in the spring of 2008; after I explained how the consumer agency would work, the guy laughed in my face. He literally leaned back and laughed out loud—and not in a nice way.

Then the world changed.

In the fall of 2008, the markets crashed. Lehman Brothers went bust, and a dozen other giant banks were poised on the brink of failure. Congress became so alarmed that a bipartisan group of lawmakers passed a $700 billion bailout for the big banks, and President George W. Bush signed it into law. The Federal Reserve started handing out money like a cafeteria lady slopping mystery meat onto plates as fast as she could. Not pretty, but plenty of it. Even so, markets continued to tumble, small businesses closed, and the unemployment rate doubled.

Meanwhile, millions of Americans lost their homes. Millions lost their jobs. And millions more lost their pensions or their life savings. Story after story came out about how Black and Latino homeowners had been targeted for the worst of the bad mortgages. There were stories about military families and seniors who had been cheated out of their homes, and stories about banks that made deliberate decisions to boost their profits by breaking the law.

The red-hot fury over how badly the banks had behaved and how poorly our government had policed those banks changed the mood in Washington. The banks suddenly had fewer friends, or at least fewer public friends. Various congressmen and senators declared that they were shocked—shocked!—to discover that banks were cheating. Gradually the idea of an agency that would protect consumers from financial predators took hold. But in a world that was still heavily influenced by Wall Street bankers and big corporations, the fight for real change was touch and go. More than once, the agency was left for dead.

We kept fighting, though, and in the end we won. In 2010, I sat in the front row of a crowd of people as President Obama signed the Dodd-Frank bill into law and, as part of that bill, created a brand-new Consumer Financial Protection Bureau. An idea that had been laughable before the financial collapse became the law of the land. Now, a decade later, that tiny little agency has already handled more than 2.2 million consumer complaints and forced the banks to return $12 billion directly to the people they cheated.

## A ONCE-IN-A-GENERATION CHANCE

The first lesson I took from the fight for the CFPB was this: you don't get what you don't fight for. That agency didn't happen just because it was a really good idea. It happened because we fought for it.

The second lesson I learned was that during a crisis, the door to change opens just a crack. What had been impossible becomes hard-but-maybe-possible. That's the moment to fight with everything you've got.

I'm not naïve. I know that the headwinds will always be fierce and that change will always be hard. But a crisis like the financial crash in 2008 or the pandemic in 2020 shakes up the embedded order. In a crisis, people are forced to stop saying "This is how it's always been" and consider a new thought: "This is how it could be."

After four disastrous years, the election of 2020 was another one of those moments when the door to change opened. And what made change possible? An enormous, vital, incredibly powerful force: voters.

Turnout for the election was huge. Two-thirds of America's eligible population voted in 2020, the highest percentage in more than a century. An estimated twenty million new voters turned out. Millions of young people voted. Millions of people of color voted. Millions of people—Republicans, Democrats, Independents—mailed in early ballots, found local drop boxes, showed up at the county clerk's office, or stood in line on Election Day to vote. It was a massive outpouring of faith in the idea that voters—not a group of rich, distant power brokers—controlled this country.

And even after the main event—the presidential race—was over, people kept on voting. The Georgia runoff two months later brought 4.4 million voters to the polls, more than double the number who showed up for Georgia's Senate runoff in 2008.

Voting is the beating heart of our democracy. When I learned a month after the 2020 election that more than 158 million people had voted, I felt a lot better about our country's health. Each state's final vote tally was heartening, but it was also the visible final step of a very long battle. The massive turnout—in the states and across America—was a victory for all the advocates, volunteers, and organizers who had busted their tails for years to get out the vote and fight for a better nation. And here's the best part: I am confident that most of those who got in the fight in 2020 will stay in the fight for years to come.

And that puts us at this pivotal moment in history. The four corrupt and shocking years of Donald Trump's presidency were topped off by a pandemic, an economic collapse, a national demand for racial justice, and a violent insurrection. For Trump's entire tenure, crisis piled on crisis piled on crisis. Now we have a once-in-a-generation chance to build something new, to shake off who we were and decide who we want to become.

This remarkable moment is an opportunity for change but not a guarantee that it will happen. It is a rare chance to think hard about the policies we want to change, especially the policies that touch our lives every day and set the boundaries for much of what happens to each of us.

As a candidate, Joe Biden may not have looked like a progressive fire-brand, but he and Kamala Harris ran a campaign promising the most aggressive economic, social, and racial changes in U.S. history. They won by more than seven million votes, receiving more votes than any presidential ticket in the history of the republic—and they accomplished this feat while running against an incumbent president. Measure their victory however you like, but there's no question that it was a mandate for change.

Our country's voters demanded a new approach to governing, and the most obvious power to make it lies with the new president himself. New administrative rules and executive orders can redirect significant parts of the federal machinery to work better for families. New cabinet secretaries and agency directors can use existing legal powers to put policies in place that will get our country moving forward again. With courage and determination, President Biden, Vice President Harris, and their team must use every tool available—administrative and legislative—to improve the lives of millions of people.

But change doesn't stop there. For the first time in more than a decade, Democrats will have control of the House, the Senate, and the White House. When Republicans held a similar position in 2017, they delivered on one big promise: a $2 trillion tax cut that mostly benefited rich people. Democrats now stand at that same threshold, and we, too, can keep a promise—except instead of delivering more wealth and power to the already-wealthy and already-powerful, we can build on an America that works better for everyone else.

The 2020 election also proved that the country's states are much more than helpless bystanders in a time of great upheavals. During Trump's tenure, many states bucked his administration and enacted policies that made a lot of positive change. And on Election Day, several states quit waiting for the federal government and made some very progressive moves. Florida voted to raise the minimum wage to $15. Arizona voted to increase taxes on wealthy people to help fund public education. Colorado voted for twelve weeks of paid family leave for most workers. The values and plans that drive progressives at the federal level can also spark change locally.

The door to change is open. Now is the moment to act. Now is our chance to make the changes our nation so desperately needs.

## IT'S PERSONAL

When I ran for president, I followed up nearly every rally and town hall with a selfie line.

After my speech and the Q&A were over, people would line up, often with family or friends, and we'd take a picture together. The pictures were fun. Or silly. Or sober. I was happy to do whatever the next person in line wanted.

As much as I loved the selfie lines, there was a good reason not to do them: time.

The math was straightforward. If I stopped doing selfies, I could complete my town halls faster. And if I had more time, I could travel to more places, do more town halls, and meet more people. But even though I wanted to go lots of places, I really didn't want to give up taking selfies.

As the crowds grew, getting through the selfie lines began to take three or four hours. Soon the math got even more brutal. When I was pinned down in the Senate for days on end during the impeachment trial in January 2020, the need to travel to more places on the few "off" days intensified. Other candidates worked the rope lines, shook a few hands, and moved on; why couldn't I? Well, I tried, but after a few times, I went back to taking selfies.

The reason was simple: I loved them.

Working my way through selfie lines grounded me in the richness and passion of our democracy. The lines included old people and babies, groups of teenagers, longtime friends, whole families. People using wheel-chairs and strollers. People who couldn't push their way to the front of the rope line. The final selfies after an event would frequently be taken as the venue was being swept out and someone was turning out the lights. Just before we headed for the door, the off-duty cops who had provided security and the crews that set up the stage and ran the sound equipment would often ask if they could have a picture, too.

Sure, I understood that taking selfies cost a lot of time. But the selfie lines were about more than campaign pictures and moving along to the next event. They gave me a chance to feel, heart to heart, the deeply personal need for change.

In a selfie line in Indiana I met a delightful little girl who got her pinkie promise and danced off the stage. Then her mother quietly explained that this beautiful child had brain cancer. "Please, please, please fight for health care."

In Iowa I met a farmer whose family had worked the same land for five generations. He said he and his brothers had been thrown deep into debt by the one-two punch of Trump's idiotic trade wars and the unrelenting pressure coming from the giant agriculture outfits. One brother had declared bankruptcy and another had killed himself. "We're running out of time."

In Nevada I met a veteran with diabetes whose sister and niece were also diabetic. He got his insulin from the VA so he was covered, but his sister and niece didn't have insurance. When money got too tight to pay for their prescriptions, the three of them shared his insulin, juggling decisions about who needed it most and who could skate on the edge of collapse just a little longer. "Couldn't we just get the price down?"

In South Carolina I met the mom of a shy third grader who needed extra help with reading but who was stuck in the back of a class with more than thirty kids because the school district had been forced to lay off teachers. "Doesn't my kid matter?"

I met a woman who feared that her son, who was in prison on a drug charge, would not survive to make it home to her. A small business owner who had just closed his doors forever. A lively young woman disowned by her parents and her church because she loved another woman. A teacher who paid for crayons and paper out of his own pocket. Two teenagers who had been the targets of online racist bullying. Dozens of women (and a few men) sporting their NEVERTHELESS SHE PERSISTED tattoos. A woman who had just buried her mother in her PERSIST T-shirt.

I met mothers who had lost their children to gun violence. Children who had lost their parents to opioid overdoses. Young people crushed by student loan debt. Seniors unable to get by on Social Security. People with disabilities who couldn't find housing. Children who understood that storms and wildfires signaled a coming climate catastrophe. Dreamers who had nightmares about federal agents coming in the night.

Meeting people in selfie lines was draining, exhausting, and overwhelming. It was also one of the best things I've ever done in my life.

Over the course of the campaign, we took well over one hundred thousand selfies. And it was in those selfie lines that the intimate, immediate impact of policy was driven home with the force of a body slam. People came with their stories. They didn't use the word "policy," but in just a few words, they explained precisely how health-care policy or student loan policy or trade policy had plowed through the middle of their lives. Hundreds of times a day, the selfie lines drove into my brain the simple fact that Americans are profoundly affected by federal policies. And they taught me again and again how important it is that we get our nation's policies right.

I loved those selfie lines for another reason, too: they gave me hope— hope that, despite all that is broken, we can make democracy work in America.

The people I met in selfie lines were wrestling with real problems—no mistaking that. But as wrenching as some of their stories were, almost every one of them carried a kernel of optimism. People stood in line, often for a long time, to get into my events. Once inside, the town hall itself could run for two or three hours—there were several speeches, an extended Q&A, a fervent pitch for volunteers. And after all of that, people lined up again, sometimes for three hours or longer, to take a selfie and tell me their story. No one would do all that if they didn't believe that real change is possible.

Over and over and over, those selfie lines offered a glimpse of the determination and commitment that we'll need if we're going to fight to make change happen. When the faces of real people crowd your imagination, when the stories about their lives become a part of how you see the world, that's when policy becomes personal.

## WHAT DO YOU BRING TO A KNIFE FIGHT?

Nothing we do will be easy. No one with power will give it up readily. Our battles will be hard. Sometimes we'll find ourselves in a knife fight, and we'll need our sharpest weapons.

But more than anything, the toughest fights will demand that we bring our whole selves. We must bring energy and determination. We must bring clarity of purpose and a richer understanding of our common goals. We must bring a deep-down commitment that will sustain us even when the fight looks impossibly hard.

This book is not a campaign memoir. It is not a rehash of big public events. It's a book about the fight that lies ahead. It's about the plans we need—no surprise there!—but it's about much more than plans.

It's about the passion and commitment that underlie those plans, and the human connection that will keep us in this fight until we see real change.

I write knowing with absolute certainty that if we fail to make major changes, we will plunge our nation and our planet into an abyss from which we cannot escape. I also write with a deep thrum of optimism that we are in a moment when extraordinary changes are possible.

Much is broken in this country. More than seventy-four million Americans voted to return Donald Trump to the White House, even as he left our government, our reputation, and even our faith in each other torn and ragged. In January 2021, his followers stormed the Capitol in an effort to stop the peaceful transition of power that has been a hallmark of our nation from its creation. But even in the darkest hours, I have never stopped believing in the strength of our democracy. Even when hatred has flared and hissed, I have never stopped believing in our capacity to create a better country based on the values we share. I believe right down to my toes that we can build a nation that expands opportunities—a nation that works, not just for the rich and powerful but for everyone.

As I lay sleepless under the covers on election night, I thought about why the fight for change matters so much to me. Why do federal laws and policies wake me up in the morning and keep me up at night? Why do I wade into one battle after another? Why do I get back up after a god-awful loss, ready to charge ahead again?

Because for me, like the thousands of people I met during my campaign for president, this fight is personal. I bring the pieces of who I am to every battle. I'm a mother and a teacher. I'm a planner, a fighter, and a learner. And I'm a woman. Together, these pieces furnish the foundation for everything I do. They are the lenses through which I see much of this world. They drive me to fight for millions of other people. They make me strong.

The stories in this book come straight from my heart to yours. I share them in the hope that they will give spark to the battles you wage and keep you grounded in the righteous fights.

# ONE

# A Mother

I first walked into a classroom as a bona fide teacher in September 1970, and by January or so, I was settling in. The butterflies I'd felt in the first few weeks were gone. I'd figured out lesson plans. Figured out the supply closet. Figured out parent conferences, the drop-offs and the pickups. And figured out the pecking order in the all-important teachers' coffee room.

I was a first-year teacher at Riverdale Elementary School in Riverdale, New Jersey. I loved these children, and I loved this work. Finally, here I was. Twenty-one years old, doing exactly what I wanted to be doing.

I grew up in Oklahoma, the baby girl in a family of boys. Like every other girl I knew, I was sure I would go to high school, learn to drive a car, get married, and have kids. I knew the plan. Living that plan was what it meant to grow up.

But I had one more part to my plan: teach school. Since second grade, I had wanted to be a teacher. When my teacher, Mrs. Lee, had put me in charge of extra reading practice for a handful of second graders, I was hooked. There would be no stopping me.

For years, I lined up my dollies—Terry Lee, Suzi, Sammy, Toni,

Nursey, Lady, the Storybook Dolls, and all the rest—and taught school for hours and hours. Of course, Sammy was always the bad boy and the Storybook Dolls were empty-headed, but I wasn't discouraged. I kept right on teaching.

The road had been bumpy. My mother didn't want me to go to work ("just marry a man who is a good provider"). We didn't have money for college ("college is for other people"). I found a way to go to college anyhow, but I got married at nineteen and dropped out ("I always knew you would"). I found a commuter college that I could afford, but my husband got transferred before I could graduate ("his job is important").

But I never gave up my dream of becoming a teacher. I'd done well at that commuter college, and when my husband was transferred to New Jersey, I finished up with correspondence courses. I got my diploma in the mail—the first in my family to get a college degree. Now I had a big dog named Thor and a medium-sized husband named Jim and I was a full-fledged teacher. Woo-hoo!

I'd even figured out how to look like a teacher.

I had always looked young—I mean really young. In high school I was routinely mistaken for a much younger kid. In college I was twice mistaken for a sixth grader. I was tall and skinny, with a figure like an ironing board. And even at twenty-one I wasn't doing much better. I had long, straight hair—the fashion of the time—but I decided it made me look even younger. So when I interviewed with the principal for the job at Riverdale, I wore a short, curly wig that I'd bought for $19.95 at Sears. I thought it gave me an older, more professional look. Every morning when I got ready for school, the last thing I did was twist up my long, straight hair and pull on the wig. I looked at myself in the mirror. There I was, outfitted in my skirt and blouse, pantyhose and heels, and I thought, "Betsy girl, *you* are a teacher."

Jim was older than I was. When he finished college and snagged a job at IBM, his folks gave him a graduation present: a shiny Brittany Blue Mustang with a white vinyl top. It had a big throaty engine and a light rear end that made it fishtail even on modest turns. It guzzled gas and the insurance was more than we could afford, but Jim didn't care. I sometimes thought it was possible he loved that car more than he loved me. But that was okay—the car was a beauty, and I got to drive it!

Riverdale Elementary was a big old brick building in northern New Jersey. It was a long drive from our house in Rockaway, so I got up extra early on school days. We left Thor to protect the house (or so we told him), I dropped Jim off at IBM, and then I hit the curvy back roads, slipping and sliding my way to school. Sometimes, even in the dead of winter, I lowered the windows, let the cold wind blow, and just laughed out loud.

I had work that mattered, work that touched other lives. Most of the children I worked with were very young, four- to six-year-olds, with special needs. Several had little or no language. Cerebral palsy. Profound hearing loss. Developmental delays. But these children weren't defined by what they couldn't do. Like students everywhere, they were learners. We sang and played word games. We identified pictures and practiced the b-b-b sound. We laughed over silly jokes. Every child, every class was about a little spark—some connection that brought a girl or boy a little closer to mastering the world around them.

I had watered this dream for so long, and now here I was. And it was even better than I'd imagined. Yes, I *was* a teacher. Okay, just barely, but I was in the door.

And then, in February, I started feeling tired, really tired. My doctor had me pee in a cup, and the next day his office called to say that I was pregnant. The baby would come in the late summer.

Huh.

I'd always figured I would have kids. After all, just about every woman I knew had kids. All except Aunt Bee, one of my mother's sisters, and that was always described as "sad." So, yeah, eventually I'd have kids. But now?

For weeks, I didn't think much about the changes that were coming. I still rolled out of bed every teaching day and headed off to Riverdale. But by the end of the day, I was so tired I would nearly doze off on the drive back home. More than once, I'd hit the front door, let Thor out, and fall asleep on the couch. Sometimes Jim and Thor left me there until morning.

By the time the spring flowers were in full bloom, I was back on my feet. The exhaustion had passed; I was ready to tackle the world. My teaching reviews were good, and in April my contract was renewed for the next academic year. I could see the whole plan beginning to unfold. Things were just going to get better and better.

I started getting ready for the baby. Painting a bedroom. Buying a crib. Thinking about who would take care of the baby while I taught school. By late May, I could still fit into most of my clothes, but only barely. I began to look like an ironing board with a bump.

I hadn't made a big deal out of being pregnant. Except for the other teachers, I didn't know a lot of working women, and beyond knowing that I'd have to arrange for childcare during the next school year, I didn't think much about how having a baby would affect my job.

One day, the principal asked me to come by his office.

This was the office where I'd been interviewed for the job the summer before. High ceiling, tall windows, two heavy wooden chairs across from the principal's desk. I don't think I'd been back there since I'd been hired. The place made me a little jumpy.

*Oh, come on*, I thought. *You're a teacher now. Sit up straight. Smile. You love your kids and your kids love you.*

In came the principal. He gave me an absentminded hello, then got straight to the point. "Are you expecting a baby?"

I was stunned. Yeah, the bump showed, but why was he asking me about this? The baby was due in August. I figured this was between Jim and Thor and me. This guy never talked to me about anything, so why this?

But he was waiting for an answer. "Um," I said. "Yes."

And in the space of a couple of minutes it was over. My job was gone. The principal told me I could finish up the last few weeks of the school year as long I didn't "look too pregnant," and then I was to clear out. He would hire someone else for next year. He stood up and wished me luck.

I sat in the parking lot, in the Brittany Blue Mustang with the big engine, tapping my fingers on the steering wheel. Dazed, I just stared into space, the tears dropping off my chin and onto my blouse. Soon the school year would be over. No more teaching. No more off-key songs and silly jokes and the b-b-b sound. No more little sparks. Just like that, my dream crashed and burned.

And sure, in the end everything worked out for me. Three months later, Amelia was born, a gorgeous baby with a cheerful disposition. Five years later her colicky-but-bright-eyed brother Alex came along. Eventually, I headed back to school, got a law degree, and became a professor. So I did fine.

But motherhood—well, motherhood changed everything.

## NO PREGNANT WOMEN

I know that when women write about motherhood, they often wax poetic about having a baby. And for me, too, it was a profound experience. Here was this little creature I hadn't even known the day before she was born, and now, after holding her in my arms for the first time, I would have gladly died for her. I remember lots of dreams about fires and floods and how I always, always saved my baby.

The changes weren't all sunny. I remember the crushing sense of responsibility and the fear that if I got this wrong, this tiny little person would be hurt. I remember the endless hours of crying—the baby's and mine. I remember feeling desperately alone.

So yes, motherhood changes everything. But we spend so much time talking about how it changes the soul or the body that we often don't pay enough attention to how the world outside the home can impose changes in the life of a new mother. And in 1971 in Riverdale, New Jersey, those changes weren't good ones.

Part of the reason they weren't good—at least not for someone like me who still wanted to teach school—was because of the law. The collective decisions that we make together—or at least make through our elected officials and the judges they appoint—create laws that help shape the ways in which motherhood changes everything. That's true now, and it was true five decades ago.

In 1971, the principal at Riverdale Elementary was perfectly within his legal rights to fire me for being pregnant. The Civil Rights Act of 1964 had banned hiring and firing based on race, color, religion, sex, or national origin. But the courts were clear: it was just fine to hire and fire employees based on whether a woman was pregnant. In fact, a few years after I was pushed out the door, the law went a step further. In 1976, the Supreme Court ruled that pregnancy discrimination didn't count as sex discrimination and thus did not violate the Civil Rights Act of 1964. Employers knew they faced no accountability for pushing pregnant women out of schools, offices, and factories.

That is exactly what principals and managers and small business owners all around America did. And women like me mostly bowed our heads and moved on. We "left" our jobs and didn't raise a fuss— and most of the men concluded that everything was just fine. Later, when I ran for president and talked about pregnancy discrimination, plenty of women shared stories from the same time period about hiding their pregnancies and losing their jobs. For some, the anger was still very raw.

In fact, employers didn't just dump women when they got pregnant; they also pried into whether they *might* get pregnant. Job interviews routinely included questions about family plans. Some men felt entitled to ask about whether a woman was using birth control and, if so, what kind. A lot of managers were quite open about not hiring young married women. Why? "Because you just have to get rid of them when they have kids."

But women were stirring. The women's movement had begun to take root in the mid-1960s, and with it came demands for equal treatment. Women were reading Simone de Beauvoir's *The Second Sex* and meeting in consciousness-raising groups. Newspapers published stories about protests, sit-ins, and episodes of bra-burning. Demands for equal treatment got louder and more public. In the summer of 1970, women marked the fiftieth anniversary of getting the right to vote by launching a national strike.

Laws began to change. In 1972, Congress passed the Equal Rights Amendment; if ratified by thirty-eight states, the ERA would become a part of the Constitution and guarantee equal legal rights for all citizens, regardless of sex. Congress also passed Title IX, which barred sex discrimination in education and opened up women's sports. The following year, the Supreme Court decided *Roe v. Wade*, protecting a woman's right to abortion. And then, in 1978, Congress responded to the 1976 Supreme Court ruling by finally passing the Pregnancy Discrimination Act, which amended the Civil Rights Act to prohibit discrimination based on pregnancy.

Changes anchored in the law set the stage for more changes, although these changes came very slowly. So for forty more years—until President Obama signed the Affordable Care Act into law—many insurance companies could say, "Sure, we'll cover a knee replacement or high blood pressure medicine, but if you get pregnant, you're on your own." A study of more than thirty-five hundred individual insurance plans offered in 2009 found that just 13 percent included maternity care.

And not until 2015, in *Young v. UPS*, did the Supreme Court inch toward declaring that pregnant workers should be treated similarly to other employees who are unable to work and that employers were required to make "reasonable accommodations" for pregnant women who continued to work, just as employers did for other disabled workers. Up until then, a shift manager could tell a pregnant woman that if she couldn't cut it anymore lifting heavy packages or standing on her feet for an entire eight-hour shift, she'd be sent home without pay—even if other workers with disabilities were accommodated.

The changes took decades, but at least the world had moved since I sat crying in the parking lot of the elementary school in Riverdale, New Jersey.

So we're all good, right?

Not quite.

After an initial burst of enthusiasm, the ERA stalled out. And the picture today is still bad enough to make me grind my teeth. Despite long-standing laws requiring equal pay for equal work, women on average continue to earn a lot less than men, while women of color have been left even further behind. For decades, sexual assault victims have been treated so badly by the police and the courts that many refuse to report even the most despicable conduct. Sexual harassment in the workplace is still too often accepted as the norm.

And now—even now—a lot of pregnant women who want to work face a hard uphill climb. "Hell, I'm young and personally know two women who faced workplace discrimination because they were pregnant," one woman told me. "It happens. Believe women when they tell you!" When asked about pregnancy discrimination by a reporter, one woman said she had needed to hide her pregnancy five years earlier. "It was just the worry that I was going to be seen as less reliable because I was a parent," she said. "There's no good time to have a baby."

In 2018, the *New York Times* completed an in-depth study of pregnancy discrimination and concluded: "Whether women work at Walmart or on Wall Street, getting pregnant is often the moment they are knocked off the professional ladder. Throughout the American workplace, pregnancy discrimination remains widespread. It can start as soon as a woman is showing, and it often lasts through her early years as a mother."

Other pregnancy issues continue to surface, some related to the impact of systemic racism and discrimination. Medical experts say that most pregnancy-related deaths are preventable, but they note that Black women are three to four times more likely to die from complications of pregnancy than white women, and Native American women are twice as likely to die. The differences are even more acute when the women are matched for income, education, and age. For example, deaths during childbirth are five times higher for Black college graduates than for white grads. Policy changes on access to health care, treatment protocols for pregnant women, training programs for health-care professionals, and even the way we reimburse hospitals for obstetric care could address these differences and help eliminate the disparities.

Discussions about policy can sometimes seem to have little to do with individual lives. But fighting to improve laws and policies can pay off in real change. In 1971, I walked out of the principal's office resigned to my fate. What happened to me was so routine that it wasn't worthy of even a passing comment.

But I changed and the world changed. Today schools don't lay off pregnant teachers—at least not so openly as they did years ago. Many companies offer generous benefits and excellent conditions for pregnant women, nursing mothers, and parents with toddlers at home. And when pregnant women are treated badly, many women fight back through their unions, in court, or even on social media. The path for a pregnant woman at work still isn't easy and it's rarely a straight line, but five decades after I was fired for being pregnant, we know how to make change—a lot of change.

## AFTER THE BABY COMES

About six million women get pregnant in the United States each year, so the laws about pregnancy touch a lot of people. After the baby comes, the changes mothers face just keep piling up. Right now, there are about twenty million children under the age of five who need someone to care for them when their parents go to work. And there are another thirty million or so school-age children who are too young to be left on their own when the adults in the household are at work. Every one of these children needs someone to look after them.

So the arrival of a child changes everything. And not just for the mom and the dad: the birth of children ultimately changes the country, too.

Consider one example: productivity. In Washington, economists and think-tank gurus love to talk about how to increase productivity and boost the gross domestic product—how to make the country richer. They churn out papers and hold conferences. And they tend to have the same answer: add more machines. They argue that we can be a more productive country if we have more robots, more computers, and more equipment of every kind. So we have all these provisions written into our tax code to encourage businesses to spend more money on machines.

But a closer look at the numbers shows something else about productivity. When women started entering the workforce in the 1970s, it led to a *huge* boost in productivity. The biggest change was not that some women had jobs—women like my Aunt Bee who had no children were often in the paid workforce decades before the 1970s, as were millions of domestic workers and women working low-income jobs. No, the big change was women with young children who shifted from staying home to getting back to work.

A giant wave of women swept into the workplace and ultimately rebuilt our economy. Economists have studied this phenomenon in all sorts of ways, but I'll just pick one statistic from a detailed study conducted a few years ago. The study found that if not for the thirty-eight million more women who entered the workforce between 1970 and 2009, our economy today would be 25 percent smaller—*25 percent*.

Think about what it would mean if our economy were 25 percent smaller. Fewer jobs. Lower pay. Fewer homeowners. Not so many televisions, iPhones, or sneakers. Smaller retirement funds.

All those women who entered the workforce boosted our GDP. It should come as no surprise that when more people work, productivity goes up. And, year by year, that's exactly what happened—for a while. But in 1999, women hit their peak participation in the workforce, and then the growth stalled out. More mothers stayed home. Now, even before the pandemic, the proportion of women in the workforce has actually been shrinking.

That's an *American* problem, by the way. In Canada, Europe, Japan, and dozens of other countries, the number of women working continued to rise. And America's failure to increase women's workforce participation has had a profound effect on our economy. Standard and Poor's estimates that if the United States had simply kept pace with countries like Norway, our economy today would be $1.6 trillion bigger. If that bigger economy had translated into higher wages, the benefits would have echoed through our economy. Families would have more money for a new car. Or a chance to save for a down payment on a house or a college fund. Or a shot at wiping out credit card debt.

Why do more women in Norway or Canada or Australia work? Did those countries outlaw colic or invent a machine to supervise homework? Are men more liberated? Nope. Once again, it was policy. Take just one example: Among 37 of the highest-income countries in the world, the United States is the *only one* that doesn't offer paid family leave. In fact, 184 nations offer a median of ninety-eight days of leave to support women when they have babies. And paid leave is just the tip of the policy iceberg. We could do much more to support women's participation in the workforce, including government-funded long-term care, pay transparency, fair scheduling, and policies that support labor unions. Dozens of countries—from Albania to Zimbabwe—can manage to support pregnant women and mothers of young children, but not the United States.

For all those super-duper smart economists and fancy think-tank gurus who want to increase productivity in the economy and produce better outcomes for all America, here's a little advice: instead of giving companies more tax breaks to replace more workers with more machines, you could figure out how to give more women a better chance to contribute their time and talents.

## GOING BACK TO WORK

I was one of those women in the workforce in the 1970s—right up until I got pushed out of my teaching job. And if that had happened a generation earlier, or even a decade earlier, that might have been it for me.

But by the time Riverdale Elementary showed me the door, other doors were beginning to crack open for women who wanted to work. In 1972, shortly after Amelia's first birthday, I hatched a crazy plan to go to law school. Me—someone who couldn't even make it through college without dropping out, changing schools, and finishing up with correspondence credits. Now I was determined to go to law school.

The very idea made my heart beat harder.

Over the course of a year, I got ready. Entrance exams. Check! Law school applications. Check! Acceptance at Rutgers, a terrific state school with low tuition. Check!

I was lining everything up. I persuaded Jim to trade in the Brittany Blue Mustang with the big engine for a much more practical Biscay Blue Volkswagen Beetle with an engine that sounded like a sewing machine. I practiced the commute to Rutgers, learning the route from our house in Rockaway to the law school building in downtown Newark. I shopped for a warm coat and a sturdy book bag. I even scoped out where to park for cheap.

I figured it all out until there was just one more thing left on my list. One tiny, little, small, easy thing: childcare. Amelia was about to turn two, and in order for me to go back to school, I needed childcare. I only needed it for about five hours a day. Hey, how hard could that be?

I found out just how hard. I spent weeks visiting all kinds of places. I drove all over the county only to learn that there were very few options. At one place, the kids looked miserable. At another, the room where they took care of the kids smelled funny. A couple of places seemed okay, but the cost was way outside my budget. And nearly every place—smelly or not—already had waiting lists that ran months into the future.

I started to get just a little sweaty. Jim didn't say I shouldn't try to go to law school, but he sure didn't encourage me, either—and it wasn't in his plan to take over more at-home duties. My mother was more direct: "Stay home with your baby. It's your job." I already felt bad enough about the prospect of leaving little Amelia with someone, and if childcare was going to be a big problem, then this hill might be simply too steep to climb. I felt myself slipping. I started to think that despite all my check-lists and planning I might have to give up on this off-the-wall idea of getting a law degree.

Finally, less than a week before classes were due to start, I found a small place that was just getting set up. Run by a cheerful lady working on her own, it had a nice play area and no waiting list.

Only one problem: as I was filling out the application, I saw that she only took children who were "dependably potty-trained." Hmm.

Amelia was still in diapers, but I couldn't let that stop me now. This was my last chance. Dependably potty-trained. Check!

Now I had about five days to get my not-yet-two-year-old dependably potty-trained. The details are better left unsaid, but I can reveal that the path that eventually led to my becoming a professor of law and United States senator turned at one point on bribing a toddler with M&M's.

In hindsight it seems pretty funny that I was so clueless that I thought I could potty-train a toddler in a couple of days. And it's even funnier that I actually pulled it off. But the part that isn't funny is how razor-thin I'd cut it. I came within inches of missing my chance to go back to school—all because of childcare.

I made it to law school. I made it through the terrifying first days when I was sure I didn't belong there. I made it through the commute even when the roads were icy or a thunderstorm blew the little blue VW sideways on the roads. I made it through the worries about the cost of tuition and fees and books. I made it through all those things, but childcare *never* stopped being an issue. For me, as for so many working moms today, it was a weight I carried around with me every day.

And that burden never got lighter. Amelia woke up with a fever. *Do I need to miss classes?* Amelia cried every morning at drop-off. *Do I need to find a different place?* The center informed me that it was raising its rates. *Can I afford this?*

By the time I walked across the stage for my diploma three years later, Amelia and I had cycled through one childcare arrangement after another. I was also pregnant again. Enormously pregnant—and thus enormously unemployable. This time, there was no job for me. No office. No junior associate title. No heading off to work each morning to practice the tradecraft of law.

Instead, after Alex was born, I hung out a shingle in front of our house and practiced law out of our living room. If someone needed my help, I shoved the toys under the couch and invited them in. For the next year, I spent most of my lawyer time working for my neighbors: drawing up wills, handling divorces, and suing someone over a car accident.

It wasn't long before I was back where I belonged: in a classroom. On short notice, Rutgers needed a teacher for a legal writing class, and they asked me if I wanted to step in. Want to? I was over the moon. I made it work by trading babysitting duty with my next-door neighbor. Then Jim's job in New Jersey wound down, and soon we ended up in Houston. Jim was still working for IBM, and I landed my dream job: an entry-level, tenure-track job teaching law at the University of Houston. By this time Amelia was six and Alex was one.

I loved being a teacher more than ever. I knew that this—teaching— was what I was meant to do.

I did everything I could to make every other part of our lives work, too. I taught Sunday school and made cookies for bake sales. I got dinner on the table every night, even if most nights dinner was late and the kids were fussy. My first year of teaching law was a blur of washing dishes, bathing children, doing laundry at eleven at night. Then I would start to prepare my class notes for the next day, and I'd fall into bed sometime in the early hours of the morning.

Jim saw my teaching job the same way he'd seen my decision to go to law school: if I wanted to do this, that was okay, but it was on me. A lot of men back then would have believed that it was entirely within their rights to say, "No, you've got to stay home and take care of the kids," so I thought his approach seemed pretty fair. Fair, because on top of teaching law school, it was a woman's job—my job—to handle childcare and do the housekeeping and cooking and a dozen other things.

Day after day, I gave it everything I had. I worked my mother job and my teaching job. It was hard, but I could do hard. It was exhausting, but I could do exhausting. Once again, though, the thing that eventually sank me? Childcare.

In the space of our first few months in Houston, I went through the whole list. It was the same old round of jumbled solutions. Day care center. Babysitter. Sharing with a friend. Home care. Another day care center. Once again the costs were staggering, many of the options involved long drives, and nothing ever fit together right.

I was lucky to have a job that didn't require me to be in an office five days a week, eight hours a day. I was lucky that I could do part of my work from home, part of it late at night. But when I had classes, I *had* to be there—no calling in late, no substitutes. A room full of first-year law students was waiting for me, and class began at ten a.m. sharp.

As the school year went on, I still careened from one disaster to another. The neighbor who had agreed to fold her kids in with mine announced one Friday afternoon that "it just isn't working, so don't bring them back on Monday." A day care center abruptly closed. A babysitter got sick. Each one of these disruptions nearly tipped over my already unsteady boat. And no matter how hard I searched or how far I was willing to drive, finding a stable arrangement for two young children proved to be nearly impossible.

One morning near the end of my first semester of teaching, I bundled both kids into the car, dropped Amelia off at school, then headed back home with Alex so he could finish his breakfast before the babysitter came. We'd cycled through the usual spilled cereal and poopy diapers, but things were moving along. I had my hair brushed, my papers packed, my car keys in my hand. I was ready to go. My drive to the University of Houston took about forty minutes with traffic, and the babysitter was due at eight thirty. It was eight thirty-five. Eight forty-five. Nine o'clock. Nine fifteen. By now, I was standing in the driveway, jiggling the baby on my hip.

When I saw her car turn the corner, I ran out to the street. I yanked her door open before she came to a full stop. She was upset and kept repeating, "I'm so sorry. Trouble at home. I'm so sorry." I shoved Alex in her arms and ran for my car. I cried all the way to school.

A couple of months later, after I'd bathed the kids and put them to bed and started another load of laundry, my seventy-eight-year-old Aunt Bee called long-distance from Oklahoma. Aunt Bee and I had always had a special relationship. I was named after her ("Bessie" became "Elizabeth"), and she loved to tell the story of how she had carried me home from the hospital in the sweetest pink blanket covered with the tiny rosebuds that she had embroidered on it.

She asked how I was. "Fine," I said in a kind of high, thin voice. And then, in the middle of a sentence, I started to cry. I couldn't hold back any longer. It was too much. I'd come to the end.

I told Aunt Bee I was going to quit my job. I hadn't even thought of quitting until it fell out of my mouth. But once I said it out loud, something inside me broke. I cried harder and harder.

Aunt Bee didn't try to calm me down. She didn't tell me it would be all right. She just let me cry myself out and then said, "I can't get there tomorrow, but I can come on Thursday." She showed up at the Houston airport two days later with seven suitcases and a Pekingese named Buddy. She stayed for sixteen years.

Now, if every working mom in the country had an Aunt Bee, we'd be fine. But think about that. I went on from this job to write twelve books, get tenure at Harvard, build a consumer agency, beat a Republican incumbent to take a seat in the Senate, and run for president of the United States. Woo-hoo! And yet childcare—childcare!—nearly knocked me out. Childcare, or the lack of childcare, nearly sent me packing *twice*. Could I have gotten back in the game later, after Amelia and Alex were old enough to go to school or maybe once they hit high school? Maybe. But maybe not.

Childcare can be a bone crusher.

For a lot of moms and dads, having no childcare isn't about not getting the job they want; it's about not getting the job they need. It's about not getting the job that pays the rent and puts food on the table. The job that keeps their family from being tossed onto the street. The job that provides the link to health insurance. The job that makes it possible for them support an elderly parent.

Here's the part of the story that makes me blindingly furious, the part that makes me want to spit nails: Forty years after Aunt Bee saved my skin, this problem hasn't gotten better. If anything, it may be worse. More than 80 percent of parents with children under five struggle to find childcare. And those who find care often can't afford it. The average cost of childcare for one child soaks up between 9 percent and 36 percent of a family's total income. Infant care is even more challenging, costing 27 percent to 91 percent of the average income of a single parent. Even today, too many working moms come to that critical moment when the childcare puzzle becomes impossible to solve and they are forced to pass up the promotion, move to part-time work, or drop out of the workforce altogether. And all because they can't get past the exact same hurdle that almost tripped me up so many years ago: childcare.

## FROM MOTHER TO MOTHER TO MOTHER

In February 2018, I agreed to speak to Annie's List, a Texas organization that promotes progressive women who run for public office in the state. As the plane flew low over Austin, I thought about a long-ago trip when relatives from all around Texas and Oklahoma gathered for a family reunion at Aunt Alice and Uncle Claud's little house in Austin.

I had turned ten that summer, and what made the reunion extra-special was that my girl cousins, all three McCallister sisters, would be coming from Victoria, Texas: Suzan, a smart-as-a-whip, mischievous kid who was just my age; Sally, a tomboy who was bit younger; and little Janie, a thin child with huge brown eyes and a soft smile who trailed around behind us older girls.

Over the long weekend, we swam in the freezing water at Barton Springs, put on talent shows in the backyard, and slept on the floor in Aunt Alice's back bedroom. Because I didn't have any sisters of my own, my time with the three McCallister girls was especially sweet.

It was a grand trip, although not without mishap. Aunt Alice burned her forearm taking a bubbling hot Frito pie casserole out of the oven. One of the boy cousins killed a snake. Aunt Max said that she thought Aunt Alice had "picked up a few pounds," which sent my mother and all three of her sisters into the front bedroom for a marathon of trying on each other's clothes. All the girl cousins joined in. Sally and Janie paraded around in the aunts' scarves and high heels. I got to try on Aunt Alice's fake mink stole. Suzan put on Aunt Alice's ample brassiere and stuffed it with socks. Little girls and grown-up girls giggled until they got the hiccups and had way too much fun.

I was still smiling at the memories of that weekend when the plane landed in Austin—and still smiling the next day when I arrived at the auditorium and found it filled with about twenty-three hundred people, mostly women who wanted to run for office or wanted to help women run for office. This event was a fundraiser, so there were lots of pleas for money, but the crowd was happy to be there and happy to be part of making change happen. Annie's List had been named after the first woman elected to statewide office in Texas just one hundred years earlier. These women were ready to push the envelope a lot further.

I bounced out onstage, bright red jacket and big smile. This was a perfect group to talk with about why America needs more women in public office. I started with good, solid economic policy—if more women can finish their educations and more women can work, then our GDP will go up and our country collectively will be richer. (Cheers!) And what do we need to invest in to make that happen? Childcare. (More cheers!) And if we really want to get any of this done, then by golly, we needed some new leaders—some new *women* leaders! (Wild cheers!)

But the speech wasn't all numbers and rallying the troops to put more women in public office. I also talked about Aunt Bee. I told the story of nearly ending my career before it got started. I talked in very personal terms about what it meant not to be able to find good childcare that I could afford—the juggling, the stress, and, most of all, the overwhelming sense of failing my babies, failing my job, failing at everything.

The lights were bright in my face, and the auditorium was dark, but as I told my story I felt something shift. The room got unnaturally quiet. I thought I heard someone start to cry.

Plenty of women had their own stories. Mamas who had quit their jobs. Mamas who hadn't finished their educations. Grandmothers and aunts and sisters. Even a few daddies. They all had stories of how crazy expensive childcare was or how it just wasn't available in rural Texas. They all wanted to figure out how to make change.

My cousin Jane was there. She had come with more of our cousins to see the speech. Jane was now an elementary school principal in Austin. She was tall—taller than I am—but she still had the huge brown eyes and soft smile that she'd had as a little girl.

Suzan was gone—she had died of cancer eight years earlier. I told Jane how much I still missed her. Sally lived in Corpus Christi, and we'd had a good visit the year before when she'd made a trip back east. Jane and I laughed about our family reunions, about a herd of little girls playing together and making our own fun.

Jane now had two grown daughters of her own, and she told me she worried about what might happen if they become mothers. Even now, Jane said, it's just so damn hard.

In our family alone, it's been the same story for generation after generation. Of the aunts, only Aunt Bee—the one with no children—got some training and brought home a paycheck in her twenties and thirties. In my generation, all the women ended up working, but only after a series of bumps and near misses that all centered around childcare. And now, as we thought about our own daughters, we knew that childcare would be the for-sure hurdle they would face if they had children.

What's wrong with this country? How can we value mothers so little? Talking with Jane that day, I was sick to death of decades of lip service and no real change. More than ever, I felt certain that we needed new leadership.

After I hugged Jane and the other cousins goodbye, I thought about what I'd just said onstage. If we need more women in the workplace to be a more productive country, we also need more women in positions of leadership to make change happen. If we want good policies that profoundly affect the lives of mothers, then we need more mothers to run for office, mothers who will get those policies enacted into law, mothers who understand what's broken and who won't give up until we fix it. That's a darn good reason for more women to run for office.

In fact, I thought, that's a darn good reason to run for president of the whole United States.

## A DOUBLE CRISIS

When I ran for president, I heard a lot of wrenching stories about working mothers and their childcare problems, but the COVID-19 crisis drove home the need for childcare with a ferociously sharp point. As the virus spread across the country in early 2020, about one-third of the workforce was deemed "essential," so those workers were still out on the front lines during the worst waves of the pandemic. Doctors, nurses, and emergency techs. People who mopped the floors and cleaned up hospitals, police stations, and drugstores. Stock clerks who unloaded groceries and cleaning supplies and put them on the shelves. Long-haul truckers who kept the food supply chain working. Local gig workers who made sure meals and groceries were delivered. Transit and sanitation workers. Police and firefighters. Millions of people who kept our country functioning, putting their own health and their own lives on the line while the rest of us sheltered in place.

In early April, just as wave after wave of coronavirus cases were hitting the United States and hospitals in hot spots were worried about being overrun with sick and dying people, I set up a conference call with a big group of Massachusetts nurses. Times were really tough—they were working long hours, there were no known COVID-19 treatments, and too often they were watching their patients die alone. I'd also heard terrible stories about the shortage of face masks and other protective gear. Nurses in some areas were creating their own makeshift gowns out of garbage bags and washing and reusing masks. And let's be clear: if nurses can't do their jobs, if they get sick or can't spend long hours attending to desperately ill patients, then the whole health-care system breaks down and all of America is at risk. Taking care of our nurses is literally a life-or-death matter for the rest of us.

I thanked the nurses and said I agreed with everyone in our country who had been calling them "heroes." There were some polite responses, and then I asked the obvious question: What do you need so you can do your jobs? The first answer came from a nurse who uttered a single word: childcare. Another chimed in, saying, Yeah, we need childcare. And then the dam broke, with the nurses talking over each other. One after another talked about how, with the onset of the pandemic, childcare arrangements had fallen through. Babysitters couldn't come. Childcare centers had closed. Classes for children had moved online. After-school activities had been canceled. The always-tricky and always-stressful task of arranging childcare had become so much harder exactly at the moment when the need for these parents to be in the workforce was at its most desperate.

Much as I had done years earlier, these nurses had pieced together different solutions to the problem. Some had moved in with their own parents so the grandparents could watch the kids. Others had asked the babysitter to move in with them. Some had a partner who was now staying at home and trying to juggle working remotely with providing full-time childcare. These women were dealing with death every day, and yet one mom after another said that managing their constant worry over their children was their biggest challenge.

Their employers saw the problem as well. As the number of infections rose in Boston and Worcester, for example, both cities turned their convention centers into hastily built field hospitals to deal with COVID-19 cases. I spoke with hospital CEOs and frontline administrators who said that although everyone was working hard, they were struggling to find nurses to keep shifts fully staffed. They cited childcare as the single biggest stumbling block, and some even created on-site centers.

The same was true for other employers who were trying to keep their people on the front lines so that, say, grocery stores could stay open or bus lines would run. Everyone agreed that these workers were essential: we needed them to keep our health-care system and our food distribution system and our entire economic system going. But one in five of those who couldn't work cited childcare as the reason. And for millions more who were still showing up to work, childcare was the rickety arrangement that could end at any moment. Without adequate childcare, an economy that was already under great strain faced the very real possibility of breaking down entirely.

Meanwhile, the working mothers who were trying to manage from home weren't doing great, either. The old routines were gone, and millions of moms and dads were now trying to work remotely—not to take a vacation or simply shelter in place, but to *work* from home. Childcare centers, schools, and after-school centers were mostly shut down. Occasionally the fallout could be amusing—a naked child would run through the background during a business video call or a baby would spit up while a parent tried to focus on a conference call. But a lot of it was just plain exhausting. Everyone patched together their own special arrangements, but the internet was loaded with announcements made by moms who had reached the end of their ropes and were declaring, "I quit." I knew exactly how they felt.

The burden was enormous. On top of all they were doing before the pandemic, working parents found that the increased demands of staying at home with children meant that, on average, they saw their total workloads increase by twenty-seven hours a week—nearly the equivalent of a second job.

And who did most of this childcare and schooling burden fall on? Who was buried under a ton of bricks while trying to manage work and children? Mothers. Of course it was mothers; it's always mothers. Mothers disproportionately carried the childcare burden before the pandemic, and when the burden got heavier—when childcare providers closed and there were fewer childcare slots and there was no in-person education—mothers took it on. Research showed that before COVID-19, even among dual-earning couples, mothers were spending twice as much time on parenting responsibilities as dads. Once COVID-19 hit and the burden of supervising children's schooling shot up, mothers' share of the work actually increased. And for single moms, the story was even worse—in many cases, they took on 100 percent of the care.

As women slipped behind men in hours logged for their employers during the lockdown, their career prospects inevitably dimmed. When businesses reopened or employers made clear that they expected employees with kids to work remotely—even without adequate childcare and with many schools still shuttered—more women were squeezed out of the workforce. And as the pandemic wore on into the fall and winter, as schools remained closed and the demands of online learning increased, even more mothers were pushed out. Experts speculate that without sufficient childcare infrastructure, the impact of the COVID-19 crisis on working moms could last a lifetime, cutting into their earnings and their eventual retirement savings.

With childcare, as with so much else, the coronavirus yanked back the curtain that has for generations covered up a national disgrace.


## THE ECONOMICS OF CHILDCARE

From 1970 through 2019, adjusted for inflation, wages for middle-class workers have barely budged. Yet if many people have been making about the same income for decades, the costs of all kinds of basic expenses have gone up. Housing costs are up over 60 percent, health insurance expenses have more than tripled, and the price of a college degree has increased by 500 percent.

For families trying to stay afloat in a choppy economic sea, it's tough out there.

But here's what makes it even tougher: between the time I was a new mother and the time I was a new senator, the cost of childcare went up over 900 percent. *Nine hundred percent.* In nearly half of all states, child-care costs are higher than the cost of in-state public college tuition. All across the country, that's a giant boulder that rumbles toward working women and then flattens so many families. For single parents, for parents working near the bottom of the income scale, and for parents trying to go back to school, the cost of childcare often stretches families' paychecks way past the breaking point.

Think about the consequences of skyrocketing childcare costs. Today, about two-thirds of mothers with young children have jobs. That's millions of parents scrambling to make sure that someone is taking care of their baby when they head off to work.

The basic economics are harsh: providing good childcare is

expensive. Ideally caregivers should have substantial training, and childcare centers should have a high ratio of caregivers to children, a facility with plenty of space, lots of playground equipment and art supplies, food on site, and hours that begin before parents go to work and don't end until parents are on the way home. But those are just the basics. For children with special needs or for parents who work late shifts or overtime, the centers need more staff and more training.

Meanwhile, fixed costs for childcare centers are high—teachers, buildings, equipment—but children get sick and parents move, so week-to-week revenues can be bumpy. And they can't just charge whatever it takes to produce first-rate childcare because too many families simply can't afford it. So the centers struggle to keep costs down. They rent older buildings, underpay their workers, and run at the highest ratio of children-to-caregivers the law will permit. They don't do this because they are bad people; they do it to try to keep their doors open for all the parents who desperately need them.

Producing high-quality, readily available childcare is really expensive—and that was true before the COVID-19 crisis drove up costs for every one of these centers. If parents found it difficult to find a center for their child before the coronavirus, by the time the pandemic was in full swing it became close to impossible. One study estimated that in early 2020 four young children were vying for every childcare slot. More than ever, the bare-bones economics of providing childcare kept the number of slots low and the number of scrambling parents high.

And yes, it *is* parents—both women and men. But let's not kid ourselves. More often than not, it's women whose career opportunities are limited when childcare is hard to find or challenging to afford. It's women who get pushed out of the workforce. It's women whose experiences paint the picture of what the childcare crisis really is: a crisis of lost productivity. But whether raising children is undertaken by women or by men, it's a significant commitment that can knock anyone back. The COVID-19 crisis has made plain the urgent need to fix this problem so no one gets knocked back.

There is a pretty obvious way out of this box: put more taxpayer money into childcare. We don't ask the parents of a fifth grader to come up with the full cost of getting that child through the school year. Instead, we tax everyone and provide free education for all fifth graders. We make that collective investment. So why not the same for childcare? That's what Iceland does. And Sweden. And Denmark. And Austria, Bulgaria, Mexico, Estonia, and dozens of other countries. All of them put a bigger share of their budgets into childcare than the United States does.

Before someone strikes up the band to play several verses of "why-should-I-pay-for-that-if-I-don't-have-kids?" it might be good to remember that every American taxpayer is helping pay for the new robots that GM just bought to improve efficiency on the factory line. Every American taxpayer is helping pay for the new fully automated 5G cell phone radio plant that a Swedish company is building in the United States. Every American taxpayer is helping pay for every piece of equipment that is boosting corporate profits. It's all happening through the tax code.

The tax code is a truly staggering document. It is long and complex, partly because laws passed by Congress are supplemented by legal cases and even more detailed regulations. The special breaks designed to encourage businesses to buy more property and boost productivity are scattered throughout reams of technical language, but it all boils down to the same thing: if a business decides to buy computers, farm equipment, rental property, furniture, oil drilling equipment, SUVs, or just about anything else, that business can get a tax break. Companies' depreciation write-offs totaled $659 billion as recently as 2014, and that's just one of the many kinds of deductions available to support businesses. Every dollar of these deductions is a dollar our country spends subsidizing the purchase of equipment by businesses. And every one of these purchases is designed to increase the profits of the company—profits that are passed along to its shareholders.

These tax deductions for depreciation may be good investments that help boost productivity, but $659 billion is a lot of money. Just to put that in context, I recently put together a plan to provide childcare and preschool for every one of our country's children. It covered all the expenses for about 70 percent of families and capped the expenses at 7 percent of income for the rest. The total annual cost? Seventy billion dollars. That's a plan that would boost productivity, too.

For that same $70 billion, the plan also included a pay raise for every childcare worker and preschool teacher in America. Currently, childcare workers earn about $10.70 an hour, and six out of seven get neither health insurance nor retirement benefits. More than 90 percent of these workers cannot meet their own financial needs, much less support someone else in their household. Many would be a lot better off working the counter at McDonald's or gathering up shopping carts at Walmart. Taking care of children should be a professional-level job, and caregivers should be paid on par with public school teachers with the same training.

But it's not only about money—it's also about respect and fairness. Almost all childcare workers are women who work for barely-above-poverty-level wages so that other women can go to their jobs. More than 93 percent of childcare workers are female, disproportionately Latinas and Black women. Paying these caregivers more would make it possible for them to build some security in their own lives. Investing more of our tax dollars in childcare would also permit childcare centers to raise standards and decrease turnover.

Increased federal spending would dramatically change the economics of childcare, which would encourage more caregiving centers of all kinds to spring up. Childcare today is offered by nonprofit organizations and for-profit companies; it is provided in homes, churches, shopping centers, recreation centers, and even extra space in office buildings and government agencies. But virtually every one of these centers runs into the reality that parents can't pay for the kind of care their children need.

Even with high demand, there are far too few centers. The economics just don't work. A single caregiver can't manage twenty babies or tend thirty two-year-olds. The costs of insurance, specialized equipment, long hours of operation, cleaning, and billing are piled on top of the salary expenses. Centers try to pinch pennies, but the high cost of running even a well-managed childcare center means that it must charge an amount that quickly outstrips what a working parent can pay. It should be no surprise that childcare centers aren't springing up all over America and that millions of parents are struggling to find decent care that they can afford.

One other bit of context. We often focus on the caregiving aspect of tending children so parents can work, but built into every childcare experience is a powerful educational element. That holds true for babies who are learning new words, toddlers who are learning their colors, and pre-K kids who are learning the skills that will make them great readers. High-quality childcare is early education.

We should also remember that early learning is one of the best long-term investments our nation can make. A tax deduction to replace a janitor with a robot may boost profits for the company's owners and investors, but it's hard to estimate the long-term public benefit. By contrast, the benefits of high-quality early childhood education can be measured for years in better performance in school and higher graduation rates. Studies also show that high-quality early childhood education reduces obesity and depression in adults; it also reduces the likelihood of arrest or substance abuse years into the future. More than one childcare expert has argued that for every nickel invested in early childhood, we save dollars down the line in problems that never happen and opportunities that open up.

It's all about choices. Our country has decided to spend hundreds of billions of dollars every year to encourage businesses to purchase equipment in the hopes that this investment of tax dollars will increase productivity. If businesses choose to replace people with robots or to build automated factories that cost people their jobs, the law makes no distinction. As a country, we accept that cost because we place a high value on increasing productivity.

Our decision not to invest more in childcare and early childhood education is also a choice. Sure, our government provides some tax breaks for childcare, which helps some middle-class families. We fund some wonderful programs, like Head Start. But overall, the needs wildly outstrip the supply. And that leaves mothers standing in driveways crying because they just can't hold it all together.

## POLICY IS PERSONAL

It wasn't a huge group—maybe fifty people—but the room was too small and everyone was jammed together. Lots of elbows. Everyone talking at once. People inching around each other to say hello to someone they knew. It was the summer of 2018 in Washington, and a group of progressive activists was hosting an evening event to provide yet another possible candidate for Congress a chance to meet people.

This kind of event always reminds me of a baseball tryout. People mill around talking for a while, then the candidate is called to the front of the room to speak for a few minutes, and then the questions start coming. Each query is like the pitch of a baseball, and everyone watches while the candidate tries to hit it. If people like what they see, they'll tell the groups they represent that they should support the candidate. If not, they'll move on.

Unlike a baseball tryout, though, the questions come at the candidate from all directions. It's like getting pitches from not only the pitcher but the catcher, the first baseman, and a guy eating a hot dog somewhere in the third row of the bleachers. The people who ask questions really know their stuff, so fluffy answers don't cut it. And the range of topics is always broad. In the space of twenty minutes, a candidate might be asked about public land policy, incarceration rates, highway funding, and nuclear waste storage—all by people who are experts on those topics. People also ask nuts-and-bolts political questions about the competition for the seat, fundraising, and relationships with the local press.

The experience can be nerve-racking, but Deb Haaland, the woman in the batter's box that evening, was very solid. I'd met her before and I liked her, but I hadn't ever seen her in action. She was impressive—tough and capable, and she really knew her stuff.

Then someone asked about childcare. She paused. In an instant, she was no longer the policy wonk who was ready with an answer on how federal law should work in this area or how budgeting should be revamped. Instead, she told a story about her own life. Suddenly policy was very personal, and the crowded room got quiet.

Deb was born out west. Her family—both her mom and her dad—were in the military, so she moved a lot as a kid, attending thirteen schools in the first twelve years of her education. Still, her sense of place runs deep. She is a citizen of the Pueblo of Laguna, a federally recognized tribal nation, and she proudly points out that she is a thirty-fifth-generation New Mexican. After she graduated from high school in Albuquerque, Deb worked a lot of different jobs. When she was twenty-eight, she headed off to college. She borrowed money to make it through, and she graduated just four days before she gave birth to her daughter, Somah.

Deb got smacked with the challenges of childcare almost immediately. She and Somah moved around, at times relying on friends for shelter and food stamps to put a meal on the table. Finally, to support herself and her daughter, Deb started her own business: she bottled and sold salsa. Childcare and work were woven together every day. When Somah was three, Deb decided it was time for preschool. She found a great childcare center for her daughter, but she couldn't afford it. So Deb worked out a deal. In lieu of paying the fees, Deb took on the job of cleaning the center.

As Somah grew up, Deb continually struggled with childcare. She moved around, held different jobs, and always had to be sure that no matter what else she was doing, someone was taking care of Somah or picking up Somah from school. For years, Deb performed the same kind of juggling act that millions of mothers do every day.

When Somah was nine, Deb started law school. Again she struggled with after-school care and coverage on school holidays. As for her social life, Deb told me that she'd hired a babysitter once—and she had to save up for it. Mostly, though, she had one simple rule: "If Somah couldn't come—I didn't go."

I knew from the start that Deb's commitment to expand access to childcare was bone-deep—and I also knew I was all in to help her get elected. Later, when she won her congressional race in the fall of 2018, I celebrated. (I celebrated again in December 2020 when she was named

Joe Biden's secretary of the interior.) Once she arrived in Washington, we spent more time together, and I came to appreciate her deep love for her family and her quirky sense of humor. She has an organizer's enthusiasm for getting people engaged and a wonk's determination to get the policies right. And best of all, she came to Washington to get stuff done.

America needs a national childcare plan. It can't be a little nibble around the edges—we need a full-blown, big-deal universal childcare and early education plan that will cover all our kids. When I decided to put together a bill that would accomplish this, I needed a partner in the House to help drive it, and Deb was the obvious choice. Together, we pulled in experts, met with childcare providers, and talked through all the details. In the summer of 2019, we introduced the Universal Child Care and Early Learning Act.

Our bill was endorsed by dozens of educational groups and economists, child development experts, and teachers. Even so, we knew it didn't have much chance of passing as long as Mitch McConnell controlled the Senate and Donald Trump was in the White House. But we also knew that it was important to lay out a bold plan, recruit as many allies as we could, and fight for a bill that will change the lives of millions of children, teachers, and parents. And that's exactly what we will keep on doing.

When we introduced our bill, Deb said that "childcare and early learning should not be a luxury that only people with money have access to." She talked about the difference we could make with our bill and about what it means to open up opportunities for more moms and dads. "I know what it is like to struggle to make ends meet as a parent." She knows, and she doesn't forget.

For Deb—and for millions of other women—policy is personal.

## OUR CHOICES

I can think of nothing more personal than carrying and raising a child. Nothing more intimate. Nothing more private. And yet the circumstances under which pregnancy and child-rearing are carried out are deeply affected by a series of decisions made collectively by our elected representatives and judges. Policy touches the most intimate parts of our lives.

Policy is not only personal, it is also deeply important. Laws barring pregnancy discrimination didn't change everything in a blink, but they moved mountains. They gave women legal rights, and those legal rights gave women the opportunity to find lawyers, get their unions involved, and build alliances with each other. Those legal rights created different expectations for the next teacher or factory worker or Walmart clerk who got pregnant. And those changes in the law and in personal expectations helped change the world.

Our collective failure to invest in childcare illustrates the other side of the story. What happened when a woman couldn't find or couldn't afford dependable childcare? Consider generations of women who needed the income from a job, women who hoped to build a career, women who wanted a chance to compete, women who struggled to survive. How many women of my generation, women without an Aunt Bee, were knocked off track? How many women of my daughter's generation were knocked off track? And how many women of my granddaughters' generation will be knocked off track if we don't change the policies around childcare?

Of course, it's not just moms whose lives are affected. Many dads cut their hours short or change jobs or choose a different career because they can't find care for their children. Many older siblings don't stay after school for band practice or join the swim team because they need to get home to watch their younger brothers and sisters while their mom is at work. And plenty of grandmothers quit their own paying jobs to help sons or daughters raise their own children. Our national failure to provide universal childcare reverberates through the whole family.

Working mothers boosted America's GDP in the latter years of the twentieth century, but by 2000 the struggle for childcare forced many of them back home. In the wake of the 2020 pandemic—which shuttered even more childcare centers and slashed our GDP by trillions of dollars—it's more obvious than ever that we simply can't afford to continue our shortsighted approach to childcare. No one knows exactly how much poorer our nation will be—25 percent? 35 percent?—if we don't change our policies to make it easier for parents to work, but it will be poorer. And no one can calculate how much less resilient our country will be if a significant portion of our essential workers can't find childcare, but it will be less resilient. Regardless of whether any one of us is directly affected or not, making the necessary investment in childcare matters to all of us.

## THE AMERICA WE WANT TO BE

I love being a mom. I can't imagine a life without Amelia and her brother, Alex, or one without grandchildren Octavia, Lavinia, and Atticus (yes, their mother took Latin in high school). I can't imagine it—and I don't wish for it.

But I don't kid myself: being a mom makes other things in life a lot harder. And it is even harder than it needs to be because of the policy decisions our country makes—decisions about pregnancy, childcare, and a whole lot more.

But none of this is written in stone. I ran for president because I know—I *see*—that policies we make are policies we can change. An America that once said it was okay to fire women for getting pregnant changed into an America that said pregnant women can keep their jobs and told a shift manager that he needs to provide a stool for a pregnant woman so she can sit down occasionally.

Yes, it's hard to change policy. It takes time, and meanwhile people have lives to live, kids to feed, work to do, dogs to walk (that came from Bailey). Besides, for every policy we have now, there's a group embedded somewhere that loves it and has no interest in changing it. Pregnancy discrimination worked just great for school principals and business owners who ran their schools or their stores like private kingdoms and who didn't want to have to deal with anything they didn't already know all about—like pregnant women. The decision not to invest in childcare sounds perfectly sensible to someone who doesn't have kids and doesn't think much about what that means for our economy overall.

Some of those who say mothers should stay home are moms themselves—and good for them if that's the choice they make in their own lives. But deciding that our country should not invest in childcare so other moms can't make a different decision is just plain wrong. It's a personal choice, just like learning to swim or going to church, but it needs to be a real choice and not just a pretend choice—and that means building real childcare options so all mothers can decide for themselves.

And let's admit it: even a world in which people try-try-try to be gender neutral, men just don't face the same headwinds as women when it comes to raising children. The overwhelming majority of our fellow citizens think that of course men should work full-time after the baby comes. For every dad who says, "I'll get up with the baby," there are a lot more dads who honestly and truly think they are sharing the childcare duties fifty-fifty but in fact aren't even coming close. Before dads start insisting otherwise, it might be useful to look at an example from the COVID-19 crisis. With millions of school-age children doing their schoolwork at home, 45 percent of fathers said they were doing most of the work supervising the lessons. Sounds great, but mothers saw things a little differently. They reported that dads were doing most of the schooling about 3 percent of the time.

How we approach change will determine how much and what kind of change we get. Changing policies about pregnancy and childcare would be huge. The futures of millions of children would be improved, and the mothers whose lives have been stressed to the breaking point by bad policies would see some relief. It's a righteous fight.

We could stop there. If we joined three dozen other high-income nations and invested in universal, high-quality childcare, I'd shout "Hallelujah!" and dance my best victory dance.

But I'm not stopping there.

Nope. I started with pregnancy discrimination to show that we *can* change, and I started with childcare to show *how profound* that change could be. But there's so much more we can and should do.

I didn't quite realize it when my children were young, but I learned about politics as a mother. I learned firsthand about how policies touch every corner of our lives. If the law had been fair to pregnant women in 1971, I might have stayed on as a special ed teacher and built a very different life.

Instead, my life took an unexpected turn. Now I'm in the fight to make change happen so that the next mom can say "Motherhood changes everything" and only be talking about how happy she is to hold a newborn miracle in her arms.

# TWO

# A Teacher

It was early in the morning, the first day of a new semester. The classroom was a small amphitheater, with the students seated at long tables on risers, stepped up in a semicircle. The teacher's place was in the well, with a table to work from backed up by tall chalkboards and plenty of chalk. The faint smell of disinfectant hadn't yet dissipated, even as the students filled the room.

I walked in at exactly eight o'clock, dropped my books on the table at the front, and started asking questions.

I always posted the first-day reading assignment ahead of that first class: Warren and Westbrook, *The Law of Debtors and Creditors*, pages 1–12. That way all the students could do the reading and we could dive right in—I didn't want to waste a single moment. Anyone who hadn't done the reading would get the message fast: this class isn't for you.

I looked out at the room. There were about seventy-five second- and third-year Harvard law students. People slumped over their books, half asleep, clinging to enormous cups of coffee like life preservers. Faces aimed down, with furtive glances up at me—glances carefully designed not to draw my attention. The overall vibe was "Please don't call on me."

But this class wasn't a spectator sport. It was more like an exercise class. People get better and stronger when they sweat hard.

Time to make them start sweating.

This was a course on bankruptcy, so I started by discussing a series of problems about debtors in trouble and creditors bearing down on them. Soon we were in the thick of it. I was in rapid-fire mode—glancing down at the seating chart, cold-calling on students, pushing back on their answers, moving on quickly.

As I swung into a new section, the first student up stumbled badly. He missed the legal references entirely. Next.

ME: Mr. Seliga, why doesn't the bank just send someone over to grab whatever valuables the debtor has? Maybe the family car? Or her grandmother's wedding ring?

SELIGA: Uh. . . . Yeah, uh. Maybe they were too busy?

Even worse. I didn't say anything. I just moved to another student.

I glanced to my right. Aisle seat, front row: Ms. Perkins. Curly hair, round face. Sitting up straight and looking me square in the face.

ME: Ms. Perkins?

PERKINS: The creditor won't go get the property because the law prohibits it. (An answer offered up with just a hint of self-satisfaction, knowing she'd certainly done better than Mr. Seliga.)

ME: How so?

PERKINS: [Long explanation of various laws that were applicable to our problem.]

ME: (Thinking to myself, Hmmm, she's pretty good. So let's ratchet up the questions.) Really? What if the banker shows up and threatens to take the property? What will the debtor likely do?

PERKINS: (A little less confident.) Well, uh, the creditor can't do that.

ME: Really? The bank can't threaten? Are these criminal statutes? Is the sheriff standing there?

PERKINS: No, but the law says they can't take the property without permission.

ME: Are we sure the debtor will know that? Will this deep-in-debt file clerk have her personal lawyer standing nearby to advise her?

PERKINS: But the law . . .

ME: *Think, Ms. Perkins. Think!*

PERKINS: I *am* thinking. This is the best I can do.

ME: No, Ms. Perkins, you can do a lot better.

I peppered her with a few more questions. She got hopelessly tangled up, but somewhere in the middle she started to see another layer to the problem, a glimpse of how the laws written in the books were one piece of the puzzle, but only one piece. In real life, some people know the rules and some don't. Some people can afford a lawyer and some can't. Some people will be embarrassed or afraid and give "permission" for all kinds of things. In other words, Ms. Perkins had started to master a central insight of the course. Simply put, what happens in life intersects with the laws on the books in complex ways—and a smart lawyer has a good understanding of how leverage works in the real world.

I went on to another student. And then another. By now, everyone looked wide awake, except maybe Mr. Seliga, who seemed to be contemplating life in an alternate universe.

I called on about forty-five or fifty people that day, some for a quick answer and some for much longer exchanges. Back and forth, occasionally hitting some of the folks who had talked earlier. Weaving ideas together. Trying out different theories. Pushing roughly on the students who hadn't prepared well. Pushing more gently on the students who were prepared but terrified. Pushing hardest on the once-confident students like Ms. Perkins.

When class was over, I was exhausted. I'd felt like I'd been leading a pack of runners in wind sprints for an hour and a half. I scooped up my books and headed back to my office. I guzzled a big glass of water and wandered around the halls for a bit, waiting for the adrenaline to wear off.

Late that afternoon, I had office hours. A handful of students showed up. Students from previous semesters—would I write a recommendation for a clerkship? Students trying to get into the current class—could

I help with a scheduling conflict? Students from today—could I explain again one of the statutory sections we'd covered in class? And then there was Ms. Perkins.

She looked terrible.

She began by saying that she knew she'd done a really awful job in class.

I thought, *Here's an A student who isn't used to getting banged around.* I suppressed a smile. I knew what was coming next—what always came next. She will politely ask me not call on her because I make her nervous and she can't think. Then she will say that she promises she will do the work and she's sure she'll learn a lot, but she just doesn't want to have to speak up in class.

My sympathy for this plea was exactly zero. These were not grade-schoolers. They were law students who had chosen a life of advocating for others. They had the privilege of receiving a first-rate education and they were developing skills that would equip them to represent people who really needed help, people whose lives or livelihoods might depend on their skills. Speaking up is the heart of the damn job.

Besides, this was *my* job—teaching them how to do it. How to get stronger and faster. How to use new tools. How to get knocked down and scramble back up. How to be more resilient. Every time I called on a student in class my job was to push them hard enough to make them really work at it, but not push them so hard that they were mortally wounded.

I was ready for Ms. Perkins to say that she just couldn't do this, so please don't call on her. I smiled at her, but it was a thin smile. Let's get this over with.

She took a breath, tapped the books on her lap, and said, "I'm only taking your class because I couldn't get into tax."

I thought, *Wow, that's an impressive opening line. Go ahead, spit on the subject to which I've devoted my entire professional life.* Ms. Perkins was clearly not a suck-up, but at this point, I was trying to decide whether she might be the single most obnoxious law student I'd ever met—and I'd met my share.

Ms. Perkins barreled ahead. "I was terrible, but please don't give up on me. I can do this. I just need some help."

I hadn't seen that coming, either.

Looking straight at me, she said: "I'm in your class because I want to be a teacher. I need to watch someone who knows how to teach. I heard you were really good, and besides, you're a woman, and there aren't many women teachers around here. I want to learn to teach law."

That last turn knocked me right off the turnip truck. No flattery. No pretense. Just "help me learn."

This student was definitely worth investing in.

The semester hurtled along, faster and faster. We studied the law, but we also studied the families whose lives had been turned upside down. Jobs that disappeared. Divorces. Deaths. Babies who stayed in the hospital for months at a time. Mortgage brokers who claimed that the fine print meant they could keep the down payment when a loan fell through. Payday lenders who dug their claws in deep. Families who had tried so hard, only to witness it all fall apart. Families for whom bankruptcy was their last chance to stop a terrifying economic free fall.

As we worked our way through the course, some—not all, but some—of the students came to understand the material on a very personal level. One of them was Ms. Perkins. Bit by bit, she connected the people in our textbook to the people she had known growing up. She was a child of the Iowa farm crisis. She'd watched neighbors lose their land to foreclosure. She'd seen people's furniture and dishes and bedding laid out in the yard in advance of an auction. She'd heard about the suicides.

Grades in the bankruptcy course are based only on one exam at the end. No research papers, no extra credit for being a star in class. At Harvard Law, grading is anonymous. Students get a number, and the professors grade the numbered papers. The match-up comes afterward.

When I found out that Ms. Perkins had snagged an A in the class, I wasn't surprised. She had a strong grasp of the complex statutes and intricate rules, but so did a lot of other students. What made her exceptional was that she understood what my bankruptcy class was really all about: I wanted to help these students comprehend what was broken in this country and to discover what tools we might have to fix it.

It's a tough world out there. Teachers try to get their students ready for it, whether they are little ones like my babies back at Riverdale Elementary or big ones like my students at Harvard. Yes, I made the big students sweat and I probably caused some of them to have anxiety dreams, but I never pushed them harder than I thought they could manage. And when they did manage it—when they sweated and they succeeded—they got stronger. They got more confident, better prepared to take on the next challenge. They got ready to pick up the extraordinary tools of law and use them to make the world a little bit better.

And sure, not every student used their new tools that way. Some of my law students picked them up and sold their services to the highest bidder. Some helped the rich get richer. And some just plain made me want to weep, like the student from my early teaching days in Texas who came back from a job over winter break to tell me that she had been so excited to have a chance to use the collection tools she'd learned about, and that she'd used them to "seize a family's Christmas tree and all the presents—and I did it on Christmas Eve!"

But I think most students left my bankruptcy class with more than just a handful of exquisitely sharp legal tools. I hope they left with a little more appreciation for what it means to have power. Maybe at the end of the course they had a better understanding of the role they could play when trying to help people in trouble. And, for some, maybe they got just a glimpse of how the tools they'd acquired could be used to help build a better, fairer country.

As for Ms. Perkins, she didn't just go away, happy with her grade. She came to see me on the first day of the next semester and announced that not only did she still want to teach law, now she wanted to teach *bankruptcy* law. But I was the only professor who taught an advanced bankruptcy course, and I was on leave that semester. So together we crafted an independent study project: she would help me conduct research that would allow her to see firsthand the families who turned up in bankruptcy court. After graduation, she devised a research project of her own, an in-depth look at rural families in financial trouble. She clerked for a judge and then practiced bankruptcy law at a law firm. Four years after graduation, she got another job—teaching bankruptcy law.

As the years went on, Ms. Perkins wrote books and gave speeches and called out abuses when she saw them. When the 2008 financial crisis hit, she worked with a group of state attorneys general to get a bigger settlement for families who had been cheated. Kamala Harris, then the attorney general of California, appointed Ms. Perkins to oversee an $18 billion settlement and hold the banks' feet to the fire, which she carried off with spectacular success.

When Donald Trump was elected president, Ms. Perkins put aside her life as a teacher and ran for Congress as a fiery progressive. In 2018, she fought incredibly hard to flip a district in California that was so red it had *never* elected a Democrat—and she won by 4 points. Two years later, she won reelection by a 7-point margin. In the meantime, she used congressional committee hearings—and her now-famous white board—to hold self-important corporate CEOs and slacker government officials accountable for the ways in which they had failed the American people.

Oh yeah, and the names of the students? The kid from outer space was not named Mr. Seliga, and the student who kept coming back was not Ms. Perkins. Mr. Outer Space shall remain anonymous, but the young woman from Iowa was named Porter. Katie Porter. Congresswoman Katie Porter.

It's easy to say now that Katie was special, because she was. But for a teacher like me, they are all special. Every one of them has incredible potential and terrific tools for making change. My former students have taken on tough cases, written statutes, and changed the law. They have built their own law firms and started their own businesses. One has patents for his work in intellectual property, another founded a foreign language school, and another started a successful tutoring business. Many have helped build legal systems around the world. They have volunteered in prisons, legal aid clinics, women's shelters, and state bar programs. Together they have donated millions of hours to help people who are in trouble.

My students have done a lot. I don't say this to claim credit: I think of our time together in the classroom as my chance to help them expand their opportunities. And if my dreams come true, some of them will help expand opportunities for others.

For me, that's what being a teacher is all about.

## LOTS OF PUBLIC SCHOOLS

The day-to-day of running for president is less about television interviews and big, public speeches and more about town halls and rallies across the country. That means it's also about riding in a car (or, in our case, a rented minivan) for long stretches, meeting lots of local volunteers, and eating food that someone picked up hours earlier.

A lot of our town halls were in public schools. I guess it is no surprise that I loved these schools. I felt at home. The main event would usually be in the gym or the cafeteria, and there would be a couple of classrooms set aside for our team to use. That's where I'd eat lunch or make phone calls or meet with some local activists before the town hall began.

Each classroom made me smile. Each room reflected a very specific person. One classroom was set up as a beach spot, with round outdoor tables, umbrellas, and fake palm trees—a place for kids to have fun even when the snow was piled up a foot deep outside. Another was decorated wall-to-wall with student self-portraits, poetry, and essays. One classroom was covered with encouraging messages about being your best self and not knowing what you can't do if you don't try, with handmade stars hanging from the ceiling. Another had science puzzles and challenges pinned on the walls, such as "How do flies walk on the ceiling?" or "How do plants drink water?" One classroom was outfitted entirely with beanbags and carpets instead of regular chairs.

Every classroom—every single one of them—radiated that someone cared. And that deep affection was returned: the teachers' spaces were loaded with "Best Teacher" mugs and photo frames and knickknacks. Several were stacked high with things the kids knew the teacher loved: a whole collection of golden retriever figurines, dozens of depictions of daisies, all kinds of stickers and hats and pennants from the state university.

That doesn't happen by accident. It doesn't happen by edict from some school board. It happens because there's a teacher who cares, a teacher who thinks about the students early in the morning before school starts and late at night long after they have gone home. Those classrooms were full of love, and the signs of that love were evident even when the classrooms were empty.

Being there reminded me of my own classroom back at Riverdale Elementary. I had a closet. Really. It was a big closet, but it was a closet. One door, no windows. The regular classrooms had all been taken by the regular classes, and there was no space in the old building for the kind of one-on-one and small-group work that I did. So the school emptied out the filing cabinets and supplies and put me in the closet.

I loved that closet.

I decorated the walls with pictures of animals—perfect for practicing growling or meowing, or for working on sounds like b-b-bear or d-d-dog. The table and chairs were low enough that even a four-year-old could keep her feet on the floor and feel secure. There was plenty of room for a wheelchair, and shelves on one wall were stacked with games and toys. My kids and I worked hard, but I wanted every child to look forward to coming to my classroom for our time together.

When I was running for president, I looked at all those classrooms I borrowed with a practiced eye. I saw just how much time and imagination had gone into every room. I was often knocked over by the creativity. I saw how much those teachers loved teaching, too.

Which is why the bathrooms in the schools I visited really got to me. Lots of them were old and poorly maintained. They weren't dirty—just sad. Faucets that didn't work. Chipped tile. Paint that was flaking off the walls. Water stains on the ceilings and down the walls. They were depressing.

Okay, I get it. The most important thing in American education is *not* the bathrooms. Of course not: buildings are just buildings.

But these buildings are also a tangible sign of our values. The teachers could do their best with their own rooms, the principals or the art teachers could decorate the halls, and the cleaning staff could scrub everything spotless. Bless them one and all. But these bathrooms make a statement to anyone who pays attention that the people who *own* these buildings—*us, the taxpayers*—don't really care enough about the buildings or the occupants to invest in keeping them fresh and cheerful.

And just to be clear: the bathrooms look really nice in the Senate. And at NASA. And in the National Gallery of Art. Even my local Registry of Motor Vehicles has nicer bathrooms than many of the public schools. Taxpayers don't put up with tired old bathrooms in most of our public spaces, so why are dreary old bathrooms acceptable in the places where our children go to learn every day?


## SHOW ME THE MONEY

Show me your budget and I'll know your values. At the federal level in 2020, American taxpayers put $72 billion into educating our children, less than 2 percent of all federal spending. That's soup to nuts, everything from preschool grants to funding for special education to helping our kids make it through college.

Just for context, American taxpayers put $738 billion into national defense. That's about ten times the amount that goes into education. In fact, we consistently dedicate about half of our nation's discretionary budget to defense.

We all know the basic story about how education in our country too often falls short. Teachers aren't paid enough. Schools are underfunded, and schools in communities of color are underfunded even more. School funding structures are determined state by state. Some states care a lot, and other states—well, if you judge their values by their budgets, it looks like a lot of states really don't give a damn about educating their children.

Our failure to invest is no secret. Pretty much everyone knows this, although it's worse than a lot of people will acknowledge. But knowing and doing aren't the same. Everyone in politics—Democrats and Republicans—says they care about the kids, but every plan to put more money into our schools runs up against the same objection: it costs too much money.

This issue has gnawed at me for years, chewed on my conscience like a wolf with a bone. I am sick to death of being told that America simply can't afford to do right by our kids.

In early 2019, as the Democratic presidential race was getting underway, Democrats were still pretty worked up about Donald Trump's single big legislative achievement: a $2 trillion tax giveaway that mostly went to giant corporations and rich people. Every Democrat running for president dutifully promised to roll back those tax breaks and use the money to pay for that candidate's great new plan. I was also in favor of rolling back those giveaways, but frankly there was a bit of a shell game going on. Let's roll back those tax cuts to support education. Let's roll them back for a Green New Deal. And roll them back for transportation and infrastructure. And for Medicare for All. And for housing. And. And. And.

In their dreams, Democrats spent that tax rollback over and over and over.

Worse, no one really planned to roll it all back. Some provisions would be left in place, which meant less revenue, although the question of exactly how much less remained elusive. But it was clear that few of the candidates had much appetite for proposing that we should raise major new money for major new priorities.

When I began thinking about running for president, I decided that if I got in the race I would go at this money question differently. I wanted to figure out a way to make a big national investment in our kids—not just a short-term flash of cash but an investment that would be there for generations to come, an investment that would create opportunities for kids who weren't born rich. I wanted big, structural change in education. What's the point of running for president if you're not going to fight for something that's really important?

But I didn't want to put out a plan for investing in our children without also spelling out how I would pay for it. I wanted the changes to be real—something we could do immediately and something we could sustain over time. After a lot of intense discussion with my team, I decided I wanted to propose something new: a wealth tax.

Here's the idea. Add up the value of everything a family owns—real estate, stock, cars, cash, and so on. The first $50 million in wealth would be free and clear, but on the 50 millionth and first dollar, the wealth tax would kick in—two cents for every dollar above $50 million, and three cents for every dollar above $1 billion. This means that only folks with $50 million or more in assets would pay the tax. That's the top one-tenth of one percent of our nation's families—about seventy-five thousand families.

The concept of a wealth tax wasn't complicated or difficult to understand. In fact, it's already built into how we currently finance public education. Nearly every homeowner in America pays a property tax that's based on the value of their home, and a big chunk of that tax is used to support local schools. Renters pay property taxes indirectly through their rent. The wealth tax is a lot like a property tax, except instead of focusing only on real estate, the wealth tax for gazillionaires would sweep in the stock portfolio, the diamonds, the expensive paintings, the yacht, and all the other fancy belongings.

Most of that stuff is pretty easy to value. In fact, most of the wealth of our richest families is held in stock, so for starters we would just need to look up the value of a family's stock holdings. In addition, there are plenty of specialists who value jewelry, artwork, and every other kind of expensive possession. Once all of a person's property is valued, monitoring it from year to year wouldn't be rocket science.

My team and I consulted a bunch of tax experts and looked into how some very wealthy people would try to game the system. In Europe, early versions of the wealth tax didn't take this into account and they created a mess—but it was a mess that wasn't hard to fix. Once we figured it out, we stitched up the loopholes in advance. So, for example, the wealth tax would cover all property, wherever it might be held around the world.

(Sorry, Mr. Rich Dude: no tax havens in the Bahamas.) We also planned to significantly step up IRS enforcement—we would hire ten times the usual number of people just to monitor the seventy-five thousand families who would be covered by the tax—and we built that cost right into the plan. Then, just to be ultra-conservative, we assumed that despite our best efforts we'd miss about 15 percent of the wealth these rich people had.

That's it. Two cents on the great fortunes over $50 million, going up to three cents when the fortune hit $1 billion.

By the way: Why tax wealth? The answer starts with the astonishing level of inequality in our country. America's truly wealthy are unimaginably rich, and they are not just a little richer—they are leaps and bounds and quadruple somersaults richer than everyone else. Why is the wealth gap so enormous? Why has it been growing exponentially? There are multiple reasons, but one that stares us right in the face is that the wealthy have rigged the tax code. For years, tax cuts upon tax cuts have been handed to folks at the top. Taxation of capital gains has been scaled back. S corporations—closely held corporations that generally don't pay income taxes—were created just for people pulling in big bucks. There are tons of loopholes that allow rich people to lower their effective annual income tax liability even more.

The math isn't complicated. Over decades, an unfair income tax code will produce a huge wealth gap, and a wealth gap can't be fixed just by cleaning up the way income is taxed in the future. We need—we urgently need—a wealth tax. It would help reduce the impact of several decades of a rigged system and also work as a defense against future rigging.

Wealth is so unequally divided in this country that my two-cent wealth tax would produce $275 billion a year—and an eye-popping $2.75 trillion over ten years. That's a very tall stack of money, and all of it could be invested in education. Every dollar could be invested in our kids.

As I talked with my team about this plan, I felt a little thrill: we had the basic outline of a tax plan that would produce enough revenue to make real change—big structural change. True, proposing the wealth tax would inevitably mean that my already long list of powerful enemies would grow longer. Before I ever jumped into the presidential race, I had already taken on Wall Street. And Big Tech. And Big Pharma. And Big Ag. And Big Banks. Hmmm. So why not aggravate a bunch of billionaires? Especially for a fight worth having. A righteous fight.

I thought about all those classrooms, all those teachers who cared so much about their kids. Two cents could change their world.

## SAY YES

Instead of saying *no* to every good idea, what would happen if we said *yes*? That question tickled the edge of my brain day and night. What could we buy for two cents? I hadn't been this excited since I'd picked out a wedding dress—both times.

Let's start with our babies and all those things that come with being a mother. A two-cent wealth tax would allow us to pay for universal childcare for all of our little ones. All of them. Millions of moms and dads could finish their educations or go to work. Millions of children would be cared for in first-rate facilities, places with plenty of books and playground equipment. And teachers would get the pay raises they deserve.

That same two cents would also cover universal pre-K for every three-year-old and four-year-old in America. All our children would develop reading readiness, begin to understand time and numbers, learn how to wait their turn. Every single preschooler.

We could do all of that for our babies, for their mamas and daddies, and for our teachers for a price tag of about $70 billion a year. Generation after generation of little ones would get a stronger start in life, a start that would pay off for decades to come.

What about K–12? Study after study shows that more investment in education results in better outcomes for our kids—higher incomes, a reduction in adult poverty, reduced criminal activity. Investment in education also boosts U.S. productivity, and higher productivity lowers the cost of goods and services and raises our overall GDP. Rigorous studies estimate that when we invest in preschool education, for example, the long-term return to the rest of us is somewhere between three to seven times our original investment.

The basic idea was simple: fund the constantly underfunded programs that work. In addition to providing money for childcare and pre-K, a two-cent wealth tax would provide enough money to improve public education for every child and every educator in America.

We could dramatically increase federal aid for public K–12 to make sure that every school gets the funding it needs and so provide every child with a good public education. We could start by quadrupling the funding for the Title I program. Title I schools serve a high proportion of children from low-income homes, children who often face a whole constellation of challenges. Additional funding would mean that these children would have more meaningful opportunities to learn—and more meaningful opportunities to succeed in life.

Two cents would let us do the same for special education. For decades, children with disabilities were often turned away from public schools. In 1975, Congress passed the Individuals with Disabilities Education Act (IDEA) to guarantee each student "a free and appropriate" education, and it promised that the federal government would pick up 40 percent of the cost of that education. In fact, the federal government has never come close to meeting that promise, and today it covers less than 15 percent of the cost. To make up the difference, local school boards find a variety of ways to cut costs—eliminating other programs, squeezing teacher salaries, deferring updates to school buildings. Fully funding IDEA at the federal level would put the money where it's needed to defray the higher costs of educating children with disabilities. It would also guarantee that, instead of pitting one group of children against another in a fight for too few public dollars, the resources needed to provide a "free appropriate public education" to all of our children would be available.

Two cents would also let us kick in some money to improve school buildings. Right now the federal government puts no real money into helping maintain the physical buildings, playgrounds, sidewalks, and the like. Instead, that's mostly left to local budgets—and the more stressed the local school budget, the less money there is for building repairs and maintenance. The need is real. The average public school building is forty-four years old, with the oldest schools typically located in the poorest districts. More than half the school buildings in America need significant repairs before they can be classified as "in good condition." And the most commonly identified facilities problem at these schools? No surprise: it's the bathrooms.

Finally, two cents would let us invest in innovation for every school. A wealth tax would generate enough money to give the equivalent of a $1 million grant to each public school in the country. Not each district or each bureaucracy, but each individual public school. Big city or rural community, old school or new school—a grant of $1 million. The teachers, parents, and administrators could put their heads together and decide what would help their school deliver a better education for their students. A new science lab? More reading specialists? More field trips? An extra month or two of classes in the summer to help make up for what was lost during the pandemic school closures? Ask a teacher what her school could do with a grant like that and watch her face light up.

Sharply increased federal funding would drive the kind of big structural change that attacks the unfairness of local funding head-on. Because schools are so dependent on local funding, children born in poorer neighborhoods have fewer educational opportunities than children whose families can afford to buy homes in wealthier neighborhoods. This means that year after year, school by school, there's less money for speech therapists and sports, less money for smaller class sizes and teachers' aides, less money for college counselors and reading coaches. And yeah, less money for sparkling new bathrooms.

These disparities between children whose families aren't wealthy and those born into privilege are sharpened along racial lines. The heavy reliance on state and local funding means that our country's nonwhite school districts get about $23 billion less every year than white school districts, even though they serve about the same number of children. Per-student funding varies, but the underlying reality is harsh, and inadequate school-district funding hits Black and Latino children the hardest. Bureau of Indian Education schools are also chronically underfunded. A tax on a small number of super-wealthy families would allow us to put an end to all this deep-seated inequality.

What would it cost to step up for all our children—to make sure that every single child gets a first-rate education? The total price tag for quadrupling funding for Title I schools, fully funding IDEA, improving school buildings, and investing in innovation grants for every school is $80 billion a year—just a fraction of the revenue from a two-cent wealth tax. It gives me goose bumps to think about the difference we could make for our kids.

## TWO CENTS FOR TEACHERS

Two cents would change the lives of millions of children. It would also change the lives of millions of teachers.

Running for president was sometimes a little bit like being back in school. At town halls, I got to talk about subjects I thought were really important, and a bunch of people got to ask questions and then argue or agree. These town halls were great fun in the same way that good classes were great fun—intense, challenging, sometimes funny, and sometimes aggravating, but always with lots of people thinking hard about subjects that mattered.

In the selfie lines afterward, I met teachers, lots and lots of teachers. Since I always talked about my background as a teacher and made so many policy recommendations about funding education, teachers would often call out their ties to teaching: "I taught special ed for thirty-six years!" "My mom and dad were both teachers, and now I'm a teacher!" "I also knew I wanted to be a teacher by second grade!"

But not all the greetings were cheerful.

LaTisha came through the selfie line, arms outstretched for a hug. She said, "I love teaching. I love my babies." Then she started to cry. She explained that she worked three jobs, with the second and third paychecks signed over to pay off her student loans. "But even with three jobs, I'm falling behind."

Jake and Erin were married, teaching at the same school. They wanted to buy a home and start a family. They scraped together every penny they could, and still they couldn't make a dent in their combined $100,000 in student loan debt, much less start saving for a down payment on a house. They had five jobs between them.

Andy said he was in his second year of teaching, and without his two nights a week as a security guard and his weekend job loading trucks, he couldn't make the rent and keep his car. "Sometimes I'm so tired I fall asleep with my clothes on."

I met teachers who worked as waitresses and bartenders, teachers who filled in at the 7-Eleven, teachers who did landscaping, teachers who worked in their parents' businesses, and a teacher who worked at a meat processing plant.

Nationally, about one out of six public school teachers works a second job during the school year. But for younger teachers, those who are just getting started, the rate is much higher: one in three is working a second job.

I get it: no one goes into teaching for the money. But teaching shouldn't be treated like an expensive hobby. Asking men and women to supplement their salaries as public school teachers so they can pay off student loans or pay the rent is disrespectful to the teachers and to the entire enterprise of public education. Underpaying our teachers delivers a very clear message: the public just doesn't care about them or about the critical job they do.

The low salaries—and the contempt they signal—have been a break-the-glass problem for decades. But it wasn't always this way. Back in the 1960s, public school teachers, on average, earned nearly 15 percent more than other people with similar educations. Now, even when health and retirement benefits are folded in, these teachers are making less than others with similar educations—about 10 percent less.

That extra $80 billion in federal money for K–12 public schools would mean more money for teachers, counselors, librarians, and cafeteria workers. Quadrupling the money for Title I schools would mean that these schools could offer a premium to the teachers who want to take on the steep challenge of teaching children from poor families and children who are learning English for the first time. More money for buildings and special programs would mean more room in the local education budget to increase teachers' pay.

After one of my town halls, Geri bounced up on the stage for a selfie. Cheerful and energetic, she seemed to be just the kind of person who ought to be teaching first graders. And that's exactly what she had done for four very happy years. "But I had to give it up," she said, her smile falling away. "Even with a second job, I just couldn't afford it." Her eyes filled with tears. And so did mine.

Two cents. *Just two pennies.* A two-cent wealth tax would make it possible for great teachers to stay in teaching.


## MORE EDUCATION

Investing in children is about building for the future, and that investment doesn't stop at high school. By 2018, 70 percent of America's workers were in jobs that required a post–high school education. And the trend line is clear: More than 90 percent of all *new* jobs require a college degree.

Consider earlier shifts in the American workforce. Around the turn of the last century, farmhands could do backbreaking labor all day without needing to read or write. Living in a bunkhouse and farming a small number of acres required a lot of different skills, but it didn't take much formal education. In that world, schooling was a haphazard affair provided by a mix of public and private institutions, and many of the schools were miles away from the children who might have attended. My grandmother, for instance, finished eighth grade, a respectable accomplishment for a woman born in the 1800s.

But as more people moved from the countryside to the city and more people worked in factories and shops, the need for more education became evident. People needed to read directions, understand safety warnings, and make calculations. The world was changing, and all across our country, state and local governments stepped up. Education through high school was free, and kids were encouraged—and, if necessary, forced—to spend more time in school. Legislators seemed to understand that an investment in the education of all our children would benefit all our people.

And they were right. The years from 1870 to 1970 were deemed the Second Industrial Age. As a better-educated workforce managed more complex equipment, productivity rose sharply and prices fell just as sharply. The resulting leap in Americans' standard of living was extraordinary. Life expectancy went up and the number of hours worked each week went down. Our collective investment in education paid phenomenal dividends.

Like millions of others in my generation, I am the beneficiary of investments taxpayers made in education. My public schools in Norman and Oklahoma City in the 1950s and 1960s were staffed by great teachers who (for the times) were well paid. And when I nursed the dream to become a teacher myself, the doors were open.

Of course, I managed to fumble my opportunities. At nineteen, I dropped out of college and got married. Like most newlyweds, we were pinched for cash. And besides, given that I grew up watching my mother count nickels, it seemed reckless for us to spend money we didn't have so that I could go back to school. I was sure my dream of teaching was gone.

I got a job working the phones in an office. And there I might have stayed, except that twenty miles away, right near the center of the city, was the University of Houston. At the time it was a commuter school—no fancy dormitories, no special places for students to hang out—but I got a first-rate education. My teachers were excellent and the on-campus clinic for children with speech and language disorders gave me my first chance to work with kids with special needs. And the part that made it all possible? Tuition was just $50 a semester.

I quit my day job, and by working as a part-time waitress I was able to pay for my classes. Eventually I got my diploma and headed straight into teaching.

Taxpayers opened doors for me. They invested in public education, and I had a chance. I'd grown up on the edge of economic disaster, always aware that my mother never stopped worrying about money. Now I had the chance to build my own economic security—and do work I loved. To this day, I count myself among the blessed.

I also recognize that those blessings were not evenly distributed. Segregation reared its ugly head in those years, and African American children, Native American children, and Latino children were often forced to make do with outdated textbooks, underpaid teachers, and crumbling school buildings. Even decades after *Brown v. Board of Education* promised an equal education to all, resources and opportunities for non-white children remained sharply constrained.

Even so, education remained one of the surest paths to a more secure future. I graduated from college in 1970. Since then, the need for more schooling has intensified. Millions of jobs that rely on physical strength or the ability to complete repetitive tasks have been eliminated. Computers, software, robotics, and artificial intelligence are all developing at lightning speed. Now even training that was once picked up on the job, work like welding or plumbing, often involves a sophisticated understanding of chemistry or engineering or another specialty that requires more formal training programs. Compounding the problem, in their drive to boost the bottom line, many corporations have cut their employer-sponsored training programs, expecting their employees to find—and pay for—training and certification on their own.

More education has been critical, but instead of stepping up, government has stepped back. Over the past two decades, state governments that once supported post–high school education have cut these investments. States are now spending about $10 billion less each year on higher ed than they were in the early 2000s. When state support is cut, families have to pick up the slack. Across the board, tuition at state schools has increased by about a third, and some states have raised tuition even more.

As our economy demanded better-educated workers, and as more students clamored for more help, the federal government responded with debt. It was like tossing an anchor to a drowning man. Today, about forty-three million students and former students collectively carry about

$1.6 trillion in federal loans. And even before the pandemic, a whopping 40 percent of all federal student loan debt was not in repayment—month after month of no payments at all.

At town halls, I often asked if anyone in the room had a student loan. The response was just what you'd expect: nearly every young person raised a hand. Lots of young people, just getting started—but there were so many others as well. Moms in their thirties, divorced and raising two kids. Couples struggling to take care of themselves, their kids, and their own parents. People now in their sixties who had gone back to college during the Great Recession of 2008, figuring a new degree would open doors. Grandmas who had guaranteed a student loan for a beloved grandchild. Student loan debt is *everywhere*.

This debt has created a new kind of hell. Almost 40 percent of people with student loan debt never made it to graduation. They signed up for college, took on debt, attended classes for a while, and then dropped out. Today about thirty-six million people are trying to manage a college-based debt load on a non-college income. Bankruptcy laws will generously erase credit card debt and medical bills and payday loans, but they won't cancel out student loan debt. Some borrowers just give up; they quit paying, then watch the penalties and interest double, triple, and quadruple the original debt. Meanwhile, the federal government is an extremely effective debt collector, garnishing wages, seizing tax refunds, and grabbing Earned Income Tax Credits. The government is even taking a bite out of more than 170,000 people's Social Security checks. But even as debtors are squeezed harder and harder, the interest and penalties they owe keep mounting, extinguishing any hope of ever getting out from under their debt. The big sin that will keep millions of Americans buried under a pile of debt for years or decades? They wanted a better education and tried to get one.

Even the people who make it through college often pay a high price. Two out of every three college graduates now carry student loan debt. That debt often has a profound effect on what they do next. People with student loan debt are 36 percent less likely to buy a home. They are less likely to buy a car and less likely to start a small business. They are more likely to be living with their parents. These effects create an enormous drag on our economy, one that has an impact on every one of us.

As is so often the case, race cuts a wide swath through opportunity. African American and Latino students are more likely to take on student loan debt in order to go to college, more likely to borrow more while they are in college, and more likely to have trouble paying off student loan debt when they graduate. And these effects last. Student loan debt is drowning millions, but, once again, more people of color are pulled down to the very bottom of the ocean.

Higher education has been a structural challenge for Black students for generations. In the late 1800s and early 1900s, taxpayers supported public universities and gave tax breaks to private universities, even while many of these schools barred the admission of Black students outright or limited their number to certain preset quotas. In order to build more opportunity, Congress funded some Black land grant colleges, but it fell largely to Black churches and civic leaders to raise funds to support colleges that would primarily serve those students who were denied admission elsewhere. HBCUs—Historically Black Colleges and Universities—have had particular success in expanding access to higher education.

Despite the successes of HBCUs, they remain desperately underfunded. Both public and private HBCUs have significantly more constrained budgets than their now-integrated counterparts. As the president of an HBCU in South Carolina told me, "We were started on prayer, and we're still counting on prayers to get by."

## A NATIONAL COMMITMENT

Especially when someone is just starting out in life, taking on debt can be like chaining your dreams to a giant boulder. America's collective investment in higher education benefits us all, and we can jump-start that benefit by getting rid of student loan debt and covering the costs of post–high school education for all our kids.

Here's where the two-cent wealth tax comes back in. Two cents would cover the cost of universal childcare and pre-K, which would come to $70 billion a year. It would also allow us to make a big new investment in public K–12, which would require another $80 billion a year. That still leaves more than another $120 billion a year, which we could devote to wiping out a big chunk of student loan debt and eliminating tuition at all public colleges and technical schools so that no one else has to take on debt to get an education.

Two cents would alter millions of lives. During my presidential campaign, I proposed canceling $50,000 of student loan debt for everyone with an income under $100,000. That would give about forty-three million of the approximately forty-five million debtors real relief. More than thirty-two million borrowers would be debt-free, including those who went to college for a while and then dropped out. About ten million more would see their debt drop dramatically.

Student loan debt cancellation is good for the people whose debt is canceled, but it is also good for the rest of us who don't have student loan debt. Debt cancellation would deliver a huge boost to our economy. Instead of shelling out hundreds of dollars every month in student loan payments, those who are freed of some or all of this debt could spend the extra money to buy a car or begin saving up for a home. Without the burden of student loan debt, more people can start a new business or invest more money in an existing one. And some people who never completed college may decide to go back to school.

Two cents would have another consequence: My debt-cancellation plan would help close the wealth gap for Black and Latino borrowers as compared to white borrowers. For the first time in decades, we could start to shrink a wealth gap that has haunted our country for far too long. Among Black Americans with student loan debt, the gap would close by an estimated 25 points. And the impact on the Latino wealth gap would be even larger, closing the gap by an estimated 27 points.

Under my proposal, we would treat debt cancellation the same way we do progressive taxation—we would provide more relief to those who earn less and no relief for those at the top. In effect, those for whom a college degree hasn't paid off with sparklers and fireworks would get help, while those who are now working in lucrative professions would continue paying off their loans.

Eliminating the heavy burden of student loan debt would be Act One. But this play has two acts, because if we provide a onetime cancellation of student loan debt and then do nothing else, we will push the following waves of students over the same financial cliff. So here's Act Two: Just as millions of kids in America were able to attend high school for free starting early in the twentieth century, it's now time to make public colleges and technical schools free for everyone. The money would be there. A two-cent wealth tax would allow us to remove the cost barrier to higher education for every single young person in the country. All of them.

Think about what that would mean for the high-schooler interested in becoming a plumber or an electrician—free training. Or the young mom who wants a chance to learn computer programming—free classes. Or the premed student intent on a career in public health—free undergraduate education before hitting medical school. Or the kid in elementary school who dreams of becoming a teacher someday—free college so she can teach the next generation.

Two cents would also allow us to make a $5 billion annual investment in leveling the higher-education playing field. Start with the 107 HBCUs—schools that, generation after generation, have opened doors and nourished dreams for Black students. Finally these colleges and universities would have enough money to shore up their buildings, expand their offerings, and increase the size of their faculties. With more resources, they could offer more scholarships to cover living expenses and books, and more help for scholarship students. A level playing field would make it possible for HBCUs to compete more aggressively in the effort to educate the next generation of Black leaders.

The thirty-seven Tribal Colleges and Universities in America could also use a major financial boost. These colleges are operated by tribal nations. Greater funding would expand opportunities for both technical training and accredited four-year college degrees.

Latino students face tough challenges as well. An investment in minority-serving colleges and universities would make certain that these students also have access to an education that's designed with them in mind. In addition, providing more need-based scholarships for these schools' students would be enormously helpful.

And there it is: that's how we could spend the remaining $120 billion a year that would be generated by the two-cent wealth tax. We could pay off student loan debt and put enough money into our public colleges and universities to make them all tuition-free—and we'd still have enough money for an extra investment in the colleges that serve the students who particularly need an open door of opportunity.

Access to higher education has been a burning issue for me ever since I first arrived in the Senate. I want every kid to have the chances I had, so I've attacked this problem from every possible direction. My first bill as a newly minted senator was designed to reduce the interest charges on student loans. I vividly remember the thrill as I stepped up to the long marble dais that rises above the Senate floor to submit my plan to attack the rising cost of student loan debt. The next night I appeared on *All In with Chris Hayes* to explain the bill and ask people watching the show for help to get it passed.

That was May 8, 2013, and the idea of cutting student loan debt was so radical that I was able to get exactly zero senators on board as original cosponsors. Zero.

But good ideas sometimes have a way of taking hold. Over the years, groups and individuals all across the country joined the fight. As time went on and the debt problem kept getting worse, I kept expanding the bill, moving from reducing interest payments to canceling student loan debt outright. As I introduced and reintroduced various versions, a few senators joined, then a few more, then a few more. Eventually, more and more progressive groups endorsed some form of student loan debt relief. By the time of the 2020 presidential primaries, nearly all the Democratic candidates had some kind of student loan debt cancellation plan.

But I kept chewing on the problem. Congress wasn't likely to act anytime soon, particularly after 2014 when Mitch McConnell and the

Republicans took control of the Senate and started calling the shots. So my team did more homework and found that Congress gave the secretary of education the power to cancel that debt. In other words, there was no need to get congressional approval. I started pushing—first during the primaries, and later, along with Senate Democratic Leader Chuck Schumer, after Joe Biden was elected president—to cancel this debt immediately.

It turns out that we don't have to wait for a two-cent wealth tax to pay for canceling student debt. So let's just do it. Now.

## BILLIONAIRE TEARS

During my campaign, I talked a lot about the wealth tax. I explained it on my website, I mentioned it in interviews. And in nearly every town hall I spoke about both the wealth tax and what America could buy with two cents: a stronger future for every child in this nation.

Some billionaires were good with that. More than a dozen billionaires, in fact, sent a letter to the 2020 presidential candidates endorsing a two-cent wealth tax. They thought taxing the wealthy was both fair and a good way to raise the money needed to make investments in our country.

But not all the billionaires were on board. Several of them came roaring out of their Billionaire Caves, determined to beat back the whole idea of a wealth tax. Billionaire Ron Baron generously allowed that he's fine with raising some unspecified taxes, but not with imposing *this* tax: "I hate the wealth tax." Billionaire Michael Bloomberg—who would later become a Democratic candidate for president—called the wealth tax "mean." Not to be outdone, billionaire investment banker Lloyd Blankfein called this kind of change "cataclysmic." When asked about the wealth tax, billionaire Peter Thiel said he was "scared." Billionaire Joe Ricketts said a wealth tax "would ruin what we have." Billionaire Jamie Dimon, CEO of JPMorgan Chase, got his feelings hurt, saying that my proposal of a wealth tax vilified successful people (like himself). "I think we should applaud successful people" (like himself).

What a shock: apparently a lot of billionaires wanted to keep everything exactly the same. They wanted to preserve a system in which they have more money than they could ever spend while public school teachers are working three jobs. A two-cent tax? The Billionaires Club was certain that it posed an existential threat.

Perhaps the most distressed billionaire in the club was Leon Cooperman, who is mostly known for paying millions of dollars in fines for breaking the law on insider trading. He explained to one interviewer that I represented "the worst in politicians as she's trying to demonize wealthy people because there are more poor people than wealthy people." His passion runs deep. He explained that he believed that the rich should pay more taxes, but not *this* tax. "This is the f****** American dream she is s******* on." Oh dear. Did I hit a nerve?

Poor Mr. Cooperman became so unhinged on national television that he finally broke down and cried. And that's the origin of the slogan on my favorite coffee mug: BILLIONAIRE TEARS. Such a sweet drink.

A slew of Republican pundits jumped in to defend the beleaguered billionaires, along with Democrats like Larry Summers, who was sure he had a better way to tax rich people. Conservative think tanks—the ones supported by generous donations from rich people—ginned up reports claiming that taxing the very rich would hurt everyone else. They threw up clouds of complaints. A wealth tax is unconstitutional. (No, it's not. See the notes.) A wealth tax wouldn't collect much money. (Yes, it would. See the notes.) A wealth tax would be complicated to administer. (No, it wouldn't. See the notes.) Some of the loudest complaints came from people like Michael Strain, a conservative commentator for the American Enterprise Institute who called a wealth tax "morally objectionable."

I understand that it's pretty alarming to billionaires and their high-dollar lobbyists when someone asks them to pay more to help support our country. Decades of lobbying and hundreds of well-funded public relations campaigns have reminded our elected officials that we should be eternally grateful to these billionaires and show our gratitude by rewarding them with tax cuts layered on tax cuts. Since 1980, taxes for billionaires have been cut by 79 percent. Perhaps the members of the

Billionaires Club have come to believe that tax cuts are a right guaranteed to every billionaire and that any attempt to take away that right would cause instant destruction of all they hold dear.

These billionaires like to tout themselves as "realists." They tell everyone they are tough men who know the score. They understand that *someone* has to pay the taxes that will make it possible for this country to function. They just think they are already paying too much.

Well, here's a little dose of *real* realism: Today, the top one-tenth of one percent in America pay total taxes of about 3.2 percent of their net worth every year. Meanwhile, the 99.9 percent pay about 7.2 percent. Think about that: Collectively, all those teachers and waitresses and factory workers and computer programmers and small business owners are paying total taxes at more than double the rate of the thinnest slice at the top. For the four hundred richest households in America, the numbers are even more obscene. They pay taxes at a lower rate than any other group—including the poorest 10 percent of all Americans. And these billionaires think that's precisely how it should stay.

Before we start to get a little misty eyed along with these billionaires, it is good to remember that two cents doesn't leave billionaire Lloyd Blankfein unable to pay the heating bill on his Central Park penthouse, his Miami Beach condo, or either of his two summer homes in the Hamptons. Two cents doesn't leave billionaire Mark Zuckerberg searching through the pockets of old jackets to find the money he needs to gas up a $1.6 million Pagani Huayra supercar. Two cents doesn't leave billionaire Mark Cuban shaking out the couch cushions for change to refuel his $36 million Boeing 757.

Billionaires know that once you have a lot of money, making more money gets easier. They spend years investing and reinvesting their fortunes, which expand as if by magic. Carefully nurtured by highly paid money managers who take advantage of every tangle, twist, and loophole tucked into the tax code, billionaires' fortunes have grown astronomically. From 2010 to 2020, the average net worth of America's billionaires increased by 80.6 percent. A two-cent wealth tax is still going to leave them plenty of room to grow their fortunes. And just to put that growth of 80.6 percent in context, the net worth of the non-billionaire part of America increased during that same time period by a whopping 1.5 percent. Cry me another cup of tears, Leon.

The fallout from COVID-19 drove this point home. Within a year, more than 450,000 Americans had died from the coronavirus, including thousands of essential workers who had taken extraordinary risks to support their families and keep our country working. In 2020, more than seventy million Americans filed for unemployment benefits, while more than fourteen million small business owners applied for help to try to keep their struggling businesses afloat. An estimated forty million people spent much of the year on the brink of getting kicked out of their homes.

But the Billionaires Club did a little better. They welcomed thirty-two new billionaires to their ranks. And in the wake of the double punch of a health crisis and an economic calamity unlike any our nation has ever experienced, the 630 members of the Billionaires Club increased their total net worth by over *a trillion dollars.*

It's time to unleash the power of two cents. It's time to fund affordable childcare, high-quality K–12 education, and free college. It's time for the billionaires to step up.

### TRANSFORMING LIVES

Town halls were the backbone of my campaign for president, but sometimes we changed things up and did unannounced drop-ins at local places. In October 2019, I headed to an unannounced stop at Dos Amigos, a local Mexican restaurant in Concord, New Hampshire. It was Taco Tuesday, and the place was crowded with families, couples, and singles—everyone looking for a really good taco.

Running for office requires a certain amount of sucking it up and doing things that feel really weird—like walking up to perfect strangers who are enjoying their steak taco with corn salsa, introducing yourself, and chatting about national politics. Sure, just a casual conversation. Perfectly normal.

Campaigning like this also requires building a brick wall around your ego.

As I moved from table to table, interrupting people in mid-bite, I got a mix of comments and questions.

Yeah, I'm thinking of voting for you. You or Bernie. Or Joe Biden. I'm just not sure.

Is single-payer really something we can get done?

Aren't you the one who wants to give everyone $1,000 a month?

Why are you so thin?

And some parts of these snippets of conversation occur with cameras rolling and reporters sticking microphones in people's faces. Sure, perfectly normal. Just like any Taco Tuesday.

After I'd made the rounds, I sat at the bar with a group of women who had heard I was there and wanted to visit. We made a tight little circle and, with beer all around, the group loosened up a little. The women— four teachers and a lawyer—talked about their lives. All loved their work, loved their partners, loved their kids.

We talked about the rising cost of health insurance and the squeeze it put on family budgets. Then we moved to childcare—how expensive it was, how the hours didn't always work, how no one had a good plan for dealing with a sick child. The women got more animated, talking over each other. They talked about how frazzled they felt, how they were pulled in too many different directions, how they always always always worried about their kids.

The lawyer said that when she had her second baby, she'd simply given up practicing law. The cost of childcare for two children was more than she would clear while working for a law firm. Now she was sidelined, and she worried that she wasn't keeping up with new developments in her field.

Then the conversation turned to student loans. These women understood the value of a good education, but they had been shocked by the price. Now they were saddled with crushing debts that they would be paying off for years and years.

"We can't even think about buying a home."

"My husband and I are both working second jobs just to try to keep up with the loans."

"It's so heavy. I sometimes have dreams—nightmares—about the debt."

"My husband's car is old, and we're scared that if it breaks down, we'll have to get something better—and fall behind on our student loans."

"Sometimes I think I'm suffocating."

These women had finished college. Some had advanced degrees. Now or in the recent past, all five had good, professional jobs. And all five were living right on the edge of a financial cliff.

After hearing their stories, I sketched out the two-cent wealth tax and explained how it would pay for childcare and cancel a big chunk of student loan debt.

As usual, I was gearing up to talk about every detail—raising teachers' salaries, providing quadruple funding for Title I schools, and all the rest. But that's when one of the women waved me off. I stopped talking.

"Let me get this straight," she said. "We could put a two-cent tax on a bunch of the richest people in this country, and I could get good childcare and my student loans would be canceled?"

"Yup," I said.

The women sat for a minute in stunned silence.

"Two cents? That's it?"

"Uh-huh."

"My God. That two cents would change my life."

And that's really the point. Two cents would change the lives of these women. In fact, it would change the lives of tens of millions of people. The lives of millions of parents and millions of children. The lives of millions of teachers and millions of people dealing with student loan debt.

The only lives it wouldn't change much are those of the billionaires whose enormous fortunes would grow just a little bit slower.

## OUR FUTURE

All those classrooms and all those kids. These are *our* kids. These are the human beings who will be our next generation of scientists and soldiers and engineers and computer programmers. These are the kids who will be called on to manage climate change and to provide a cure for the next pandemic. These are the kids who will cook our meals and push our wheelchairs. These are the kids who will be asked to keep our economy, our society, and our democracy going strong. These are the kids who depend on us today and the kids on whom we will depend tomorrow.

Making a big federal commitment to education is a way of saying that one of the main jobs of government is to ensure that no one gets left behind. And we need to make that commitment in schools, in the workplace, on farms, in cities, in communities of color—everywhere.

For decades, almost all Republicans (and a fair share of Democrats) have recited the same old "government is bad/stupid/wasteful" mantra, and they have proposed "fixing" government by cutting taxes for rich people and starving government services. Over time, that strategy has bitten us, hard, in the rear end.

America was once a country that prided itself on expanding opportunity. Yes, millions of people were discriminated against. Black people, Latinos, women, Native Americans, Muslims—it's a long list. Far too many people were denied the chance to compete on a level playing field. Even so, our faith in a vision of ourselves as stewards of a land of opportunity was grounded in an important truth. Back in the 1960s, kids had a 90 percent chance of doing better than their parents—90 percent, and that applied to *all* kids. Today, a kid's chance of doing better than his or her parents is about fifty-fifty. It's not simply that inequality is growing. It's that opportunity is shrinking.

This is all about our values. Do we think we'll build a stronger future by letting billionaires continue to grow their fortunes and pay lower tax rates than everyone else? Or do we think that scraping two cents on the dollar off the top of those fortunes and investing every penny of it in our children will be more productive? For me, the conclusion is obvious. It is smart, patriotic, and morally responsible to put that two cents toward our kids.

And if that makes Leon Cooperman burst into tears and rend his shirt and pull his hair, then that's just too bad.

This is about our future. I'm a teacher and a mother. Teachers and mothers spend their lives investing in the future. That's also a basic function of government, one that we have ignored for far too long.

It's time to take better care of this country we love. And it's time to take better care of each other.

# THREE

# A Planner

My first memory of my oldest brother is from the morning he left to join the Air Force. Don Reed was nineteen; I was three.

The memory is like a five-second home-movie fragment that plays in my head. It's 1953. We've driven to Oklahoma City, where he will report for duty. My mother and I are standing close together on a sidewalk, her full cotton skirt blowing around me. She's crying. He's halfway up some steps when he turns. Squinting in the blisteringly bright Oklahoma sun, his crooked grin makes it clear that he's ready for this adventure. He waves and gives us a quick wink. Then the memory is over.

For years, whenever Mother told that story, she always ended it the same way. After Don Reed left, she stood on the street sobbing. I looked up, patted her hand, and told her, "Don't worry, Mama. You still have me."

She also said she cried all the way home.

Don Reed was headed off to basic training at Lackland Air Force Base in San Antonio. Over the next twenty years, he was a part of my life as much by his absence as by his presence. Six days a week, my mother rushed to the mailbox to see if there was a letter from him—or later on, from my brother John or my brother David, after each of them went off to the military. The day's mail delivery was almost like a clock that organized our lives—there were the hours until the mail came and the hours after. If a letter did come, my mother was cheerful, quick to call my aunts or my grandmother to read it aloud. Her first words when Daddy walked in from work would be, "We got a letter from Don Reed today." When there was no letter, she would always say, "Maybe tomorrow."

Don Reed was dashing, a sharp dresser who used his newfound wealth as a pilot trainee to buy a black Ford convertible with a red leather interior. He also bought me my first pair of cowboy boots—yellow leather with green vines up the shafts. I still have those boots.

When I was six, Don Reed married Nancy, a tiny woman with jet-black hair and a feisty temper. She could play the piano by ear, and she, like Don Reed, loved clothes. Nancy was a swirl of bright colors, petticoats, and jewelry. She had tiny feet, and she always gave me the fanciest of her castoff high heels. I was particularly fond of a pair of patent-leather orange stilettos; they took my breath away. I paraded around in them for weeks, desperate to wear them to second grade. My mother said no, but that didn't stop me from believing that Don Reed had brought me a magical sister.

By my lights, Don Reed and Nancy led a charmed life. They wore beautiful clothes. They drove an awesome car. They went to dinners at the Officers Club. And, before long, they had two adorable little boys.

By the time I was eleven or twelve, I used to visit them for weeks at a time. They lived at Bergstrom Air Force Base in Austin, Texas, in a flat little ranch house that backed up to an enormous airstrip. Planes took off all day and all night. My job was to take care of the boys, which mostly meant hanging around the swimming pool on the base until we were all waterlogged. Nancy would sometimes take me to get my hair cut, and when it came time for me to go back to Oklahoma, she always found something wonderful in her closet that I could take home. I never cared a lot about clothes, but those trips to her closet made me feel very special.

For years, Don Reed's job was to fly B-52s loaded with nuclear weapons all around the world as part of America's Strategic Air Command.

There was talk of a job in the Pentagon, but he didn't have a college education, and, besides, he was a pilot through and through—he loved flying, not paperwork. Then the war in Vietnam heated up. For nearly six years, off and on, he flew B-52s in combat. He became a squadron leader, then a wing commander. A number of men under his command were killed; others were captured. He never talked much about his years in combat, but after they were over, his crooked smile seemed less assured.

By the late 1960s, life at home was no longer picture-perfect. Don Reed and Nancy lost their third child, a boy who was stillborn. They named him Benjamin and buried him in the family plot in Nancy's hometown.

Don Reed finished his career the way he started it—flying. The noise level in the cockpits was so high that toward the end he was nearly deaf and unable to pass his annual flight physical without help from a couple of sympathetic techs who would give him broad hints during his hearing tests. At thirty-nine he retired, ready to settle down and live full-time with Nancy and their two boys, both now teenagers.

Within a few months, he launched a small business customizing cars—stereos, pinstripes, sunroofs, whatever. He had to learn how to do the actual work, but he also had to teach himself how to run a business. When we got together for Thanksgiving that year, he was full of excited stories about managing payroll and inventory supply and customer service. His grin was contagious, and he seemed younger again.

Then Nancy got sick.

Don Reed called to say something was wrong and it was serious. He was taking her to the military hospital in San Antonio. It was 1981; Bruce and I were teaching in Austin, so we were only about an hour's drive away. We arrived right after she got the diagnosis—leukemia. We spent Christmas that year alternating between visits to the hospital and walks along the river that cuts through the center of San Antonio. Nancy died in January, with family close around her.

Don Reed buried her next to their baby.

My brother hung on until the boys made it through high school, and then he just sort of gave up. He'd lost interest in his business; eventually he closed it. I tried to engage him in various projects—a business in Austin, building a house for Mother and Daddy—but it was hard to hold his attention, and nothing came of it. He played more golf. He moved to Mexico where an informal group of military retirees had settled. He got married again but soon divorced. He went back and forth between Mexico and Oklahoma.

In time he married Judy, another American living in Mexico. Judy's children were grown, and she and Don Reed seemed to take good care of each other. They moved to Texas, then back to Oklahoma.

By the early 2000s, all three of my brothers were in Oklahoma, so we could hang out whenever I came to town. The four of us—Don Reed, John, David, and I—liked to go for Tex-Mex at Chileno's or hamburgers at Johnnie's Charcoal Broiler. Later Ray's Smokehouse in Norman became our go-to place. Bruce was usually with us, but he let my brothers have the floor. They would talk away entire evenings, telling funny stories about their cars, their dogs, and their many transgressions in high school.

But mostly Don Reed and I kept up by phone. We'd talk every few days, and the conversation often turned to politics. Don Reed was a Republican, through and through.

He grumbled that taxes were too high. I would tease back with mock amazement: "How do you expect the country to pay for jet fuel and military retirements?" He was always quick to say that military pay was too low and we ought to do better by our veterans.

He grumbled that he didn't like government. I would tease back: "But you worked for the federal government for twenty years and loved it!" I never persuaded him to think otherwise; for him, "government" was some faceless beast that had little to do with the Air Force he loved.

He grumbled that all politicians were crooks. After I became a senator, I would tease back: "That's your baby sister you're talking about, buster!" No, he always said, I was a senator, but definitely not a politician.

He grumbled that he despised "socialized medicine." And I would tease back: "You've had the best socialized medicine in the world since you were nineteen years old!" Somehow I don't think he ever associated that description with the military hospital in San Antonio and the ter-rific doctors who had cared for Nancy in her final days, and I never had the heart to push the point.

Over the course of hundreds of calls, we talked about pollution. (He hated it.) About debt, both personal and national. (He hated it.) About Russia. (He hated it.) We also talked about cars, dogs, and what bad boys all three of my brothers had been in high school. Every conversation ended the same way. "Love you, Sis." "Love you too, Brother."

By the time Don Reed was in his sixties, he watched Fox News every day—with the sound up loud. It was like the theme music to his life in retirement. In 2012, when I ran against one of Fox News' favorite senators, Scott Brown, Don Reed would sit in his living room in New-castle, Oklahoma, and follow the race—from the Fox News perspective. Months into the campaign, he was still a Republican and he still watched Fox, but he thought they lied about his sister. Funny how, according to my brother, Fox could be so truthful about everything else and lie about the one person he actually knew. Yeah, real funny.

In 2019, as the race for the Democratic nomination got underway, my Fox coverage got a little more, uh, intense. One of the network's hosts loudly proclaimed that if my plans were adopted, "American cit-izens will become serfs of the state." When I talked about protecting young Dreamers, I clearly wanted "to have illegal aliens come across this border and kill Americans." When I talked about breaking up Big Tech, I was on a "jihad" and I wanted to turn the United States into Cuba. Some commentators cut straight to the chase with the claim that I was "essen-tially a communist." Tucker Carlson added his own spin, claiming that I had gone corporate and wanted parents to raise their children "as good little servants of globalized market capitalism." (Wait, didn't Fox just declare that I was a communist?)

As the race went on, Don Reed started having some doubts about his favored news source. He admitted that once or twice he snuck over to CNN—God forbid—to watch a town hall or check out the coverage of a speech I was giving. He didn't approach a galactic epiphany, but there was obviously a disturbance in the Force.

In late January 2020, I called him from somewhere in Iowa. The Senate had been pinned down for the better part of that month with the Trump impeachment trial, which Don Reed seemed to have slept through. He was cranky when I spoke to him, and he sounded tired. Over the next week or so, he started feeling pretty sick. Pneumonia, the doctor said, and put him in the hospital in Norman. After a few days on antibiotics, Don Reed spent part of a phone call arguing with me about whether Trump had done anything wrong in pressuring the Ukrainian government for dirt on Joe Biden. I smiled. He was getting better.

Soon he wanted to go home—and Judy wanted him home. But by then Don Reed had been in bed for a long time and his lungs still weren't completely clear. His doctor suggested that he spend a couple of weeks in rehab, doing some exercises and getting his strength back. It was now late February, and I was crisscrossing the country in the lead-up to Super Tuesday. Don Reed and I talked a lot about what to do next. I was worried that he might still be too weak, that he might fall. I wanted him to be safe. Rehab sounded like a good plan. "Let the pros help you," I said. So he agreed to go to a rehab facility.

I relaxed. He began getting stronger, and before long he was finally ready to go home. On a Monday in early April the day was set—he would go home on Thursday. My brother David would pick him up.

Then the coronavirus found him.

On Tuesday Don Reed told me that someone had come in to test him. He wasn't worried because he was going home in two days. But the test came back positive. He still wasn't worried. He felt good and he didn't have any symptoms. Even so, the rehab facility wouldn't let him leave.

He couldn't leave, and no one could visit. Not Judy, not his brothers, not his sons or his sister. The phone was his lifeline to the world.

Now I started calling twice a day, morning and night. Day One after the test—all good. Day Two—all good. Day Three, Four, Five, Six, Seven—all good.

When I called on Day Eight, he said his doctor had been in and told him that maybe he'd already had the virus and "shaken it off." According to his doctor, lots of people had no symptoms, and he was doing great. Don Reed laughed. "I'm too tough. This thing isn't going to get me. I'm going home."

Day Nine—all good. Day Ten—all good.

Day Eleven—no answer when I called. So I phoned again later. And again after that.

Early the next morning, Judy called to say that the rehab center had rushed him to the hospital. She had received the news from a nurse in the hospital's intensive care unit, and then Judy had called me and the rest of the family to pass it along.

Now the news came in sharp bursts—from an overworked nurse, to a frightened wife, to me.

He's in trouble.

He won't make it through the night.

He's better.

He ate a little bit.

He's sitting up.

He's a charmer.

He's going to pull through.

He's failing again.

His fever is worse.

He's gone.

Don Reed died alone. No wife. No sons. No grandchildren or brothers or sister. I don't know if he was choking for air or if he was mercifully unconscious. I don't know if he was thirsty or cold or afraid. I just know I wasn't there to hold his hand and tell him I loved him.

## WHERE'S THE PLAN?

More than 450,000 Americans died from the coronavirus in the first year of the pandemic. More than 450,000 families were separated from a beloved relative the same way our family was separated from Don Reed. The coronavirus robbed us of the friends and family we loved, and it robbed us of our last time together.

This didn't have to happen. America didn't have to lose more people to the coronavirus in a single year than in eight Vietnam Wars put together. Multiple analyses project that if the United States had put plans in place that were as good—not better, just *as good*—as the plans in other countries, or if we had just followed the best of the state plans, then hundreds of thousands of deaths here at home could have been prevented. According to the researchers, even the most modest changes could have saved tens of thousands of lives.

Trump said that no one could see the virus coming. He lied. In 2017, shortly before he was sworn in, Trump's team was briefed about the possibility that a new virus could cause "the worst influenza pandemic since 1918." In 2018 and 2019, government officials and health experts warned him and his team about America's increasing vulnerability to a pandemic—but Trump went ahead with cuts that swept away any preparation for such an event.

Trump's lie was not borne of ignorance or misinformation. It was deliberate. By January 2020, information about a dangerous new virus in China began pouring in. In February, Trump himself told reporter Bob Woodward that the virus was "deadly." The CDC issued a warning, and intelligence agencies and the Department of Health and Human Services urged Trump to begin making plans. Epidemiologists around the world went on high alert. The World Health Organization declared an international public health emergency. And still Trump refused to act.

It didn't take a clairvoyant to know that we needed to get going. It just took a leader who could see the danger looming on the horizon and understand that we needed to move quickly to put a plan in place to deal with it.

In January 2020, as the presidential primary season was kicking into high gear and the impeachment trial pinned senators down in Washington, I put out a plan to address the coronavirus. The plan focused on preparation and training, on coordination and stockpiles, and mostly on getting our act together before the virus hit. Former vice president Biden was also sounding alarm bells, writing about the terrible risks posed by Trump's failure to develop a pandemic plan. And not long after the United States declared a health emergency, the World Health Organization issued its own plan for dealing with the crisis. As we learned more, I put out two more pandemic plans. It was so obvious that we needed blueprints and strategies for how to protect ourselves.

But Donald Trump and his administration didn't want to hear it—not any of it. In January, the president reassured America that the coronavirus was "totally under control" and that "it's going to be just fine." In February, even as he was privately telling Woodward that the virus was "deadly," he publicly promised that it would "disappear." In March, he said that the country would "be open for business—very soon—a lot sooner than three or four months," and that he was aiming for it to happen "by Easter." In April, he said COVID-19 "is going to go away." In May, he suggested coronavirus testing was "overrated."

There is so much we could have done early on. We could have increased testing, ramped up contact tracing capacity, collected better data, modified reimbursement rules, funded paid leave, helped provide childcare, and on and on and on. We could have stepped up manufacturing of masks and ventilators and stocked up on gowns and testing swabs. We could have set up plans for field hospitals and testing sites. We could have created emergency training for people to administer those tests, initiated contact tracing, and helped people in quarantine get food, medical care, and support. We could have set up new procedures for nursing homes and behavioral health centers. We could have strengthened domestic supply chains to make certain that we'd be prepared, no matter how hard the pandemic hit us.

And we could have done all of that quickly. A pandemic is like a fire. When it's small and isolated, it can be dealt with, but as it spreads and grows into a nationwide threat, it becomes a thousand times harder to manage. Delay and inaction allowed the virus to spread rapidly, and the resulting devastation cost us critical resources and precious lives.

On the day in April that my brother died, Donald Trump held a press conference and declared that he could "see the light at the end of the tunnel." He reassured Americans that "we have one of the lowest mortality rates in the world." He argued that our numbers were bad only because "we're already testing more, by far, than everybody else, every other country combined," so he really didn't need to come up with a plan. And his central complaint of the day? Because of the coronavirus, in some parts of America "you can't use golf courses."

Three months after that press conference, the number of COVID-19 deaths had more than doubled. The U.S. infection rate was ten times higher than in Europe or Asia. And Donald Trump still didn't have a plan—but at least he was back on the golf course.

My brother, who served in the military for twenty years, who made it through nearly six years of on-and-off combat in Vietnam, who survived the death of an infant son and a beloved wife, will forever be part of the coronavirus statistics. Even as I grieve, I am deep-down angry with a president who lacked the leadership, the courage, and the basic humanity to step up and develop a plan to deal with this crisis.

Plans matter. The pandemic was an unforgiving reminder that the difference between a good plan and no plan may be life or death on a massive scale. But plans are more. Plans are the essential means by which we chart a course for our collective future. How do we want our economy to function over the next ten years? How can America be a better, stronger democracy a generation from now? How do we assess the threats to our survival? And how do we not just survive but prosper?

When I was running for president, I often wondered why other candidates didn't have detailed plans for the future. It seems so obvious to me that plans are critical to our well-being. Maybe the more puzzling question is why people running for office so rarely campaign on plans—and why that's apparently okay with millions of voters.

When we're talking about government, I don't want to oversell planning. After all, there is dumb planning and misinformed planning and just plain bad planning. And everyone understands that government, just like people, makes mistakes, and sometimes those mistakes cost lives. Planning alone won't save us. But those failures and risks are precisely why our leaders should lay out their plans for all the world to see. The plans explain what problems a leader sees and how these problems can be solved.

Whether the future looks scary or bright, plans are hopes made practical. They reassure people that there's a road map that will take them to a better place, and they give people a reason to join in the effort to get there.

## TO SAVE OURSELVES

I'm a lifelong planner. I was never the "I must account for every minute of my time" kind of planner. No, I was the "Wow, here's something cool and a little outside our reach that we could do and here's a plan for getting it done" kind of planner. The way I saw it, planning expanded my range of opportunities.

From the time I was a little girl, my daddy was my favorite plan partner. I'd come up with an idea and he'd gently say he wasn't sure that it was possible. Then I'd fill in the details and pitch the plan to him again. Usually I could persuade him to give it a try.

My second-grade teacher talked about how dull the yard outside her classroom was, so I organized parents to donate plants for some flower beds, then persuaded my daddy to dig up the ground and plant all those flowers and shrubs. By ninth grade I'd noticed how shabby our bathroom was, so I used my babysitting money to buy six rolls of wallpaper and persuaded Daddy that we could teach ourselves how to wallpaper. By my senior year in high school, the cracked plaster ceiling in the living room was becoming a real embarrassment, so I talked Daddy into helping me tear it down and staple up ceiling tiles.

Daddy didn't go along with every plan. He nixed the party I planned in seventh grade that would have involved digging a giant hole in the backyard and roasting a whole pig. (I still think that would have been a great party.) And sure, I enjoyed spontaneous fun as much as anybody. But planning opened up all kinds of adventures.

Years later, my children noticed that I loved nothing better than a good plan. They didn't always share my enthusiasm for planning, however.

Amelia, for example, was slow to wake up in the morning, while I was ready to go the minute my feet hit the floor. One day when she was a teenager, I overhead her talking on the phone in the next room, clearly sympathizing with a friend who seemed to be complaining about her mother. "Oh, that's awful," Amelia murmured. "Just terrible." I was feeling a little smug. How nice that Amelia's friends complained about their mothers to her. Yes, other mothers really could be a pain.

After a few more "un-huhs" and "hmms" of sympathy, Amelia pulled out a topper, one that was clearly intended to put her friend in her place by describing the horrors that she herself had endured. "I know that's rough, but listen to this. Every Saturday morning the first words my mom says to me are, 'Hi, sweetie. What are your plans for today?'" And then Amelia gave a deep groan that sounded as if she was trapped somewhere in the third or fourth circle of hell.

It's true that not everyone wants a plan for every situation—and certainly not sleepy-headed fourteen-year-olds on Saturday mornings. But I'm not talking about teenagers; I'm talking about how we run our country. I'm talking about threats to the survival of our nation and how we cope with an uncertain future. And yes, for that we need a strong, competent federal government to map out a lot of detailed plans.

Let's begin with the role of the federal government in making plans. One clue is right there in the preamble to the Constitution. We established this country "to provide for the common defence." (That's the original spelling.) Common defense has been a basic function of our government right from the get-go.

And what does that common defense actually cover? Most people who encounter this term probably think immediately of our military—troops, weapons, military bases. Some people might give it a second thought and also include our State Department and diplomatic corps, the people who serve as our eyes and ears abroad and help negotiate our alliances and disputes with foreign governments. And yes, both of those answers are right. Our military and our State Department do provide our common defense, and it is important that they receive the support they need to do their jobs.

But there's more. Broadly speaking, providing our common defense requires that we recognize the threats to our nation—the powerful threats that have the potential to destroy our country as surely as if North Korea hit us with nuclear weapons or Russia launched an all-out cyberattack.

In the twenty-first century, we are facing two other huge threats that require our government to provide us with a common defense: pandemics and climate change. Both could do at least as much damage as a major military attack, and both should spur urgent calls to make detailed and comprehensive plans.

The first of these threats has become terrifyingly obvious in the past year. Providing a common defense is—or should be—as much about protecting our citizens' health as it is about protecting us from terrorists or hostile foreign governments. It's about safeguarding our nation from the severe threat posed by a new coronavirus or Ebola or some other still-unknown virus or bacterium that could kill millions of people. It's about protecting ourselves from an outbreak that could trigger a collapse of the food chain or threaten our access to safe water and reliable electricity. It's about maintaining a vigilant defense against a raging disease that could bring our economy to its knees and kill people we love.

COVID-19 has been a wake-up call for millions of Americans, but the alarm bell still hasn't rung loudly enough. Even as I mourn my brother and watch the rising death toll, I know that this coronavirus is not the worst possible threat to our health and well-being. Think about the possibilities that lurk in the next pandemic. What if COVID-19 mutates into a different disease next year or the year after, and the death rate is ten times higher? What if the next respiratory virus attacks children and leaves them impaired for life? What if the next illness is waterborne and escapes our usual filtration systems so that every sip of water carries the risk of death? What happens to our economy, our people, and our nation if the next contagion is much deadlier? If we don't have a plan for the next pandemic, a life-altering catastrophe might provide tragic answers to these questions.

And then there is climate change. If our government can't provide a common defense against this most dire of threats, we may not *have* a government. I've been learning about and thinking about climate change for years, and during my campaign I discovered that I was far from alone.

## OUR COMMON SURVIVAL

I started running for president on the last day of 2018—New Year's Eve. Bruce, Bailey, and I stepped outside our house in Cambridge, met the cameras and reporters head-on, and suddenly we were locked in for a ride on the presidential roller coaster. Our team had produced a four-and-a-half-minute video in which I outlined the economic pressure on families, described the Black/white wealth gap, and called out the attack on America's middle class by bankers, insurance companies, oil companies, and other giant corporations. My main point was that I believed we had a chance to build an America that works for everyone. We worked on that video for a long time, and when I saw the nearly complete version for the first time, I teared up. The video said exactly what I wanted to say, and when I later learned that it had been viewed almost six million times, I felt glad to be in the race no matter what lay ahead.

That night, I got a small taste of what lay ahead. A few hours after announcing my run, I had recorded a short Instagram Live during which I wished people a happy new year and had a couple of sips of beer. Fox News didn't say much about the issues I raised in the four-and-a-half-minute video that I'd put out earlier that day, or the fact that I had specifically called them out for their contributions to an echo chamber of lies. Nope. They thought the image of me drinking a beer was the major news story. They were sure it was fake, and the proof was how "awkward" I was. Huh, I'd never thought about the way I drink beer. But Fox ran numerous stories about this earthshaking moment and was still talking about it a year later.

As insulting as Fox tried to be, their nasty stories actually made me smile because I realized that their news team must believe that I had a real shot at winning the nomination. In fact, after I saw their first round of attacks, I went to the fridge and took out another Michelob Ultra to celebrate.

After the presidential announcement, I didn't stay in Cambridge long. Four days later I was on a plane to Iowa, ready to start the marathon of town halls. I held town halls in school gyms and movie theaters. In big restaurants and recreation centers. In churches and fire stations. As winter rolled into spring and then summer, the town halls sometimes moved outside. I spoke to people in backyards, farms, town squares, and parking lots, often two or three times a day. Over the fourteen months of my campaign, I held more than two hundred town halls.

All the candidates for president did some version of town halls. Some spoke, shook a few hands, and then left. Others permitted prescreened people to ask prescreened questions. I usually spoke for twenty or thirty minutes, then took questions from the people who had shown up. Everyone got a ticket on the way in, and after I spoke, we drew tickets out of a basket. If someone's ticket was drawn, they could ask me whatever they wanted.

Sometimes the questions were a little offbeat. What are the implications of abandoning the gold standard? (We did that fifty years ago—seems like it worked out okay.) What are the chances of passing an improved Voting Rights Act this year? (As long as Mitch McConnell is the Senate's majority leader, the words "snowball" and "hell" come to mind.) What kind of vice president would I want—someone like Mike Pence, who looks adoringly at Donald Trump whenever he speaks? (I already have a dog.)

Because the tickets were drawn randomly and because some parents or grandparents undoubtedly passed their tickets to youngsters, a fair number of children got a chance to ask questions.

I remember a lot of those questions, and one I particularly recall was asked at a town hall in Iowa City in December 2019. We had a big crowd at the Iowa Memorial Union hall. A little girl who was maybe nine or so stood up to ask a question. She had wavy brown hair that was sensibly pushed behind her ears, a navy blue T-shirt and blue jeans, and a shy smile. The hall's main area was packed with hundreds of people, and more were standing against the wall. As the little girl started to speak, the adults looked her way, craning their necks to locate her. A television camera swung in her direction.

She stood straight, leaned into her microphone, and began. "I am

Eleanor and my nickname is Bear." The adults started to smile and chuckle, but Bear didn't miss a beat. "My question is, When you become president, are you going to stop global warming?" No beating around the bush, no sugarcoating. Bear wanted a commitment. Bear wanted to live.

I had been asked this question before, sometimes by kids and sometimes by grown-ups. But practice didn't make it any easier. It was really hard to stand on a stage and look straight at a nine-year-old who was worried about survival. Bear didn't giggle or look for the camera. She was calm and determined, and she seemed to fully understand the magnitude of the question she was asking. She searched my face for an answer, just as so many other children had done.

In a blink, I thought about how the cumulative impact of climate change will cause terrible damage to the earth by the 2030s, right around the time Bear goes off to college. It'll be even worse by the 2040s, about the time Bear starts a family. And it'll be far worse by the 2050s, when Bear herself may have a child who is nine years old.

I did my best to answer Bear's question, but each time another youngster asked me about climate change, I felt a familiar pain just under my ribs. Pain that a child was so worried about the future. Pain that I didn't know how to tell them that the adults have made a huge mess of things. Pain that everything we once took for granted—clear air, clean water, magnificent forests, thriving oceans—could all be gone before those children were my age. And if these essential features of our planet are lost, what will happen to human civilization?

Children like Bear are right to worry. We're currently on a path that could lead temperatures on Earth to rise over the next fifty years more than they rose over the last six thousand years. By the end of the century, hot zones like the Sahara Desert that currently cover 1 percent of the earth may cover almost 20 percent. Scientists believe that in some places, spending even a few hours outside "will result in death even for the fittest of humans."

Those living near the oceans will also be under severe threat. The rise in sea levels and ocean temperatures already puts millions of people at risk for chronic flooding and harsher storms. I've spent time in Massachusetts towns like Scituate and Marshfield that often flood during storms, and now these towns must respond to flood maps laying out the current risks and predictions that significant areas will be permanently underwater within a few decades. Scientists predict that by 2100, sea levels will be at least four feet higher, leaving a large amount of our coastal land permanently underwater. Food supplies will be disrupted, millions of people will migrate from place to place looking for livable land, and chaos will follow.

Climate change threatens the survival of every human being on the globe. So when we're thinking about how our government can provide for the common defense—or, more immediately, when we're thinking about the world Bear will inherit—we should be thinking about how we can do everything possible to prevent the destruction of our home planet. And that takes hard-core, no-more-time-to-waste, get-on-it-*right-now* planning.

Our nation faces enormous threats, and we need to respond to these threats with detailed, far-reaching plans. If it would help, I'd shout it from the rooftop, paint it on the side of a building, and have it tattooed on my arm: MAKE A PLAN! The action we need to take goes way past lobbying or politics or even elections. We need a government that provides for the common defense by developing comprehensive plans that will keep our children and their children safe.

## WHY DON'T WE HAVE A CLIMATE PLAN?

Bear and the other children weren't the only ones who asked me about climate change. Plenty of adults also asked me what I planned to do about the ongoing devastation of our planet. Once the questioner finished, I nearly always started my answer the same way. After a brief pause, I told the audience that I was about to say something really controversial (sort of the verbal equivalent of a drumroll). Drawing it out for a moment, I said, "Please, everybody, get set for this shocking announcement. Sit if you can, hold tight to a neighbor if you can't. Here it comes . . .

"I believe in science."

Okay, it was a shtick, but I kept doing it because everyone laughed—and then, after a few seconds, applauded. People got it.

Jokes aside, my point was deadly serious. Science is about reality, and plans are how we influence reality. Moreover, the absence of a climate plan is not an accident. Our collective failure to put an effective climate plan in place is the consequence of a deliberate strategy by corporations that make obscene profits year after year, in part because they operate without reasonable constraints. And the absence of a climate plan is, at heart, a story about corruption.

By the early 1980s, we basically knew that climate change posed an existential threat. In those days we called it global warming, and although the specific timelines and other supporting data weren't as well filled in as they are now, scientists already understood that if we continued to pump billions of tons of carbon into our atmosphere we would destroy life on our planet. The public also had a growing sense of the danger: By the end of the decade, most Americans wanted more environmental regulation, and, by a ratio of 18 to 1, we believed our government was spending too little to protect the environment. During George H. W. Bush's campaign for president in 1988, he talked often about global warming and the need to protect the environment, promising that he would counter the "greenhouse effect" with the "White House effect."

And yet, thirty years later, we still have no coherent climate plan. No National Climate Action Plan. No Get to Zero Emissions by 2030 Plan. No Save Our Planet Plan.

So what happened?

The fossil fuel industry happened. By the early '90s, fossil fuel executives and their biggest investors had figured out that if the federal government took on climate change, they stood to lose a lot of money. They knew that if Americans continued to believe in science—in particular, the science of climate change—they would demand drastic action. Coal, oil, and natural gas executives also knew that such action would cost them dearly, perhaps even bankrupt their companies. The industry could continue to fight on the policy front, arguing that the federal government should not shut down polluting plants, not pass a carbon tax, and not require companies to clean up their toxic spills—but they were losing. For every policy the fossil fuel industry executives opposed because it would cost them money, they had to respond to people who asked, "Okay, if this approach doesn't work, then what *is* your plan to solve the climate problem?"

To counter this dangerous threat, the industry devised a new strategy. Instead of fighting policy, it would fight science. Industry executives claimed that there was no such thing as climate change, that science showed a lot of mixed results, that global warming was natural, and that even scientists were divided over whether there really was a climate problem. In other words, they created doubt.

An outside observer might have concluded that fighting the science would be impossible. After all, climate science was by then solidly established. Data had been piling up for years. Scientists all around the globe were running a wide range of tests, studies were being conducted by the thousands, and projections were getting more and more accurate. Researchers demonstrated that climate change would have multiple effects—on the atmosphere, oceans, polar ice caps, rain forests, deserts, and on and on. Kids began learning about climate science in elementary school, and the media regularly ran articles about the threat posed by increased carbon in the atmosphere.

But fossil fuel executives proved that they were just as determined and just as innovative when attacking science as they were when pumping more carbon out of the earth. In short order, they built a climate denial machine. They spent billions of dollars and established more than a hundred loosely related organizations and think tanks employing thousands of people dedicated to undermining Americans' understanding of climate science. They even pulled in the national Chamber of Commerce to front for them when filing lawsuits or mounting public relations campaigns that needed a little distance from the industry.

And what did they get for all that money?

They didn't change reality, but they changed public opinion. By the late 1990s, public support for environmental regulations had dropped significantly, fueled by growing skepticism about the reality of climate change. Over the next two decades climate denial became so politically popular among conservatives that in 2016, each of the dozen-plus Republican presidential candidates downplayed, questioned, or outright denied climate change—and then the denier in chief, Donald Trump, was elected president. One of Trump's first acts as president was to withdraw from the Paris Climate Agreement. Four years later, Republican senators were still "doubting" the threat posed by climate change. Senate candidate Tommy Tuberville explained, "There is one person that changes this climate in this country and that is God. OK?" He won his race in Alabama by 20 points.

Public opinion may have changed, but the science of climate change didn't. Thirty years after the fossil fuel industry began their campaign of doubt, the climate threat is not only more dangerous than ever, it's bearing down upon us with even greater speed than expected. Scientific consensus about the risks posed by climate change is now at 100 percent. Meanwhile, the fossil fuel industry bought thirty years of unimpeded growth, thirty years during which they continued to stride the earth, drilling and pumping and blasting their way to billions of dollars in profits. And they are still at it today.

Although public concerns about climate ebb and flow, what has changed in recent years is how politically polarized the issue has become. As one report put it, "Increases in climate change belief, concern, and prioritization among Democrats have been largely canceled out by concurrent declines among Republicans." Today, about one in five Americans is a climate denier, and those deniers are really dug in.

Climate action groups have battled back, and they deserve enormous respect and gratitude. But the thirty-year fight over *facts* has cost us precious time. While the industry was pumping out almost as much misinformation as fuel, stronger regulations weren't passed, cleanups were delayed, and green energy projects didn't move ahead nearly as quickly as they could have. And in just four years, the Trump administration rolled back 125 environmental regulations and turned a blind eye to who knows how many violations.

It didn't have to be this way. Today, Denmark produces almost half of its energy from wind, and Iceland is on the threshold of becoming the first 100 percent renewable-energy country in the world. While the United States fought over whether climate science data is fake and the whole idea of climate change is just a conspiracy dreamed up by liberals and communists, other countries were doing their part to save the planet from destruction.

Yes, we need a big idea like the Green New Deal. And we need a plan—in fact, we need a lot of plans to turn the Green New Deal into a reality. A plan to produce clean energy. A plan to clean up pollution and poison. A plan to regulate emissions. A plan to invest in new green technologies. And we need good people to implement those plans. Thankfully, the Biden administration has assembled an all-star team on climate, and God bless every one of them and everyone else who is out there fighting to save our planet.

But to make the kind of change we need and to make those changes as quickly as we need to, we must address the brick wall that has stopped aggressive climate action for years. To say it simply, we need to confront the corruption of our political system. This corruption has delivered untold profits to a handful of billionaires and corporations— and it may cost us our future. So when I say that we need a plan, I mean that it can't be a plan that has been shaped by the fossil fuel industry. It can't be a plan that has been neutered by politicians looking for campaign contributions. And it absolutely can't be a plan that is so broad and so vague that we end up arguing about scientific facts for another thirty years.

That's what a plan can do—it can lay out a road map for getting things done. It can also demonstrate whether a politician has the courage to take on the deniers and the money guys who will fight them. And in this singular case, we need a plan that can unrig a system that is literally threatening to destroy us.

We're running out of time, and we need that plan *now*.

## SHE HAS A PLAN FOR THAT

When I began thinking seriously about running for president, I talked about it with my family, of course. Even the grandchildren got into the conversation. Atticus had just turned eight, and he was most interested in whether I'd have my own campaign airplane like Donald Trump. (Sorry, no.)

Our kids—daughter Amelia, son Alex, and their families—all lived in Southern California. They were enthusiastic about my jumping in, but it was Alex who really surprised me. He announced that he and his wife, Elise, and their dog, Obie, had talked it over, and they were willing to turn their lives upside down during my race for president. The three of them would move to the East Coast for a year to help out. "We can keep Bailey when you and Dad are gone," Alex said. "We can cook when you're here and check on your house when you're not. This is an amazing undertaking, and we want to help."

So they packed up and moved to a house in Medford, Massachusetts, only a few miles from our place in Cambridge.

It was great having them nearby, but once the campaign started, I barely saw them. I was away for long stretches, either in Washington for my Senate work or on the road for an endless series of town halls.

I liked the town halls, but the travel was brutal. Every day was a sprint. Up early. Scrambling for food. Two or three events and long selfie lines. Time zone changes. Lots of press. A different place to sleep pretty much every night. Fortunately, I had a lot of help. A great team to set up the events and get me from here to there. Truly amazing people who worked from early in the morning to late at night to make sure that each event went off without a hitch and that I got fed and watered and sent off safely to the next stop. They were wonderful, but they weren't family. Bruce was tied down with full-time teaching, so he was with me only part of the time. My days were busy and full of people, but oddly lonely.

And then Alex surprised me again. When he realized how grueling my schedule was, he offered to travel with me as often as possible. He frequently came along when I went to Iowa or Nevada or New Hampshire or South Carolina. He was up every morning to take an early walk with me, and he was still there for a late dinner. In between, he helped load equipment onto trucks, worked the selfie lines, functioned as pinch hitter on security, and helped out wherever he was needed. Best of all, he sat in the front row at every town hall, laughed at all my jokes, and waved at people when I introduced him.

Alex was not only generous with his time and a really good sport; he also made real sacrifices. He set aside his life for weeks at a time, and he left Elise and Obie at home, the same way I'd left Bruce and Bailey at home. Elise, who never expected to live anywhere but in a mild coastal climate, bought her first pair of fuzzy earmuffs and cheerfully took up the tasks of shoveling snow and chipping ice. After the first snowstorm, Obie stepped outside and seemed to reach a perfectly understandable conclusion: "I think I'll wait until spring to pee." No question about it, running for office is a family affair.

I have some wonderful memories from all that time on the road with Alex. In late April 2019, for instance, a few months into my presidential bid, we made another swing through Nevada. By the time the sun came up one morning, Alex and I were already out walking. Surprise fact: The Las Vegas strip looks very different at seven a.m. than at eleven p.m.

We hadn't been home for a while. I was okay for clothes. I always carefully counted out exactly how many black camisoles, pants, undies, and sweaters I would need for each trip. (Did I mention that I'm a planner?) I was always the most efficient packer on our travel team, and I pulled around the smallest rolling suitcase. Now, since we were in Vegas, I got to wear the sandals I had brought, which were just right for showing off my dazzling, Democratic-blue toenails.

It was a Saturday, hot and bright—although I'm pretty sure it's always hot and bright in Vegas. We spent the morning with various local leaders, then headed to Bonanza High School, home of the Bengals. It's a big high school, built in the 1970s, and it looks a lot like the one I'd graduated from in the 1960s.

The town hall was in the cafeteria, which I loved. Instead of an auditorium and a stage, where I'd always be farther away from the audience, the big open cafeteria would allow us to do an "in the round," with me in the middle and chairs set up in concentric circles all around me. Yeah, someone was always looking at my backside—campaigning for office is no time to get self-conscious—but the good news was that I was never very far from anyone, even in a room with several hundred people. People could see each other, and that magnified the energy.

At the appointed hour, I was introduced, and I ran to the center of the cafeteria and picked up the microphone. And that's when I saw it: the first T-shirt that said WARREN HAS A PLAN FOR THAT.

Then I saw another. And another. And another.

I knew our creative campaign team had put out a new T-shirt, but until that day I hadn't seen it. After spotting several in the audience, I paused for a second and then leaned into the idea. I said it out loud: "Yeah, I have a plan for that!"

When I first decided to run for president, I knew what I wanted to fight for, and it could be summed up in just a few words: I wanted to make this country work not just for the rich and powerful but for everyone. That meant unrigging a rigged system, and every plan we put out headed in that direction. The wealth tax. The plan for childcare. And student loan debt relief. And climate action. And anti-corruption laws. And gun safety. And—okay, you get the point.

I really did have a lot of plans and that seemed right to me. If you decided to run for president and wanted to get a ton of things done, wouldn't you need a lot of plans? And they couldn't be wing-and-a-prayer plans. They had to be serious plans. Detailed plans. Plans with enough information that anyone could see the costs, the trade-offs, and the values that they embodied.

Sure, we need plans to keep our country safe. We desperately need plans to deal with pandemics, climate change, and terrorist threats. But we need more. We need plans to combat systemic racism. We need plans to expand opportunity for all our children. Plans for honoring our promises to tribal nations. Plans for rebuilding our State Department.

We also need plans to expand real opportunity. A lot of very successful people like to talk about how much their own efforts propelled their rise. They celebrate their hard work, independence, and determination. All the good words are undoubtedly true, although they're often more than a little self-serving. But sometimes a few of these very successful people make a surprising admission: they take just a minute to point out that all their work and diligent planning paid off thanks to decades of ambitious planning by our country. The massive, if often unexciting, plans executed by our government year after year have built an astonishingly strong foundation upon which tens of thousands of successful businesses have been built and tens of thousands of fortunes have been made.

In 1994, Jeff Bezos was just a smart guy with a big dream. He started Amazon in his garage, driving packages to the post office himself. Now Amazon employs 1.2 million people and is worth more than $1.5 trillion. No doubt Mr. Bezos worked hard and was creative and had the right idea at the right moment (and a nice $245,573 handout from his parents). But he also had something else going for him—the intelligent planning that America had collectively invested in for decades.

Here's how he describes Amazon's extraordinary rise.

It happened because we didn't have to do any of the heavy lifting. All of the heavy-lifting infrastructure was already in place for it. There was already a telecommunication network, which became the backbone of the internet. There was already a payment system—it was called the credit card. There was already a transportation network called the US Postal Service, and Royal Mail, and Deutsche Post, all over the world, that could deliver our packages.

That "heavy-lifting infrastructure" that Bezos relied on to build his business and his fortune made Amazon possible. And it wasn't only the communications network, the monetary system, and the postal system—he also relied on public roads and bridges that enabled his trucks to make deliveries, police and firefighter protection that kept his sprawling business safe, and a public education system that made it possible for him to hire employees who could read. Because of the enormous investments made by American taxpayers, Bezos was able to take his shot at creating a trillion-dollar company.

Or, to say it another way, Jeff Bezos didn't get rich on his own. In fact, nobody got rich on their own.

Jeff Bezos—just like everyone else in this country, rich or poor—counted on our government to come up with the plans that made it possible to expand opportunity. No matter who we are, we all need these plans.

We also need to commit ourselves to the *act* of planning. Planning makes our democracy work. When candidates stand up and say, "Here's what I think is wrong and here's how I plan to fix it," then voters have real choices. Plans give us the chance to voice our ambitions as a nation and show us the way to meet those ambitions. And as time goes on, plans allow us to hold elected officials accountable and stay on track as we make change.

We face a crisis of trust in this country. Tens of millions of Americans don't believe we can accomplish much of anything anymore. But the plans I developed during my campaign call out that lie—and they show that we can still dream big and do great things. Look at the plans, look at who they help, and look at how to pay for them. After a while, you may find that the plans provoke only one question: Why aren't we already doing all this?

The plans we put out also showed who has power and who doesn't. Collectively, my plans were built on the idea that in a democracy, the people can decide what gets done. Of course, that profound idea made some powerful people really nervous. Tech giants. Wall Street. Fox News. Billionaire donors. When the plans are specific enough and popular enough, the possibility of real change takes on new life.

So yeah, I knew these plans would make a lot of rich and powerful people ready to declare war on me because they understood that, if I won, their power would be diminished. I also believed these plans would give a lot more people hope that our country could change. And that trade-off was just fine with me.

## PLANNING CREATES TRANSPARENCY

President Obama believed in plans, and he put a lot of political muscle behind a plan to expand health-care coverage for millions of people. Once the Affordable Care Act passed, people without insurance could get covered, and people with insurance got better coverage. It was no longer legal to cancel someone's insurance after they got sick. People who were laid off or divorced had access to health insurance. Babies were covered from birth. People with preexisting conditions couldn't be discriminated against. Kids were covered on their parents' policies until they were twenty-six. Lots of good protection.

It is hard to overstate the importance of the ACA. But it is also hard to overstate how much remains to be done.

Even with all the good the ACA does, tens of millions of people still don't have health-care coverage, and millions more have learned the hard way that their coverage is too thin or the price is way more than they can afford. Even before the pandemic, 41 percent of Americans— that's seventy-two million people—were trying to pay off old medical bills, and 42 percent were struggling to keep up with the cost of their prescription drugs. In 2019, one out of four people failed to get the medical care they needed because they simply couldn't afford it. And when the pandemic hit, massive layoffs meant loss of insurance coverage for millions more people—just when they needed it most.

The evidence of the stress that medical debt puts on families is all around us. Take a look, for instance, at GoFundMe.com. This is a crowdsourcing platform where people ask friends, neighbors, workmates, and strangers for money. Originally set up to fund "life events," the first-listed item for GoFundMe campaigns is now "medical." Each year, more than 250,000 people turn to the website for help with medical expenses, raising more than $650 million. GoFundMe helpfully breaks down the asks by category—cancer, leukemia, lymphoma, and so on. The stories are truly heart-wrenching. Even the headlines make me tear up. "Help Baby Zoe Fight Cancer." "Help Michelle Defeat Leukemia." Each headline is accompanied by a picture of a precious baby, a hopeful teenage soccer player, a serious uniformed police officer, a beloved mom, a desperate family clinging to each other.

We are the richest nation on earth, and a quarter of a million of our kin are reduced to begging friends and strangers to help pay their medical bills. Morally and economically, this is flat-out *wrong*.

I have studied our country's health-care problem for a long time, and for years I said that I thought we should do three things: improve the Affordable Care Act; lower drug costs; and move toward full health-care coverage for everyone.

In January 2018, almost a year before I became a presidential candidate, I put out a plan that was designed to improve the ACA and help more people get the health care they needed without going broke. The central idea was that Congress should require insurance companies to meet the same standards as Medicare and Medicaid on costs, on coverage, on doctor networks, and on profits. If they didn't, I argued that the government should step in and offer a public alternative. I also focused on the current tricks and traps in health insurance plans and showed how we could stitch those up—much as the new consumer agency I'd launched had stopped many of the tricks and traps in mortgages and credit cards. Later that year, I fleshed out the second part of the plan, which would reduce the cost of prescription drugs, both by permitting Medicare to negotiate drug prices and by involving the federal government directly in issuing contracts to manufacture commonly used drugs when prices were out of control.

Yes, it was a complex plan with lots of parts. And, over time, I added more parts to it, some of them developed during my presidential campaign. A plan to deal with the high rates of maternal mortality among African American mothers. A plan to combat the opioid crisis. A plan to ensure access to mental health care.

And that's both the beauty and the beast of plans: when they are detailed, they force transparency into the debate. Good plans or bad plans, they all start with a set of facts—or at least the facts the planner is working with. Next they provide a statement of the problem, followed by a plan to fix it. But a complex problem usually means that a lot of different factors are in play, so a plan for solving the problem also introduces a lot of complexity.

During my campaign, I advanced dozens of plans, but in the fall of 2019 one in particular bubbled to the surface. Unsurprisingly, health care was a huge issue, and the health-care conversation was dominated by a fierce debate about Medicare for All. There were the "I'm all-in for single-payer right now" people, with Bernie Sanders leading the charge. There were the "Don't take away private health insurance" people, and pretty much all the other candidates were riding that train.

I have long believed, and I still believe, that a single-payer approach makes the most sense. So long as private insurance makes its money by collecting premiums and denying coverage, people—patients—are going to suffer. And so long as private insurance is sucking billions of dollars in profits out of our health-care system, costs will remain high and millions of people will find themselves without help at the very moment when a health crisis hits.

I'm also a realist. I know that getting from here to there—getting from two-thirds of all Americans relying on private insurance coverage to getting everyone automatically covered—will be tough. So I put together a three-part plan that built on my original plan from 2018. I proposed that we improve the Affordable Care Act, reduce prescription drug prices, and expand coverage to everyone by implementing Medicare for All. I also put together a proposal that both showed how to pay for a single-payer plan by increasing the wealth tax on billionaires to six cents for each dollar of assets over $1 billion. We could have full health-care coverage for everyone without raising taxes on middle-class families, and I set out a timeline for getting it done.

To me, that's what it means to be a serious candidate for president— you show your plans. When Donald Trump ran for president in 2016 claiming that he would replace the Affordable Care Act "with something beautiful," I thought he should be hounded every single day until he put out a plan—which he never did. When I decided to get in the race, I was ready to slug it out over every health-care issue on the table. I was eager to talk about how to reduce the cost of insulin and EpiPens. I was prepared to explain how to make unions whole by requiring employers switching to Medicare for All to put the now-eliminated cost of health benefits into higher salaries for union workers. I was happy to debate whether we should change our health-care system by taking a couple of big steps or a lot of small steps. And start to finish, I was ready to fight for the ultimate goal of getting universal coverage for all Americans.

Show your plans.


## BORROWING PLANS

In August 2019, almost all of the presidential campaigns took a little breather before heading into the fall sprint. Bruce and I decided to hike a portion of the Pacific Crest Trail, and at the tail end of our trip, we dropped down to Seattle and had lunch with Governor Jay Inslee and his wife, Trudi. I'd gotten to know the governor while we were both running for president, and I liked him. He had dropped out of the race a couple of weeks earlier, and since Bruce and I were in the general area, I thought it might be a good opportunity for a visit.

We met Jay and Trudi at a spot the governor had picked, a restaurant with a balcony that looked over the harbor. The view was truly extraordinary and the food was terrific. But I confess that I get cold pretty easily, and we were eating outside. The weather was damp and cool; the wind was picking up. I really needed a coat. But not the Inslees: they are sturdy folk. They just smiled and behaved as if everyone eats outside even when their fingers and toes are turning blue.

Cold yes, but the conversation was warm. All four of us—Jay, Trudi, Bruce, and I—talked about climate change. We'd barely get into one subject before we were jumping headlong into another. Ocean pollution. Clean energy. Recycling. Repurposing. Recharging. Beer. Goats in the Cascade Mountains. Salamanders on the Washington islands. The next Ice Age.

When Jay got into the 2020 presidential race, he set himself apart as the candidate determined to focus on climate change. He spoke about the topic with real conviction, and he could point to an impressive number of climate initiatives that he had put in place in his home state of Washington. Although every 2020 presidential candidate declared their eagerness to fight climate change, I thought the reason Inslee had real credibility on the subject was because of his detailed plans. The package of climate plans he put out during his campaign included a lot of good ideas about both regulation and investment, and he provided a thoughtful analysis of how the different pieces of his climate agenda would work together.

Shortly after he dropped out of the race, I'd called to ask if he would object if I picked up some of his climate plans and added them to my own. He was enthusiastic about the idea, and during our lunch he made a number of good suggestions about which issues I should focus on. With his blessing, I included much of his work in my own climate plans, and if I'd been elected I would have put many of his proposals high on my agenda.

The lesson here? Another benefit of running a race with a lot of plans is that you leave a legacy. Even if you don't win, someone else may pick up one of your plans and run with it.

In March 2020, a little more than six months after my lunch with Jay, it was my turn to pass the baton. I'd come in third on Super Tuesday, and I didn't see any way I could win the nomination, so I thanked my supporters, faced the reporters outside our house, kissed my husband, scratched Bailey's ears, and dropped out of the race.

Quitting was really tough. I had put heart and soul into a presidential campaign that had lasted for over a year. Volunteers and friends and family had all made huge sacrifices to make it happen. People who could barely afford it had pitched in $10 a month. Thousands of little girls had given me pinkie promises. And then one day it was over. Losing is hard.

But good things can come even from a losing campaign. About a week after I dropped out, I got a call from Joe Biden. He had already called when I'd ended my campaign, but this time he wanted to talk policies.

After a couple of minutes of casual conversation, he abruptly said, "Elizabeth, I really like your bankruptcy plan. Are you okay if I pick it up?"

Okay? Are you kidding? I was over the moon. After all, I'd been fighting for years to get more protection for families who go broke. These families had been overlooked in every presidential race and every administration. I had a bankruptcy plan, of course, but now another candidate—one of the final two—was saying he would pick up this ball and run with it.

True to his word, Joe made the announcement the next day. Later, a group of bankruptcy professors and economists, led by Adam Levitin at Georgetown and Bob Lawless at the University of Illinois, helped hammer out the details. By late summer, we had drafted the legislative language, and in late 2020 I introduced it in Congress. Predictably, Mitch McConnell refused to bring it up for a vote, but with Joe Biden now in the White House, bankruptcy reform is officially on the president's agenda.

Change—real change, not a pie-in-the-sky slogan that promises change—starts with a plan. Whether it's green manufacturing or canceling student loans or improving health-care coverage, bumper stickers won't get the job done. We need hard-core blueprints and strategies and maps. That's what a commitment to change is all about.

## LEARNING FROM PLANS

In the rough-and-tumble scrum that is politics, plans give a candidate a chance to learn—even if the lessons can be painful.

In the summer of 2019, right in the thick of campaigning across the country, I put out a plan for small farmers. I thought it was a pretty terrific plan, with lots of detail about how to break up Big Agriculture to give smaller farmers a chance to compete. I argued for reversing decades of farm subsidies and moving instead to a supply management system similar to the one we used during the Great Depression. Because I was developing a new plan in an area in which I didn't have a lot of experience, I talked to a lot of experts and studied hard, learning about the danger posed by fencerow-to-fencerow planting, the persistence of agricultural overproduction, and the need for a right to repair for farm equipment. Along the way, I developed a pretty good understanding of the terrible stress experienced by small farmers. Half of independent farmers lose money every year, while the tens of billions of dollars U.S. taxpayers spend on farm subsidies goes mostly to giant agriculture corporations—also known as Big Ag.

After all my research, I thought I had this. So we put out a plan.

Then I heard from a group of Black farmers. My farm plan had included sections about discrimination and access, but I soon learned that I didn't know the half of it. I'd failed to understand the long-standing practices that had cost many of these farmers their land. I also knew far too little about the systemic—and ongoing—discrimination carried out by the Department of Agriculture.

The farmers wanted to talk, so I met with them and listened and asked a lot of questions. They told me stories about land theft that went back generations. They spoke eloquently about the struggles they endured every day. These were men who had worked the land all their lives, and they had seen firsthand how our government routinely undermined them and the farmers who looked like them. They didn't raise their voices, but a lifetime of hard experiences had sharpened their determination to be heard. In no uncertain terms, they schooled me on what I'd failed to understand.

They also had some really good policy ideas, layered with the kinds of details that only someone who has lived with a complicated problem can provide. I put their work to good use. In the end, I met some really good people, I learned a lot, and I put out another plan—the first comprehensive plan to address the issues facing Black farmers. And not long after my presidential campaign ended, Senator Cory Booker introduced a groundbreaking plan to begin providing justice for these farmers. I'm a proud cosponsor of the legislation, and I'm glad that we put some of the groundwork in place for this plan. This is yet another way we make change.

I love seeing good ideas build on each other. Just as I borrowed from Jay Inslee, I also borrowed from another fellow candidate—Julián Castro. I had known Julián back when he was secretary of housing and urban development in the Obama administration. He'd been a strong advocate for affordable housing, and I was impressed by his unwavering commitment to public service. When he ran for president, he put out one innovative plan after another. He spurred me on to approach areas that I hadn't dipped into. After he dropped out of the race in January 2020, he was one of my favorite people to borrow ideas from.

Julián had been the first to put out a disability plan, so we asked for his help. We looped in the people he had talked with, but because we had come to the issue later, we had the chance to build on those ideas further, asking people from multiple disability communities to help us think through a plan. The response was overwhelming. People volunteered hundreds of hours, discussing with each other and with us the wide-ranging problems facing people with various disabilities. The result was a much more comprehensive disability plan that, I hope, will serve as a basis for the next version of the Americans with Disabilities Act.

That's another part of what plans should be about. First, we highlight a problem and try out ideas for solutions. Then we test and criticize, borrow and improve. In the end, we bring people together in a concerted and collaborative effort to move our nation's plans and policies to a better place.

## CREATING TARGETS

For all my cheerleading, I realize that there are some powerful downsides to having a plan. I love developing a plan and love it even more when I meet new people and learn how to make a good plan that much better. But it can be risky to learn on the run, particularly if some of that learning is happening in public. Plans force us to make choices, but they also create targets—which we then have to defend.

One of the most obvious choices our nation makes is where we spend our money. Whenever I described the two-cent wealth tax, I also talked about how I wanted to spend the revenue the new tax would create. Child-care, universal pre-K, K–12 support, free college, money for HBCUs, and student loan debt cancellation—I knew how much all that would cost, and I explained how we would pay for it. But by providing so much detail I was also making a larger point: policy decisions are about choices. I couldn't put my great plan to build more housing units in the two-cent wealth tax bucket because there wasn't enough money. For that, I had to find another source of revenue or admit that the cost would have to be added to the national debt. Real, worked-out plans highlight choices.

Think for a moment about the federal budget. It, too, is a plan—an exceptionally large and detailed one—and it, too, is about choices. The Center on Budget and Policy Priorities is a well-respected think tank that provides nonpartisan analysis of how and where the federal government spends money. CBPP describes the big areas of public spending— defense, Social Security, Medicare and Medicaid, and what they call the safety net programs (food stamps, housing subsidies, etc.). The center does a deep dive into subcategories, like transportation and education. They even cover interest on the federal debt. But they don't have categories for public health or environmental planning and enforcement. What we spend on public health and environmental regulation is just too small to notice in the sprawling federal budget—in effect, it's not much bigger than a rounding error.

So, for example, the 2020 federal budget for the Department of Defense is $738 billion. Homeland Security soaked up $47.7 billion; the State Department got $41 billion. By comparison, the appropriation for the Centers for Disease Control and Prevention in 2020 was $7.7 billion. The federal budget for planning and enforcing our environmental regulations was $9.4 billion. In other words, for every dollar it spends on defense, the federal government spends a little over two cents on public health and protecting the earth combined.

It's not like the slack gets picked up by the states. In fact, state spending is even more anemic. The budget cuts following the 2008 Great Recession closed public health programs across the country; a dozen years later, funding levels that were inadequate before the cuts still haven't recovered. And in recent years, more than half of states have cut their environmental budgets as well.

I realize that battleships and troops cost a lot of money. But testing labs and trained nurses also cost a lot of money. I know that designing and developing the latest weapons is really expensive. But researching and tracking pathogens that could cause the next pandemic is also expensive. Just about everything the federal government aims to achieve comes with a hefty price tag. Real plans, with the price tags attached, force us to confront these costs. These price tags also force us to think about revenues and tax policies.

In November 2019, the *New York Times* ran an article titled "How Would Elizabeth Warren Pay for Her Sweeping Policy Plans?" The paper put together a very fancy online graphic to show how much each of my plans would cost. Piece by piece, the *Times* added up the cost of childcare and all the investments I would make in educating our children, the cost of my plan to attack climate change, the costs of building more housing, increasing Social Security, and expanding health care. They added in the money I wanted to spend on things like rural broadband and election security. Alongside each expenditure, the *Times* noted how I would pay for it.

I thought it was a terrific article. I loved the graphic that showed what each plan would cost and what we'd have to do to pay for it. I loved seeing how each piece compared to all the others—how, for example, all my education plans from universal childcare to canceling student loans would require about the same amount of money as stabilizing Social Security and increasing individual payments by $200. Sure, I already knew all these numbers, but the graphs were another way to engage people to show them what was possible.

Then I got a dose of reality.

Not long after the article came out, I was talking with a former political consultant. His voice was full of concern. "I was really sorry to see the hit piece on you in the *Times*."

My stomach lurched and my breath quickened. Was there something new in the *Times*? What could it be? Had I said something really stupid? Had some person I didn't know claimed to be my high school confidant and revealed my darkest secrets? After eleven months on the presidential campaign trail, it was amazing how fast my brain could invent different kinds of terrible news.

ME: (I wasn't sure I wanted to hear the answer, but I asked anyway.) What hit piece?

SENIOR SMART PERSON: The piece on how expensive all your plans are.

ME: Wait, what?

SENIOR SMART PERSON: It's really a shame. I mean, nobody wants to hear about tax increases or how much stuff costs. This is a killer.

A dozen possible responses immediately came to mind. I could have told him that we're already spending more money on health care than we'd spend on my Medicare-for-All plan—at the moment, we're just making families pay for it on their own. I could have said that nearly everything I had proposed, from providing childcare to increasing Social Security, is really popular and can be done without costing 98 percent of America a single penny. But why bother? He'd already tagged me with the two most dreaded words in Washington—"tax increases"—and nothing I could have said would have changed his mind about the political viability of my plans.

That conversation was the final straw for me. Ever since, I haven't hesitated to make the case that it's long past time to shake off this old notion that all tax increases are bad. Pretty much every time I proposed a major new tax like the wealth tax or the corporate profits tax, the political establishment would gasp, take to their fainting couches, and say that it was a dreadful idea. To bolster their pronouncements, they would immediately commission a bunch of polls, convinced the polling would confirm the unpopularity of the idea. Then the polls would say the idea of a tax increase on billionaires or giant corporations was widely popular. But the political establishment types never seemed to reach the obvious conclusion that the right kinds of tax increases were both economically responsible and politically possible.

A wealth tax is extremely popular. A minimum tax on giant

corporations is extremely popular. Closing up tax loopholes is extremely popular. For decades, Democrats running for office made promises, but most of these politicians didn't want to talk about how to pay for those promises. I made it my business to show people in my party that we could do more than talk about rolling back the Trump tax cuts. The popularity of these tax increases was not lost on the other candidates. By the time the primaries were over, Democrats across the board were finally talking about a range of plans to raise taxes on those at the top.

These plans—and the tax increases that would fund them—would make almost everyone in this country vastly better off. We would have better schools, better opportunities, less racial inequality, healthier lives, and more economic security. In fact, if I had a complaint about the *New York Times* piece, it would be that it failed to note one thing: If *every* plan and *every* revenue increase that I proposed were passed—every single one of them—then America would no longer be among the lowest-taxed countries of the thirty-seven most industrialized nations. Instead, we would join a cluster of countries in the middle. Or, to say it another way, if we collected taxes from rich people at a rate that is roughly equal to the average tax rate of other wealthy nations in the world, we could build an America that works better for nearly all our people.

## PLANS CREATE CHANGE

My team and I built our presidential campaign around plans. We had fun putting out T-shirts and coffee mugs that touted the plans, but the real power in these plans was that they showed exactly how we could dismantle an economic and political system that was working great for those at the top but leaving everyone else behind. Plans were the way I could make my central argument real—or, at least, how I could try.

I took these plans out to every corner of this country. I talked with people about the policies that were affecting life right where they lived— and talked about how we could make change together. I went to Colorado and Utah with a public lands plan that would put a stop to using our national treasure as a giveaway to mining and logging interests, and that would create a program modeled on the Civilian Conservation Corps of the 1930s to rebuild crumbling trails and clean up waste that polluters had left behind.

I went to West Virginia to roll out the nuts and bolts of a plan to attack the opioid crisis head-on. We met with a big group of people in a small, conservative town that had been flooded with opioids. I heard stories from many of these people about how they had lost relatives and friends to addiction, and people cheered when I talked about my plan for providing addiction services while also insisting on accountability for the executives who knowingly caused this problem.

I went to Indiana and Ohio to lay out plans for rebuilding manufacturing in heartland America. I went to Puerto Rico to talk about my plan to break the stranglehold that Wall Street vulture funds had on the island's economy and future. I traveled through the Mississippi Delta and Alabama to visit neighborhoods of crumbling housing and to talk about my plan for building more and better housing. I went to Long Island City, the site of a failed attempt to build a huge Amazon facility with huge taxpayer subsidies, to talk about my plan to break up Amazon, and to Austin, Texas, for SXSW, the big technology conference, to talk about breaking up Big Tech. I traveled to countless places and talked about my plans to anyone who would listen.

And here's the thing: people came to hear me out. Sometimes dozens. Sometimes thousands. They wanted to hear about my plans, and they came with questions and with challenges and, most of all, with hope.

Yes, in the end I lost. But ask me how sorry am I that I put out really strong plans on climate change? Or eliminating private prisons? Or debt relief for Puerto Rico? Or affordable housing?

How sorry am I that I ran for president and put out a boatload of plans?

Not. One. Bit.

In August 2019, we held a town hall in St. Paul, Minnesota, that drew about twelve thousand people. The selfie line was hours long, but one of the best moments came when a young man shook my hand and said that he wanted to thank me for all the plans—not any plan specifically, but all the plans together. He explained that for the second time he was running for a local office. When he'd run a few years earlier, he was told, "No one gives their plans. Just say generally what you like and what you hate, then talk about the Vikings." This time he said he was talking about plans. And whenever he got criticized, he would say, "If Elizabeth Warren can do it, so can I."

I never caught his name, so I don't know if he won or lost. But either way, I hope he feels the same way I do: putting out plans was one of the best things about running for office.

Over the course of fourteen months, our campaign put out eighty-one glorious, juicy, interesting, hard, important, imperfect plans. Plans that sparked a lot of debate and caused people to think long and hard about what's broken in our country and how to make our democracy work for everyone. Plans that people improved on and adopted. Plans that inspired people to join the campaign because they gave our supporters something to believe in. Plans that energized volunteers and raised the money to fuel a national campaign. Plans that were now on the shelf for future campaigns and future policy makers. Plans that gave us a vital framework within which to dream big and fight hard.

I lost, but I'm still smiling.

## THE FUTURE IS ON THE LINE

A big vision without a plan is just a fantasy. Exciting, but little more than a wisp that eventually blows away.

A plan is the first step on the journey to making a vision real.

When our founders came together to build a nation, they saw this new form of democratic government as a force for good. By pledging our loyalty to each other, we could provide for our common defense against enormous threats—threats that today include war, terrorism, pandemics, and environmental collapse. Long before he became a Broadway star, Alexander Hamilton explained that government—and only government—can create "the plans and measures by which the common safety is to be secured." In other words, it takes a government with a plan to keep us safe.

As COVID-19 has shown, we need plans that will ensure our health and safety. We can't wish away a virus. Nor can we forever ignore the cataclysmic impact of climate change or the threat of nuclear proliferation. We need careful plans that are patiently developed and refined, day by day, out of the spotlight. We need road-tested plans that are ready to roll out even when no one is sick, even when wildfires aren't raging and hurricanes aren't blowing in, even when terrorists and foreign dictators haven't pushed us to the brink of annihilation. If our country is to survive, we need comprehensive plans, thoughtful plans, creative plans— and we need them before disaster strikes.

A few days after Joe Biden was elected president, Bruce and I took Bailey for a walk, his last outing of the day. It was dark, and I was hunkered down against a cold November wind—knit cap, mask, gloves, puffer coat. Even so, a young woman spotted me. Well, actually she admitted that she recognized Bailey first and then figured that the humans must be Bruce and Elizabeth.

She was a student, also bundled up and out for a walk before hitting the books for another couple of hours. We chatted for a minute and took a selfie—with Bailey of course—and I was about to turn to go when she said, "Senator Warren? More plans. We need more plans."

I laughed. "Oh, eighty-one isn't enough?"

She looked at me quite seriously and said, "No, it's not. My whole future is on the line."

She was right. Her—and our—whole future is on the line. So yes, we need more plans.

# FOUR

# A Fighter

My mother used to give me advice—lots of advice. Stand up straight. Take off your glasses. Don't bite your fingernails. Don't wear yellow. Don't be smarter than boys. And don't fight so hard.

I don't bite my fingernails. I don't wear yellow. But the fight thing didn't quite work out.

Part of it is probably nature. There's a reason that as a twelve-year-old I sought out the combat of my school's debate team instead of the collaboration of the drama club (as most of the other girls had done). There's a reason that as a young mother I went to law school instead of veterinary school. There's a reason that as a law professor I didn't even consider running for elective office until it involved going to battle against a well-funded incumbent in a race with national implications.

And part of it is probably nurture. I scrambled to keep up with my three older brothers. I struggled mightily to pay for my college education because I couldn't ask my folks for money they didn't have. I spent a big part of my adult life pushing back against male professors and lawyers who talked to me as if I were an idiot (at least for the first few minutes). And, early on, I learned that no one gives you anything for free. If you really care about something, if you really want something, you have to fight for it.

By the time I entered into the political arena, that lesson had been burned deep into my brain. After the financial crash in 2008, I knew that our country's families needed a new watchdog agency to make sure the giant banks couldn't cheat them again. But even after a $700 billion bailout, the banks remained among the most powerful forces in Washington, and they weren't going to simply roll over and agree to a new agency. The choice was fight or give up. I fought.

In 2012, Massachusetts was represented by a popular Republican senator who was a favorite of Fox News and a darling of Wall Street. Democrats who already held office in Massachusetts looked at the possibility of running against him and saw that it would be a brutal fight. I had never run for public office and had no network of powerful supporters. Once again, the choice was fight or give up. I fought.

So, yeah. I own it. I'm a fighter.

## THE BILLIONAIRE CANDIDATE

In February 2020, I went to Las Vegas to fight.

The race for the Democratic nomination had been underway for more than a year, and the debate in Nevada was the ninth in a long series. It was held in the Paris, a hotel on the Las Vegas strip, complete with its own version of the Eiffel Tower, the Arc de Triomphe, and a 95,000-square-foot casino. We were assembled in a big theater with a fancy stage, bright lights, and lots of red, white, and blue. Notwithstanding the French theme, the night's vibe seemed to be Vegas Goes Patriotic.

NBC was handling the coverage. By then the field had narrowed: the first debate had been held almost eight months earlier, and back then, in June 2019, a total of twenty candidates had debated over two nights. Of that unwieldy group, only five now remained: Joe Biden, Bernie Sanders, Pete Buttigieg, Amy Klobuchar, and me. And tonight we had one new candidate: Mayor Michael Bloomberg.

While the five of us—plus a gaggle of other candidates—had spent endless months campaigning, traveling across the country, holding town halls, answering reporters' questions, and battling back and forth in debate after debate, Mayor Bloomberg had a different plan. He had skipped the months of meeting people face-to-face, hearing about their lives, and listening to them describe what worried them about our future—you know, the democracy part. After waiting until late November 2019 to announce his run, he had simply vaulted over the country's first four primaries in the apparent belief that he could score a lot of big victories on Super Tuesday in March and then begin his march to the nomination.

Over the space of a few months, Bloomberg spent nearly a billion dollars of his personal fortune in a massive effort to promote himself in states that would vote in later primaries. His campaign plan was all about television ads and carefully controlled events. He didn't answer queries from people who felt that it's their civic duty to attend candidate forums; he didn't lean in for anxious hugs from people who had lost their health insurance; he wouldn't talk to little kids who were worried that our planet was dying. Because he entered the race so late, he didn't have to put out the same financial disclosures as everyone else, and he also didn't make his taxes public, which nearly every other Democratic candidate did do. In fact, he didn't even expect to win the most votes; instead, it was widely reported that he planned to woo the party leaders and capture the nomination in some sort of brokered convention. He made no secret of his intention to let everyone else fight it out, then swoop in and pick up the nomination as the man who saved the country from Joe/Bernie/Elizabeth/Pete/Amy/anyone-not-Bloomberg.

This scheme was not a pipe dream. A billion dollars buys a lot of advertisements, a lot of consultants, a lot of social media, and a lot of outreach to influencers. In the political world, a billion dollars also buys a lot of attention from the party officials and the press covering the race. And Bloomberg undoubtedly hoped that a billion dollars would buy a lot of love.

The power of that billion dollars was lit up in flashing red lights. Since jumping into the race less than three months earlier, Bloomberg had rocketed from less than 1 percent in the polls to about 16 percent. By the time we took the debate stage in Las Vegas, he was just about tied with

Biden. Pundits hailed his strategy as "genius." Some were already predicting that he would walk away with the nomination. After making no real connection with voters, after enduring no real scrutiny of his record, a lot of people were certain that Bloomberg would carry the Democratic Party's flag and take on Donald Trump in the general election.

I thought this was totally, completely, absolutely wrong.

The influence of money in politics was already strangling our democracy, and Bloomberg threatened to finish the job. In my view, if the only way to successfully run for president was to be a billionaire or suck up to billionaires, then our whole democratic system would crumble. Handing over the nomination to one of the country's richest men—a guy who wasn't even making a pretense of campaigning—undermined our democracy. If it turned out that my party's nomination was for sale to the highest bidder, then we would be helping to build an America that would work even better for the billionaires and even worse for everyone else.

Besides, this particular billionaire candidate had some very serious problems: his poor treatment of women, his racist stop-and-frisk policy as mayor of New York, his decision around the time of the 2008 financial collapse to blame communities of color for predatory mortgage lending. He had a number of other ugly stains on his record, too. It was a long list.

Just before that night's debate began, I joined the other candidates and walked out onstage. My assigned spot was right next to Bloomberg's, and as I stood waving to the crowd, I took a quick look at the rows of seats right up front. In the twisted, made-for-television logic of the debates, spouses and significant others are given assigned seats next to each other, making them sitting ducks for the cameras trying to catch occasional reaction shots. I saw that Bruce was tucked in next to Diana Taylor, Bloomberg's longtime partner.

The lights were bright. The audience was settled in their seats. Once the cameras stopped clicking, the six of us hustled to our podiums and got ready for the debate to begin.

The first question from Lester Holt, one of the debate's moderators, was about how the eventual Democratic nominee could beat Trump.

Holt directed the question to Bernie, who listed several policy proposals. When Bernie finished, I tried to speak up, but Holt went straight to Bloomberg and asked him if Bernie could beat Trump. The mayor was ready. "I don't think there's any chance of the senator beating President Trump," he said, and then offered his reasons.

When Bloomberg wound down, Holt turned to me. "Senator Warren?"

This was the moment: it was time to challenge the billionaire and tell him why he didn't belong in this race. "I'd like to talk about who we're running against," I began. "A billionaire who calls women 'fat broads' and 'horse-faced lesbians.' And no, I'm not talking about Donald Trump. I'm talking about Mayor Bloomberg."

For a microsecond, the audience went completely silent; then it gasped. It was as if a thousand people simultaneously sucked in their breath and then coughed it out in a single bark.

I pushed forward.

"Democrats are not going to win if we have a nominee who has a history of hiding his tax returns, of harassing women, and of supporting racist policies like redlining and stop-and-frisk. Look, I'll support whoever the Democratic nominee is, but understand this: Democrats take a huge risk if we just substitute one arrogant billionaire for another."

There was some rumbling, and then the audience in the theater started to recover. Even though they had been warned ahead of time not to make any noise, people began to applaud—not everyone, but some. I heard the clapping, though of course I had no idea how the huge audience at home—a record-breaking nearly twenty million people, as it turned out—was responding. But I had laced up my gloves and I wasn't going to quit until I'd finished what I started.

The moderators directed a new round of how-to-win questions to other candidates, then came back to Bloomberg and asked him to comment on what I'd said. Instead of taking the opportunity to respond to my attack, he simply ignored everything I'd said about his treatment of women, stop-and-frisk, and redlining. He seemed to think that the objections I'd raised didn't deserve even a passing comment. Instead, he launched into a speech about why he was the party's best candidate. He used a lot more words, but he basically said that he'd win the nomination and the presidency because he was a great manager and he was rich.

The moderators then turned to the others onstage and asked questions about why they believed they could beat Donald Trump.

I was stunned. For an instant, I couldn't absorb what had just happened. I had just outlined three huge concerns about the candidate who, at that moment, had the most money, was running the most ads, and was shooting up in the polls—three concerns, any one of which should have disqualified him as the Democrats' candidate in 2020. And yet, nothing. No response. What I'd said had simply been swallowed up. The format of this televised forum allowed Bloomberg to ignore every charge I'd made, and apparently the moderators were fine with that. The debate would just roll on.

Like so many women in so many settings, I found myself wondering if he had even heard me.

Twice more over the next thirty-five minutes I looped back to Bloomberg. He still made no response.

At last one of the moderators asked Bloomberg about women's claims of a hostile work environment and a lawsuit against him for sexual harassment. Bloomberg again rolled out a canned answer. His company and his foundation employed lots of women, he said, and he took great pride in the fact that his company had received an award for being a great place to work.

He might as well have waved a red flag at me. After studiously ignoring everything I'd said about how he treated women, did he say he'd made mistakes and he was sorry? Nope—he said he was proud. Proud! He muzzled these women with nondisclosure agreements so they couldn't talk about their experiences in public, and then he said he took great pride in what he'd accomplished.

I was done with waiting for a moderator to call on me. Whether they called on me or not, I would simply jump in. I picked my moment and then, looking straight out at the audience, I said, "I hope you heard what his defense was. 'I've been nice to some women.' That just doesn't cut it. The mayor has to stand on his record. And what we need to know is exactly what's lurking out there. He has gotten some number of women—dozens, who knows?—to sign nondisclosure agreements both for sexual harassment and for gender discrimination in the workplace."

Then I turned directly to him. "So, Mr. Mayor, are you willing to release all of those women from those nondisclosure agreements, so we can hear their side of the story?"

By this point, I didn't wonder how the audience in the theater was responding. I didn't think about the millions of people watching at home. I didn't even care about any of the other candidates on that stage. I only cared about the women who were legally barred from telling their side of the story because Bloomberg had enough money and enough power and enough lawyers to shut them up—over and over and over.

Yes, the fifteenth richest man in America thought he knew exactly what he could get away with. He thought he could silence any woman who'd ever worked for him while he ran for the highest office in the land. He thought no one would seriously challenge him. He thought his money and power insulated him from ever having to talk about the unacceptable things he had done.

He was wrong.

I asked my question—or, more accurately, threw my punch—and this is how the fight played out:

BLOOMBERG: We have a very few nondisclosure agreements.

ME: How many is that?

BLOOMBERG: Let me finish.

ME: How many is that?

BLOOMBERG: None of them accuse me of doing anything, other than maybe they didn't like a joke I told. And let me just—and let me— there's agreements between two parties that wanted to keep it quiet and that's up to them. They signed those agreements, and we'll live with it.

ME: So, wait, when you say it is up to—I just want to be clear. 'Some' is how many? And—and when you—and when you say they signed the [agreements] and they wanted them, if they wish now to speak out and tell their side of the story about what it is they allege, that's now OK with you? You're releasing them on television tonight? Is that right?

BLOOMBERG: Senator . . .

ME: Is that right? Tonight?

BLOOMBERG: Senator, the company and somebody else, in this case—a man or a woman or it could be more than that, they decided when they made an agreement they wanted to keep it quiet for everybody's interests. They signed the agreements and that's what we're going to live with.

ME: I'm sorry. No, the question is . . .

BLOOMBERG: I heard your question.

ME: . . . are the women bound by being muzzled by you? And you could release them from that immediately. Because, understand, this is not just a question of the mayor's character. This is also a question about electability.

We are not going to beat Donald Trump with a man who has who-knows-how-many nondisclosure agreements and the drip, drip, drip of stories of women saying they have been harassed and discriminated against. That's not what we do as Democrats.

After the debate, Chris Matthews of MSNBC said he "never saw anything like it. It was the Roman Colosseum. It was boxing in the 1950s. . . . [Elizabeth Warren] kept punching the spot and it kept bleeding and bleeding. [Bloomberg] had no way to stop it."

Some people thought it was too brutal. But that's the thing about taking on someone whose wealth and power have insulated them for decades. The fight won't be pretty—and yes, there will be a lot of blood and teeth left on the floor.

Over the next couple of weeks, Bloomberg's poll numbers started dropping and his billion-dollar campaign went up in smoke. Thinking back on that no-holds-barred debate, I hoped some number of women who had been handcuffed with an NDA and some number of Black men who had been stopped, frisked, and thrown up against a wall believed there was just a little more justice in this world. Because that—calling the powerful to account—was what this fight was all about.

## MONEY MONEY MONEY

Ever since I entered the public arena, I've been fighting against a particularly powerful enemy: money. Battling the power of money in politics isn't the reason I got into politics, but it's been a constant theme from the start.

In the summer of 2011, Harry Reid, Chuck Schumer, and a handful of other people were encouraging me to run for the Senate. They thought I had a shot at knocking off the popular incumbent Republican in Massachusetts, but they also knew that I was a complete novice. I'd never been around political campaigns, and what I knew about running for office wouldn't fill a thimble, which made the idea of jumping into the race kind of hard to think about.

The senators made sure I met with people who knew how successful campaigns worked—meaning people who could teach a first-time candidate about the importance of money. My first in-the-weeds conversation about running for office was with a political Wise Man who started our talk with a hard truth: it costs a lot of money to run for the Senate. And for someone like me, who would be running against an incumbent who was very friendly with rich guys on Wall Street, the race would take even more money. That conversation went something like this:

ME: How much money?

WISE MAN: An amount you can raise.

ME: How much money?

WISE MAN: We can help you raise the money.

ME: How much money?

WISE MAN: Maybe $10 million.

ME: What! *Ten million dollars?*

WISE MAN: Well, maybe $20 million. Um, possibly $25 million. Not more than $30 million.

At that point, my heart quit racing. My breathing slowed down. The numbers were so astronomical, so completely absurd, that I didn't even need to think about this. I couldn't possibly raise that kind of money, so there was no point in even trying. I was not going to be a candidate for the United States Senate.

Turns out I was wrong on both counts. I did become a candidate for the Senate. And I could raise that kind of money.

That's the darkest part of the story: money really was a huge barrier. If I wanted to run for office, I would have to raise an unimaginable amount of money. If I couldn't do that, I couldn't run.

And there was only one way to raise lots of money: I would have to ask for it.

I hated asking for money. Hated it. Growing up, my family never talked about money—maybe because there were so many times that we didn't have any. When my daddy was "between jobs," my Uncle Travis would slip a few dollars to my mother and sometimes press a dollar bill into my hand. No one ever said a word about it. My daddy would have died before he'd admit that we needed help.

Eventually, while working with families struggling with bankruptcy, I had learned to talk about money—but that was someone else's money. Now I needed to ask for money for my own campaign.

It was embarrassing. Awkward. Icky.

And it wasn't just money. I needed many kinds of help—advice, public support, volunteers. I suspect that launching a rocket is a little like launching a campaign: it takes a lot of power just to get it started. So as soon as I decided to become a candidate, I sat down at my kitchen table and started calling people. Please help me. Please. By the third phone call, I realized that the people I was calling were evaluating whether to support this long-shot race. I began to feel a little like a used car that someone was circling—maybe they would drive me home, maybe not. The questions I got were humbling.

Are you going to change your hair/makeup/clothes/voice/look? (Thanks for such a helpful idea!)

What does your family look like? (My husband is handsome, and my dog is even handsomer.)

I don't give money to people who are going to lose. What do your polls look like? (I'm way behind, but I'm staying in this fight, and I need help now so I catch up and win.)

How can you beat him? The last woman lost. (Yeah, well, we're not all exactly the same.)

And after asking for help again and again and again, I got good at it.

I wasn't particularly clever, but I made clear in every call that I was running for the Senate because I truly believed we needed to make change in this country, and then I explained exactly what I thought those changes should be. I told everyone I called that my first contribution to change would be to oust a Republican senator, and I promised I would bust my tail to get it done.

At first, I really disliked sitting down to call people for help—and I particularly dreaded asking for money. But as the days rolled by, I realized that my team was rapidly outgrowing my kitchen. In fact, we had the beginnings of a real campaign organization. People were turning their lives upside down to help—moving, quitting jobs, uprooting families—and more help was coming in every day. To make the organization part of this campaign work—office space, campaign staff, supplies, and (eventually) advertising—we'd be racking up a lot of bills. I figured that if so many people were willing to come work for me, and if hundreds—thousands?—more would eventually volunteer to help me win, then I could damn well suck it up and ask people for advice, for support, and for money.

## WHO HAS INFLUENCE?

But from the beginning, we thought about other ways to fund our campaign. Not long after the political Wise Man came to see me in the summer of 2011, I also met with Adam Green and Stephanie Taylor, cofounders of the Progressive Change Campaign Committee, an organization dedicated to promoting candidates who will fight for big, bold ideas. Adam and Stephanie introduced me to a whole new way of thinking about a campaign.

Calls were heating up for me to run, but I still hadn't decided whether to take the plunge. Not only was I shell-shocked by the huge amount of money I would need to raise, I was also alarmed by the warnings about how personal and how ugly the race would be. The day Adam and Stephanie came to see me in Cambridge, classes at Harvard were about to start and I was preparing my first lessons, getting geared up to head back into the classroom. The idea of a Senate race seemed far off.

I made iced tea, and we sat on the back porch and talked about popular ideas such as expanding Social Security and strengthening banking regulations—progressive ideas that couldn't get a foothold in Washington. Adam and Stephanie had founded the PCCC two years earlier, and they had already been in several big battles, including the fights to expand health care and to establish the Consumer Financial Protection Bureau. They believed that progressives needed a way to counter big-dollar donations, and they'd become adept at building online support for progressive candidates with small donations.

Stephanie told me about the PCCC donors—people who gave $3 to advance an issue or support a candidate. We talked about how many of these folks lived on modest budgets and needed that $3. But they made a political contribution because they cared about the future of our nation and they wanted their voices to be heard. They believed that the PCCC family wanted someone like me to get in the race, and they would help me if I ran.

Online contributions might sound like a no-pressure, easy way to raise campaign money, but it sure didn't feel that way. For me, the pressure was more intense than talking to well-to-do donors. From that first conversation with Stephanie and Adam, I thought about the responsibility of taking $3 contributions from people who wanted to make change. I assumed these people needed that money, and if I was going to ask them to give it to me, then I needed to fight the most effective and tireless fight I possibly could. I knew I'd carry this kind of commitment with me for life, so I'd better deliver on it.

When I ran for office that year, there were three main models of funding a Senate race: 1) ask lots of rich people and PACs for money; 2) hope that a super PAC would support you; 3) finance the campaign with your own personal fortune. We decided to try a fourth model: launch an online small-dollar fundraising effort.

I wasn't the first candidate to rely on online fundraising. At the presidential level, both Howard Dean in 2004 and Barack Obama in 2008 had raised record amounts online, and during those races, MoveOn and other groups had also raised significant amounts of money in the form of small political contributions from supporters. But this was a Senate race, and these races hadn't yet attracted that kind of strong engagement.

Even so, our team began talking seriously about whether we could support a substantial part of our operations by asking people for help online. We started out tentatively, explaining who I was and why I was running, and then asking people if they could help. Within weeks an army of small online donors rode to my rescue. People pitched in $3 and more. People held bake sales and sold handmade jewelry. Kids offered their saved-up allowances. We asked supporters to vote online in a contest that would determine the slogan for our first T-shirt, and they picked THE BEST SENATOR MONEY CAN'T BUY. I still knew very little about politics or campaigns, but before long I started to believe that I might have what it takes to run against a guy who already had nearly $10 million in the bank.

By the time the 2012 race was over, 350,000 people had contributed to my campaign, more than any Senate campaign ever. More than half of our contributions were $25 or less. Collectively, small-dollar donations added up to $19 million, also a record at the time. And the Wise Man's estimate that I would need to raise "not more than $30 million"? I blew past that and eventually pulled in $42 million. And because the race went down to the wire, I needed every penny of it.

Our campaign used a mix of approaches—I made the phone calls and attended the fundraisers, but we also spent a lot of time and energy asking small donors for help. Those donations mattered hugely. Because I could spend less time on the phone asking for money, I could spend more time with voters across the state and more time talking with people about a government that worked just fine for those at the top, but not for everyone else.

I remain deeply grateful to the people who contributed to my first campaign. And I'm grateful to the people who volunteered, knocked on doors, and made phone calls—to everyone who helped power a campaign for someone who had never run for office before. All those people—nurses, musicians, retirees, lawyers, janitors, teachers, students, dancers, shop owners, and so many others—lifted me up and made me a better, stronger candidate.

Although I raised a good amount of money from small donors, I also followed the Wise Man's playbook and raised a lot of money from wealthy people. Many of them were contrarians, people who weren't looking out for themselves so much as they were fighting for others. People who said they hoped I would raise their taxes. People who said they wanted to be part of the fight to end childhood hunger or reduce our nuclear arsenal. People who had worked in finance and thought that better regulations were critical to the safety of our economy and our nation.

I was fortunate to receive support from these donors. But what worried me was that every other Senate candidate and every sitting senator had inevitably spent an enormous amount of time scooping up money from millionaires and billionaires and giant corporations, and I am certain that many of those donors—not all, but many—were *not* contrarians who were working against their own interests. Many were wealthy people who wanted the government to help make their lives just a little cushier, and they found a welcoming home with politicians who were ready to deliver. I have no doubt that the candidates who pocketed their money were grateful to these donors, and I'm equally sure that this gratitude gave the already rich and already powerful huge influence in Washington.

Over time, a democracy in which political campaigns are funded by a small number of people who can contribute a lot of money looks very different from a democracy in which campaigns are funded by a large number of people who can contribute only a modest amount of money. The former works extremely well for those at the top, while the latter at least has a chance of working well for everyone else.

The well-to-do have strong collective influence, but the true giants on the Political Money Playground are the ultrawealthy. Over the past decade, just ten people—ten donors and their spouses—have injected more than $1.1 billion into super PACs and other organizations that support their favored candidates. Ten families have a voice in Washington that drowns out millions of families who also need a government on their side.

Ever since my first campaign, I've focused on small-donor contributions. But corporations have taken a different tack, and they have exercised much of their power through secret channels. Although some have supported candidates directly, many more have hidden their political connections by washing their money through secretly funded nonprofits and industry trade associations. One study highlights the repellent truth that many so-called charitable donations by corporations are in fact designed to promote the donor's political agenda. The total amount of these donations is huge—over a billion dollars a year in 2014 alone— and they don't count as identified corporate political contributions. Of course, that calculation does not include the money corporate executives contribute themselves—and the checks they gather up from all the other executives in their company, and their spouses, and their buddies at the country club, and on and on.

Unions donate money to candidates, too, although every union official I've ever met makes clear that the union's money comes out of the hard-earned paychecks of their members. These leaders see it as their responsibility to make sure that union money helps candidates who they believe will help working people. Even with lots of people working together, the money unions contribute to campaigns doesn't hold a candle to the money contributed by businesses. In the 2018 elections, for example, for every $1,000 contributed to political campaigns by unions and worker groups, businesses contributed about $16,000. Citizen groups are in the fight as well: environmental groups, health-care advocacy groups, and many others have jumped into the political arena, supporting candidates who support their issues. Even so, the playing field remains wildly tilted, sloshing waves of money toward any candidate willing to become allied with a handful of corporate clients or help out a few billionaire investors.

Sure, I wish that campaigns were publicly financed, but they aren't. And until that changes, the people who do the funding matter. As long as the three groups funding campaigns are the wealthy, the wealthier, and the wealthiest, then—surprise!—the interests of the wealthy, the wealthier, and the wealthiest will be well tended to. Only when funding itself becomes more democratic will we have a much better chance of electing officials who are willing to pass a wealth tax or tackle climate change head-on.

By stitching together small-dollar contributions, we also have a chance to elevate activists who donate their energy and organizing skills and deep-down passion. I think, for example, of my friend Ady Barkan. Ady and I met in 2012 when he organized protests at Federal Reserve meetings to force the economic gurus to pay a little less attention to the well-being of Wall Street and a little more attention to the well-being of America's families. A brilliant advocate and organizer, Ady drew lots of new volunteers into the fight. When Ady was diagnosed in 2016 with ALS and his body began to fail him, he doubled down, traveling to several states even after the disease began to attack his mobility and he started to use a wheelchair. Undaunted by his disease, he later testified before Congress using computer-assisted speech. He waded into fights over tax cuts for the rich, Supreme Court nominations, and the Affordable Care Act. In doing so, he took on megabanks, health insurance giants, and billionaires.

I love Ady's courage and his willingness to jump into every David-versus-Goliath fight, but I want a level playing field so that Ady and all the other activists who put themselves on the line aren't constantly battling the well-funded armies representing billionaires and giant corporations. I want to beat back the influence of money—the driver of so much of the corruption of our government—so that Ady and the activists and the volunteers they pull in can win more fights.

When I ran for the Senate in 2012 and again in 2018, I talked constantly about corruption. At every town hall or local meet and greet, I tied the substantive issues to money. If someone asked about climate change, I explained how the billionaire Koch brothers made big political contributions, funded lobbying networks, and launched ad campaigns to block even the smallest effort to regulate carbon. If someone asked about gun safety, I noted that although the overwhelming majority of Americans want sensible gun regulations, the gun industry pours millions into groups like the National Rifle Association and ultimately has such a stranglehold on Congress that we can't pass even the most modest gun safety laws. If someone asked about health care, I talked about Big Pharma and insurance industry contributions and lobbying campaigns that paralyze our government and hobble our health-care system. And there are so many places we're falling behind. Among the ten highest-income countries in the world, our nation has the lowest life expectancy, the highest infant mortality rate, the highest HIV/AIDS rate, and the highest obesity rate—despite the fact that we spend about twice as much on health care as other countries. Why? The short answer is the corrupting influence of money in politics.

In both of my Senate campaigns, I argued that money is choking our democracy. And when I decided to run for president, I was determined to build on what I'd learned about the power of small-dollar donations. I wanted to launch a campaign that didn't rely on selling access to my time. I wanted my campaign to be about making democracy work for everyone—even in the way we funded the race.

## CHANGE WHAT'S POSSIBLE

As 2019 and the primary season got closer, rumors began flying about various people who were likely to run. There was a lot of talk about how a number of would-be candidates were already lining up corporate executives and industry lobbyists and their millionaire friends to help them out. By now I was no longer the naïve political newcomer: I understood that "help them out" was a polite way of saying "raise more money than anyone else in the race."

I carved out a different path. This was a Democrat-versus-Democrat primary, and I decided that during the primary season I would not hold a single big-dollar fundraiser. I would not make a single call to a rich person to ask for money. I would not take a dime from a PAC or a lobbyist. In short, I wouldn't sell access to my time. In this campaign, everyone would be welcome and my asks would be different. Please volunteer. Please make whatever contribution you can. Please be a part of a movement.

In February 2019, shortly after formally announcing my run for president, I stepped out publicly and swore off selling access to my time.

Time. That was the heart of it. The decision not to solicit money from high-dollar donors changed how I spent my time. True, a number of people contributed the legal maximum to my campaign, but I spent no time—not one minute—asking them for contributions, organizing special events for them, going to receptions at their homes, or providing special access of any kind. My team never scheduled me to fly to Aspen or San Francisco or Miami Beach so that I could meet with wealthy donors.

It also changed my focus. No one in my campaign ever asked if a policy might offend our generous friends from this industry or that business sector, but it was more than that. Because I didn't spend days on end attending fundraisers in rich enclaves, I had time to travel to Kermit, West Virginia, population 406, to talk with people about my opioid plan—and thus test-drive it with people who had been directly affected by the crisis. I had time to go to the Mississippi Delta to see crumbling homes and oversubscribed affordable housing firsthand, and talk with people about my plan for a major investment in housing. I had time to visit a national forest in Utah to meet with people who understood the need for better land management, a crucial component in the effort to fight climate change.

I also had time to work on plans—lots of plans. Plans that could improve our lives. Plans that could strengthen our communities. Plans that could help us build a better nation.

I didn't give up talking to donors, but this time I talked to a very different kind of supporter. Instead of going to fancy cocktail parties, I reached out to people directly. I wrote e-mails and tweets. I called people who contributed $3 or $5 or $10 to say thank you and ask what was on their minds. I talked to bartenders, sales clerks, and social workers. I called people while they were eating dinner, watching movies, or walking their dog. Once I spoke to a man while he was working on top of the Jefferson Memorial (he was repairing the roof). I loved those calls: they gave me a chance to thank some of the people who were willing to invest their hard-earned money in an effort to build a country that works for everyone.

But this wasn't just about how I wanted to run my own campaign. I also wanted to push our party to change its approach to campaigns. I was inspired by what Barack Obama had done in the 2008 presidential primaries: he'd said no to contributions from PACs and federal lobbyists. At the time, he was widely derided as naïve and unrealistic, but it was part of the reason he created a lot of energy—and that energy powered a hugely effective campaign. By 2020, every candidate in the Democratic primary made an up-front pledge not to accept money from corporate PACs.

Now we could take the next step. We could use the primary as a chance to make our party more appealing by fueling the candidates' campaigns with grassroots volunteers and small-dollar donations. If we did that, we would significantly strengthen our party in advance of the general election. We'd build grassroots organizations that would help our candidates up and down the ballot, which in turn would help us get Democrats elected in state houses and city elections. We'd build the kind of participation that would open up the electoral process and give more women and more people of color and more outsiders a chance to run campaigns and run for office themselves. A Democratic presidential primary that featured candidates who had built organizations that tapped into the energy of the people could carry us to victory in November 2020, help us win state and local elections, and thus set the stage for a generation of election wins.

I wanted the other Democratic candidates to give up high-dollar fundraising—and I fought for it. I talked about fundraising at nearly every town hall and debate, and I raised it in press interviews and roundtables. In the debates, I threw a roundhouse punch at billionaire Bloomberg, and I talked about Mayor Pete's closed-door dinner in a billionaire's wine cave.

Unfortunately, few of the other candidates showed much enthusiasm for reforming our campaign practices. Most rejected corporate PAC money, but otherwise they pretty much kept right on raising money the same old way, using some combination of big-dollar phone calls, pricey fundraisers, and some small-dollar online fundraising. In all, they pulled in tens of millions of dollars from the usual sources—and that was just in a Democrat-versus-Democrat primary, not a no-holds-barred, the-house-is-on-fire general election.

Even so, I'm glad I refused to rely on the usual fundraising playbook—really glad. Fundamental change doesn't happen in a single race or a single campaign season. In 2008, Barack Obama showed the Democratic Party that we could engage more people in funding elections. In 2012, my campaign broke records with the number of donors and the number of dollars for a first-time candidate in a Senate race, supercharging a campaign against someone who had access to buckets of Wall Street money. In 2016, Bernie proved that a lot of energized volunteers and small-dollar donors could power a national campaign. In 2020, I took the next step by raising all my money through grassroots donations.

By the time the primary season was over, I had raised more than $115 million. That put me well behind Bernie, who raised $214 million, most of it coming from a grassroots program similar to mine. But together, the two of us raised far more money than every other candidate during the contested primary. Neither Bernie nor I won, but we showed people that campaigns don't have to depend on never-ending efforts to beg rich people for money.

That point was made even clearer later in 2020 when small-dollar donors got engaged in races up and down the ticket. Grassroots supporters were already fired up, and after the death of Ruth Bader Ginsburg, contributions for Senate races poured in. Once the nomination was locked in, the Biden-Harris ticket set records for grassroots donations. And in the Georgia runoff for Senate, both Democratic candidates pulled in tens of millions in small-dollar contributions. It has taken years of work, but the stranglehold of big-dollar funding has begun to loosen just a bit.

Near the end of the presidential primary season, the whole money business took an unexpected turn. A stunningly generous woman put $14 million into a super PAC to pay for ads promoting my candidacy in Super Tuesday states. I had met her a few times back when I was running for the Senate, but as far as I know, she didn't have any business interest to promote or a big chunk of family money that she wanted to protect with a tax loophole. She just wanted me to win.

By this point, every other candidate who participated in the Las Vegas debate—Joe, Bernie, Pete, and Amy—also had a super PAC or similar outside support. Only the billionaire, Mike Bloomberg, who probably had more money in the back of his sock drawer than all the super PACs put together, did not have a super PAC. I am convinced that this woman believed in what I was fighting for. And I'm sure that all the other primary candidates who benefited from super PACs supporting them felt the same. But I will keep up the fight for a world in which no one can engage in this kind of spending on behalf of anyone—including me.

## CORRUPTION UNDERMINES OUR DEMOCRACY

Campaign contributions provide the most visible evidence of the influence of money in politics. They get considerable attention from the media. There are legal ways to trace some of them. They loom large in the minds of novice candidates and people who would like to run for office but don't have a personal fortune to finance themselves. But in Washington, campaign contributions are only the tip of a gigantic iceberg of buying influence.

An entire industry has grown up around the business of attempting to influence Congress. Paid lobbying is nothing more than taking money from a client who wants to persuade elected officials to act in ways that benefit that client. So much money flows to lobbyists from big corporations, billionaires, and even foreign governments that the industry now rakes in about $3.4 billion annually. But that figure captures only the work that formally falls within the narrow, legal definition of lobbying. More telling, perhaps, is the fact that there are more than ninety-two thousand trade associations that exist to advance the political interests of their members. Thousands of public relations firms. Specialized think tanks with a pro-industry point of view. Bought-and-paid-for experts. The list goes on and on. And all these associations are focused on spending bundles of money to influence our government to help their clients.

Washington is awash in money. Most of that money comes from the rich and powerful, and it has just one purpose: to help these privileged people get richer and more powerful.

I've seen firsthand the many ways that money rigs the game in Washington, but my experience has also been borne out by careful research. One rigorous study analyzed 1,779 policy issues over the course of decades and identified the relative influence of economic elites, business-oriented groups, organized interest groups, and regular people. The study's conclusion? "The preferences of the average American appear to have only a minuscule, near-zero, statistically nonsignificant impact upon public policy." Read that again: the concerns and opinions of the average American have a "near-zero" influence on what actually gets done. In the study's words, "It makes virtually no difference whether an overwhelming majority or only a small minority of average citizens favors policy change." Elected officials listen to the rich people, interest groups, businesses, and organizations that can help them get elected and reelected. Do they listen to real people? Not at all.

A corrupt system lies at the heart of nearly everything that is broken in Washington—and everything that isn't getting fixed across our country. Giant corporations and wealthy investors have learned that if they can persuade lawmakers to do their bidding, they will get even wealthier. Inequality is not an accident of the past four decades. It was carefully nurtured by thousands of decisions by legislators who helped out their rich friends and let everyone else fall behind.

I've had a seat in the Senate for eight years now, and from where I sit I see the influence of money in every issue that matters, from health care to education to climate change. I could follow the money trail as it winds through a dozen different issues, but I'll illustrate my point by focusing on the country's housing crisis. This issue is personal for me, not least because when I was a little girl our house was proof to my family that we had made it into America's middle class.

The first house I remember was at 115 West Haddock—the last row of houses on the edge of Norman, Oklahoma. (Yes, we were the Herring family living on Haddock Street, and I was on the receiving end of plenty of fish jokes in my childhood.) Our street was gravel, and behind our house and beyond the back fence was a patchwork of wheat fields that stretched as far as you could see. My daddy would spend hours working in the backyard, and sometimes he'd call me outside to show me something in the small tool shed that was in the back corner of our yard. He'd point to a long, translucent skin that a rattlesnake had sluffed off. The message was clear: don't go in the fields.

The house was in a development, and its streets were dotted with nearly two hundred perfectly spaced similar houses—small ranch houses dropped down on the cold-in-the-winter, hot-in-the-summer, wind-always-blows prairie. Each house had a paved driveway and one—exactly one—skinny little tree in the corner of the front yard. Like most of the houses, ours was a two-bedroom, one-bath ranch, but in our case, the garage had been converted to a bedroom for my three brothers. After years of renting, buying this 1,150-square-foot house was a big step up for my mother and daddy. This was their chance to build something, their chance to be part of the American dream.

My folks had no money to improve the place, but they made up for that with their hard work. They drove to my Uncle Roy's farm to dig up blackberry bushes for the backyard. They scavenged saplings from the side of the road during trips to visit family in Eastern Oklahoma, and then carefully nursed them as they took root along the side of the house. They bought leftover and dented cans of paint to give the place a little color. My mother tried to make draperies for the windows, a disaster that left her in tears and required my Aunt Max to come to the rescue.

In truth, our house on West Haddock was small and ordinary, but my parents treated it like something precious. I remember how excited we were when, after years of scrimping and saving, my parents could finally afford to put carpet in the living room. And for our family, that house was a crucial building block, because it provided the foundation for our next house, a nicer place in Oklahoma City.

I could tell more stories about that first house, and they would be close cousins to the stories that tens of millions of other Americans could tell about their homes. All these stories share the same theme: they remind us at a gut level how important housing is.

Whether families buy or rent their homes, the data stack sky high on this: People with adequate, affordable housing are healthier and better able to take care of themselves. Children who grow up in stable housing do better in school and in life. Housing affects the jobs you can get, the schools your children can attend, and the kinds of communities you can live in. That's why it's so important for the government to get housing policy right.

Housing has long been an important issue, but now America faces a housing crisis of epic proportions. According to a recent study conducted by the Federal Home Loan Mortgage Corporation, the United States would have to build another 3.3 million new homes just to cover the minimal housing needs for American families. That's homes of all kinds—single-family homes, duplexes, triple-deckers, condos, townhouses, apartments, and mobile homes. The main consequence of this housing shortage is exactly what economists would predict: people are paying a bigger and bigger chunk of their paychecks for housing but getting less and less for their money. When families and individuals can't pay, they double up, couch surf, land in homeless shelters, or wind up on the street.

The COVID-19 crisis made a bad situation much worse. Because of the coronavirus, overcrowded housing in cities became downright dangerous. Any place where housing costs were high and people doubled and tripled up became a high-risk COVID-19 contagion spot. On tribal lands, where lack of adequate housing means Native American families are often crowded into small homes, social distancing was essentially impossible, creating another housing-COVID nexus.

Over the past twenty years, the housing squeeze has intensified. Basic economics pinpoints the underlying causes. Houses deteriorate over time, and eventually some become unlivable, shrinking our housing stock. Meanwhile, our population increases and people move around, creating both a nationwide shortage and intense localized shortages. And here's where the economists tap their chalk again: more people bidding for fewer houses means that prices go up.

So why haven't Americans built enough new housing to meet the demand? The first reason is that most private developers are no longer building the 1,150-square-foot house I grew up in. Instead, developers have migrated to 4,000-square-foot starter mansions and luxury condos with access to gyms and infinity pools. There's an obvious reason for this change: those giant houses and big-ticket condos are more profitable to build. Anyone who's in the market for a house with five bedrooms and an all-marble kitchen—and who has the money to pay for it—is in luck. There are plenty of places to choose from. For everyone else, not so much.

The second reason for the shortage is local government. Cities and towns have put a lot of restrictions in place that make it difficult to build new housing—restrictions like minimum-acreage zoning, minimum sizes for dwellings, and enough other rules to choke even the most determined builder. The result is fine for those who already own property, but these restrictions have driven up costs sharply for anyone trying to buy or rent.

And there's one more big reason: The federal government has changed its approach to housing. From the 1930s through the 1970s, the U.S. government built millions of housing units, mostly aimed at families of modest means. By increasing the housing supply, prices stayed lower for all renters and buyers, particularly those with moderate incomes. But in the late 1970s, federal policy changed, shifting to rental assistance that relied on giving cash or vouchers to renters, and then turning them loose to find their own housing. The unspoken premise was that "the market" would respond to the shortage and build enough new housing units to solve the problem.

Reliance on the supposed magic of the market was so intense that in 1999 Congress actually passed a law known as the Faircloth Amendment, requiring that not a single new unit of public housing could be built unless an existing unit of public housing was destroyed or sold to a private party. In fact, since the 1990s, the federal government has made the crush even worse by destroying nearly a quarter of a million public housing units and replacing only about half of them. Now, even with a growing population, even with an increasing squeeze for adequate housing, it remains the policy of the U.S. government to keep a tight lid on the number of public housing units.

The magical market that would provide housing for everyone turned out to be an illusion. Today, the housing shortage is so severe that about four hundred thousand additional young people, who in earlier generations would have had their own places, are doubled up with family. But as people struggle to deal with the rising cost of housing, the squeeze is felt in all age groups.

Every year Congress talks about what to do—or, at least, the Democrats in Congress talk about what to do. The suggested fixes are all variations on a few familiar ideas. Increase federal vouchers. Offer more tax credits. Subsidize landlords. They all follow the same basic approach: give people a little more money and that will solve the housing problem. I'm all in favor of giving people some help on housing, but these approaches take us right back to the failed promise of the magical market.

By itself, the market will never solve the problem. Too many people need help, and the gap between what housing costs and what people can afford to pay is too big. In many places, increasing housing vouchers or finding another way to give renters and buyers more cash just provides an opportunity for landlords and sellers to charge more. Instead, we need a bigger, structural solution. Only by dramatically expanding the supply can we make housing more affordable.

To me, this is much more than a topic for political debate: it's an existential issue. I believe that housing is a basic human right. In the same way that we work hard to build an America where everyone has access to food, medical care, and education, I believe we should also ensure that families and individuals have safe, affordable housing. There's a trio of critical issues here—health, housing, and economic independence— and the deep interconnection among them means that we cannot afford to ignore the role housing plays in the overall security of the American people.

## A FIX THAT REALLY FIXES

That little house on West Haddock has been a North Star for me during my time in the Senate. In 2018, I started developing a plan to invest $500 billion and build about 3.2 million new housing units. The plan wasn't about just one kind of housing. It was about rental housing and homes people could buy. It was about housing for poor people and homeless people. It was about housing for middle-class families. It was about housing for seniors and people with disabilities and people who needed group homes. It was about housing in inner cities, housing in small towns, and housing in farming communities. It was about housing on millions of acres of tribal lands. The plan was about acknowledging that housing is a basic human right and putting some serious federal muscle behind a commitment to create the housing Americans need.

My team and I decided that before we rolled out the plan, we should ask some independent economists to take the idea for a test drive. If our numbers were off or there were effects we hadn't thought about, better to learn this in advance instead of having to backtrack and issue a giant "oops." The econ nerds aren't easy to impress, but after crunching the numbers they were enthusiastic. Mark Zandi, who had been

John McCain's economic adviser, told us that by approaching the housing problem from the supply side, the plan would cut rents across the board by about 10 percent. He also said that the surge of construction would produce up to 1.5 million new jobs—good, union jobs that can't be shipped overseas.

The plan would have yet another beneficial effect. As the supply of new houses increased, the cost of buying a home would drop. More people could afford to step up from renting and buy a place to live. Maybe the houses wouldn't be 4,000 square feet and have marble bathrooms, but they would allow people to build wealth over time, provide a nest egg for their retirement, and perhaps pass along a wonderful gift to the next generation.

My plan also had a critical feature designed to counter decades of racial discrimination. Housing made it possible for millions of middle-class families to get a handsome return on their investment, so it is no surprise that the federal government subsidized the purchase of homes—for white people. That opportunity was denied to Black families through what's known as redlining. For decades, the federal government literally drew red lines on maps that identified communities of color, then decreed that government-sponsored mortgages would not be available for homes in those neighborhoods. My plan created assistance for first-time home buyers in these neighborhoods—support that would acknowledge that legacy of discrimination and help to close the Black/white wealth gap.

The plan had a number of other important features. It would offer substantial money to communities that were willing to modify their laws to increase density, modernize building codes and materials, and lower building costs. It would ban discrimination against LGBTQ people— discrimination that is currently legal. Every bell and whistle in my plan was designed to expand housing in ways that would be life-changing for millions of Americans.

But I didn't stop there. I also proposed a simple way to pay for the plan. Borrowing from history, we would shift the estate tax thresholds back to where they'd been during the George W. Bush administration, and we'd also establish a more progressive tax rate beyond those thresholds. That's it; that's all we'd need to do. According to IRS data, this would affect the tax rates of about fourteen thousand wealthy families. Requiring them to pay their estate taxes at the same thresholds that were in place in the 2000s, and instituting more progressive rates above those thresholds, would generate enough income to build housing for more than three million people—and help ease the housing squeeze for millions more.

Once my team and I put the finishing touches on the plan, I got pretty excited about it. I couldn't wait to start talking about the plan with some of the other senators, and I was all but certain that it would be an easy sell. Nearly every senator has areas in his or her home state where families are stretched to the breaking point by housing costs. Nearly every senator is eager to bring good construction jobs to his or her home state. And paying for my plan would be a snap. What's not to love?

When I made my first pitch to a colleague over lunch one day, the senator practically finished my sentences. When I began talking about how important it was to deal with the lack of affordable housing, he waxed eloquent about how my plan would make a big difference in parts of his state and how people back home really cared about this issue. In fact, he was so eager to hear more that he jumped right to the bottom line and asked how I would pay for the plan. I explained, and the conversation came to a screeching halt. Ask rich people to pay a little more in taxes? Not gonna happen, my colleague said. You'll never get this passed. You'll never even get a vote.

Why? Because those fourteen thousand families have the resources to make sure it never passes. The minute the plan goes public, the word will go out: Call your friends, call your lobbyist, call your favorite senator. Lean on them hard. Shut the plan down. Strangle it before it tries to walk. Kill it before it even crawls.

My colleague in the Senate was instantly dismissive, but not everyone responded the same way. Good friends elsewhere in Congress loved the idea as much as I did. As I developed the proposed legislation, Cedric Richmond took the lead on the bill in the House. He was enthusiastically joined by Elijah Cummings, Barbara Lee, and Gwen Moore. They were committed to the cause, but everyone knew it would be a tough uphill climb—not because the housing wasn't needed but because the way to pay for it would nip into the fortunes of the richest fourteen thousand families in our country.

For me, this story—one of many I could tell—offers a vivid example of how deep the corruption runs in Washington. Our government can't even consider new housing for 3.2 million families if it means that fourteen thousand super-rich families would have to pay a little more in taxes. Let's break those numbers down: For each wealthy family that would pay a little more in estate taxes, 228 modest-income families would have a new place to live. Meanwhile, millions more families and individuals would benefit from lower rents, would have a chance to buy a home, or would get a job building some of the millions of new houses.

In a healthy democracy, my housing bill shouldn't be hard to pass. Sure, I get it that my colleagues in Congress might think they have a better solution for the housing crisis or a better way to pay for my plan. But those aren't the objections holding back this bill. The only real objection is that a handful of rich people with a lot of political power would hate the idea of paying more in taxes. In fact, our elected representatives are so in tune with the wealthy in this country that nobody even needs to *ask* them about a bill like mine. The equation is simple: in the upside-down world of Washington, D.C., a few thousand very rich people are far more important than millions of not-rich people.

I haven't given up on the housing fight—in fact, with a new administration in Washington and a lot of allies who are very determined, I think a big, bold investment in housing is possible. But there's no disputing that getting something like this done—providing relief that is desperately needed by millions of Americans—is far harder than it ought to be.

And that's only one issue. During my years in the Senate, I've seen a lot of other good plans hit a brick wall. Plans to shore up Social Security. Plans to cancel student loan debt. Plans to support renewable energy. Plans to stop furnishing weapons to terrorists halfway around the world. Plans that would change a lot of people's lives for the better. All shot down because these plans would anger rich people who didn't want to pay more taxes. Or enrage oil company lobbyists. Or infuriate defense industry executives.

Corruption stands in the way of every single policy that would help us build a more just America. Corruption is a cancer that is eating away at our democracy.

## BEATING BACK THE INFLUENCE OF MONEY

I decided to run for president because I believed that our government was no longer serving the large majority of people in this country. Presidential politics is famously a blood sport, but corruption made me ready to get in the fight.

When I picked up the microphone at my very first town hall in Iowa, I talked about a corrupt system. I tried to tie the pieces together: the reason government doesn't work for you is because it's too busy working for the wealthy and well connected who spend big bucks to twist outcomes in their direction.

From the start, I hoped my campaign could lift up a bunch of issues like childcare and student loan debt and a $15-an-hour minimum wage and climate change and expanding Social Security. These issues are popular— really popular. They're exciting to talk about, too. But to make any real change, we have to tackle the corruption in the system. We have to take on the billionaires who don't want to pay more in taxes, the polluters who don't want to face more regulations, the corporations that don't want to pay their workers more. By talking about these issues, I wanted to shine a light directly on the corruption at the heart of our democracy.

The approach I used to finance my campaign was step one in my effort to fight corruption. But I knew we needed to do more: if we're going to fundamentally change the way political campaigns are funded and run, we need different laws. Yes, that means overturning *Citizens United*, the infamous 2010 Supreme Court decision that allows unlimited political spending. I'll fight for that, because corporations and billionaires should not be allowed to buy elections—period.

But we don't have to wait for a constitutional amendment. Even in a *Citizens United* world, we can reduce the influence of money on our elections. We can improve laws covering contribution disclosures so that voters can see where a candidate's money is coming from. We can insist that all campaign contributions be made public within twenty-four hours, not three months. And we can outlaw all corporate contributions to candidates for the House, the Senate, or the White House. If we established these three simple rules, all perfectly legal in a *Citizens United* world, we could move the needle on the influence of big-dollar spending on elections.

Step two in my effort to fight corruption was bigger—a lot bigger. During the campaign I released a comprehensive anti-corruption plan that identified hundreds of ways in which money makes its power felt in Washington. I also showed how we could change the laws to put a stop to each one of those ways. At nearly every town hall, in nearly every stump speech, in almost every interview, I talked about the corruption that threatens our democracy. Even more important, I described tough, realistic plans that would root out this corruption.

Any good anti-corruption plan should start with eliminating conflicts of interest.

Donald Trump's conflicts during his presidency—his personal conflicts, the conflicts of his family, the conflicts of his sleazy friends and bootlicking toadies—were the stuff of jaw-dropping legend. In 2018, for instance, Trump saved a large state-owned Chinese business from collapse, and later it became clear that this was just a way to say thank you to China for granting first daughter Ivanka Trump a slew of trademarks that allowed her to market her products in the country. Of course, that was a mere drop in a bucket the size of the Grand Canyon. Citizens for Responsibility and Ethics in Washington counted more than 3,400 conflicts of interest by President Trump. During his tenure, Trump generated substantial revenues (at taxpayer expense) by visiting his own businesses more than 500 times. Meanwhile, Trump and other White House officials used their public platforms to promote Trump businesses 426 times.

No one is as grotesque as Trump, but less obvious conflicts should also be barred. The law should be changed and it should apply to every administration, Democratic or Republican. Tax returns for every single person who files to run for federal office—the White House, the Senate, and the House—should be automatically put online. How many years of returns? Let's follow the example set by Barack Obama and require a minimum of eight years for anyone running for president.

It's also time to tighten the conflict of interest rules and make them apply across the board to presidents and to their cabinet officials and agency heads. That no-conflicts rule should also apply to senators and representatives. After the primary season ended, Joe Biden and I issued a joint call for a no-conflicts rule. No member of Congress should own individual stocks, nor should they have an ownership stake in a business.

During the pandemic year of 2020, the two Republican senators from Georgia seemed to be in competition to see who could profit more from being in "public service." Senator David Perdue made 2,596 stock trades, including 61 trades in a single company whose fortunes would be dramatically affected by congressional decisions that were being directly influenced by Senator Perdue. Senator Kelly Loeffler got private briefings on the spread of the virus, then bought stocks in companies that manufactured protective equipment and produced telework software whose value would rise in a pandemic. The Republican Justice Department investigated but declined to prosecute Senator Perdue, while the Senate ethics committee said Senator Loeffler's actions violated no rules. How could anyone think this was okay? If these actions didn't violate any rules, then it's time to change the rules. And if the public officials investigating senators can't enforce the rules, then we need to bring in some independent enforcement officials who have a real backbone instead of overcooked spaghetti.

For public officials who cry because they are required to put their money in broad-based mutual funds or blind trusts, pass a box of tissues. For elected officials who squirm about the public seeing their tax returns, hand them a hankie. And for any politician who believes that no-conflict rules are too burdensome, offer a glass of warm milk.

Because if all this seems too tough, then the solution is simple: don't run for office. The American people should never have to worry about whether the decisions made by public officials are driven by public interest or by their own personal financial interests.

While we're at it, let's ban those same senators and representatives from becoming lobbyists once they are no longer in office. It's time to put a stop to the slimy business of lobbying firms vacuuming up high-ranking government officials just to get their contacts and their access to the Senate Dining Room. And the same rule should apply to cabinet officials, to the heads of agencies, and—yeah, I guess we need to say it—even to the president and the vice president.

It's also time to block the revolving door between Wall Street and Washington. Consider just one example. Candidate Trump talked about draining the swamp and focused particularly on Goldman Sachs, but newly elected President Trump changed his tune. He made Gary Cohn, the former president of Goldman Sachs, his top economic adviser. On his way out of Goldman, Cohn received the promise of a staggering $285 million from the firm. Nice, but the money came with a catch: Cohn wouldn't get the big bucks if he joined the Red Cross or started teaching in a rural elementary school or just retired. Nope: he could only collect this boatload of money if he left the firm to work in the White House.

Why did Goldman Sachs think it was so important to encourage Cohn to go to the White House? Easy answer: his job would allow him to rewrite America's economic policies. After cashing that $285 million check—which I call a "pre-bribe"—Cohn helped draft changes to our nation's tax laws and then ram those changes through Congress. And in the first year alone, the new laws gave Goldman Sachs a tax break worth over $300 million. That's $300 million in tax revenues that weren't available to pay for pre-K or to raise Social Security payments or clean up our air and water. But hey, Goldman investors loved it, and in the company's view Cohn more than earned his obscene payoff.

There's so much more we could do to end the corruption—or at least beat it back. We could expand the legal definition of lobbying so that none of it happens outside the public view. We could bar political contributions from lobbyists. We could ban foreign governments from using U.S. lobbyists. We could require experts who testify before Congress to reveal who paid for their research.

And while we're at it, we could attack corruption in our courts. Let's begin at the top: Justices of the United States Supreme Court are bound by no rules of ethics. None, zero, zip. That means they can take all-expenses-paid trips to "seminars" at lovely vacation spots or fancy hunting lodges and pal around with people who have cases that will eventually come before the Court. That's just plain wrong, and it should be illegal.

All this is just a start—if we wanted to, we could do a lot more to reduce the influence of the rich and powerful and start to level the playing field. But none of these changes will happen on their own. There is no industry or corporate group advocating for any part of this agenda. On the contrary: the pushback to these kinds of proposals will be ferocious. After their time in public service, many congressmen look forward to raking in multimillion-dollar salaries as lobbyists and top executives for industry associations. Corporate CEOs, meanwhile, like picking senators and presidents—and getting more tax breaks, less antitrust enforcement, and whatever else is on their wish list. And their lobbyists like handing out checks to elected officials, who very much like cashing them.

My anti-corruption plan is long and detailed—because it needs to be. And the fight to get it adopted won't be easy. But if we don't root out a significant amount of the corruption in our government, then other changes involving health care and climate and housing, changes we desperately need, will remain impossible.

## THE FIGHTERS

Mike Tyson once said that everyone has a plan until they get punched in the mouth. For some people, the plan is never to get punched in the mouth, but those people aren't fighters. The real fighters are willing to look down and see that the blood and teeth on the floor are their own—and then lift their heads and take another swing.

As a law professor, I participated in my share of heated exchanges.

But when I started a big political fight over establishing a new consumer agency, real money and real power were at stake, and it was a whole new world. In the midst of that fight, *Vanity Fair* noted that I "was called incompetent, power-hungry, ignorant, a media whore." At a televised hearing, a Republican congressman called me a liar. *Bloomberg Businessweek* featured me on the front cover, with words like "smug," "liberal," "entitled," "arrogant," and "know-it-all bureaucrat" splattered across my picture like rotten tomatoes. One community banker defended me, but he seemed a little taken aback by the vitriol, saying, "It was like she was the Antichrist." And what exactly had I done to provoke such responses? According to *Vanity Fair*'s reporter, all of this was triggered because "Warren fought back . . . by speaking out in public."

I won the battle for the Consumer Financial Protection Bureau, and I could have quit there. I could have kept my head down, retreated to my teaching job, not run for the Senate—and later, not run for president. When I decided to run for office, I did it eyes wide open. I had a pretty good idea of what was coming my way. I knew I'd get involved in hard, sometimes brutal, fights, and I knew that everything about my life would be fodder for nasty attacks. But there was an upside to diving into the ring. These were the fights that could make real change. If we won, we wouldn't make just nibble-around-the-edges change, we'd make transformative change, the kind that people could feel every day. These would be righteous fights—the kind worth fighting.

Even so, every once in a while an unexpected kick knocked a few teeth loose. During the presidential debate in Las Vegas during which I took on Bloomberg, Jennifer Rubin, a columnist for the *Washington Post*, tweeted, "Mean and angry Warren not a good look."

And there it was, the same damn remark made about every woman who ever stood up for herself and threw a punch. Repeat after me: fighting hard is "not a good look."

I shouldn't have been surprised because my mother had warned me. She'd given me her best advice on how to make sure that everyone thought I looked good. No glasses, no biting my fingernails, no wearing yellow. And no fighting.

I heard her. But I also watched her. I watched her fight to hang on to our house when my daddy was out of work. I watched her tell the story of fighting a knot of self-important local cops when they threw my then fourteen-year-old brother John into the Norman jail. I watched her fight for me when I needed stitches and the receptionist at the doctor's office balked because we were behind on paying our bill. I watched her fight when she was afraid, when she was humiliated, and when she was just plain exhausted. I heard my mother's advice, but I watched her fight for our family.

It's a tough world out there. And when the stakes are high, the rich and powerful aren't going to give up even a fraction of their riches or their power just to be nice. If we want to create more opportunities for our children, if we want to save our planet, if we want to narrow income inequality, if we want to reduce racial injustice—if we want any or all of these things, we will have to fight for them.

Because no one is going to give up *anything* without a fight.

# FIVE

# A Learner

THE JUDGE: Why are you asking about race?

ME: Because it might be important.

THE JUDGE: But people may not want to say.

ME: It's all voluntary. We're asking about sex and age and other stuff. No one has to answer any of the questions.

THE JUDGE: Yeah, but this study is about bankruptcy, not about race. Why are you asking about race?

ME: Because race might be important.

Back in the 1980s and 1990s, long before I got into politics, I studied families that go broke. I looked closely into what had gone wrong for so many people. For me, it was personal: when I was growing up, my family had teetered for years on the edge of a financial cliff, sometimes slipping a little, sometimes clawing our way back. I don't think any child ever quite recovers from a deep sense that the whole world might soon break apart.

As a young law professor, first at the University of Houston and then at the University of Texas, I taught bankruptcy law. I led my students through many lessons on finance, court systems, and how to read complex statutes. I was a teacher, but I was also a learner. I wanted to know more about the people who washed up on the shores of the bankruptcy courts and how the legal system dealt with them. I wanted to understand what drove them into bankruptcy and whether bankrupt families could tell us more about risk and failure throughout our economic system. For me, one of the best parts of being a teacher was that I had a great excuse to continue being a learner.

From the time I'd started studying bankruptcies in the early 1980s, the number of filings had been skyrocketing. In those days, the standard explanation for the financial troubles facing millions of American families was plain old overspending. If Americans were struggling financially, it was because they were spending too much time at the mall and buying stuff no one really needed. Dial back on Nike and Gucci, and the problem would disappear. Case closed.

Maybe that was right, but I needed to learn more, to see some real evidence. And there was no good way to know what was really driving this surge of bankruptcies unless we got more information about the people who were going broke.

To dig into this work, I teamed up with two remarkable people. Dr. Teresa Sullivan was then a young sociology professor at the University of Texas at Austin. (Later, she served as provost at the University of Michigan, president at the University of Virginia, and interim provost at Michigan State University.) Professor Jay Westbrook had already spent eleven years in practice in Washington, D.C., and been a partner in a very prestigious law firm before coming home to teach at UT Austin. My coauthors gave our little team the chops to conduct serious empirical work and data analysis (Terry) and achieve a deep understanding of the legal system (Jay). My job was persistence.

Our first project together in the mid-1980s had gone well. In a careful and detailed empirical study, we collected a huge amount of information straight from the public records. This was possible because in order to file for bankruptcy, a person had to practically get naked, at least on paper. Name, address, previous names, previous addresses, co-ownerships. Homes, cars, boats, jewelry, furniture, appliances, rugs, tools, collectibles, guns, sporting equipment, dogs and cats, savings, retirement accounts, security deposits, cash in your wallet, upcoming tax refund, alimony or child support, gifts given or received—all of it listed and given a dollar value. Same for debts: how much, down to the penny, owed on credit cards, mortgages, payday loans, student loans, business debts, leases. Every creditor had to be identified by name and address—banks, hospitals, dentists, family members, everyone. How long had these debts existed? What were the interest rates? Were the debts secured? The lists were as exhaustive—and exhausting—as generations of lawyers could make them.

To make sure the bankrupt debtor was telling the truth, the system had lots of checks. Each creditor listed in a bankruptcy petition would receive a notice from the court and a request to verify the information the debtor had listed. A trustee would be assigned to administer an oath requiring each bankrupt person to swear to the accuracy of the lists and submit to potential questions about each item. Finally, to make sure everything was all buttoned up, the person filing for bankruptcy had to sign a statement saying they understood that they could be liable for perjury if they got anything wrong. A bankruptcy file is a whole financial life laid bare.

Every weekday, people trudged up the courthouse steps, clutching reams of forms that they'd carefully filled out, usually with a lawyer's help. Showing up to declare themselves flat broke, they were generally perceived as losers in the great American economic game. Those completed forms made their lives a matter of public record, there for any nosy neighbor or future creditor or bullying brother-in-law to see. Bankruptcy can be terribly painful on many levels.

Terry, Jay, and I had used that public information to better understand what had gone wrong in people's lives, and we'd written a groundbreaking book about the bankruptcy system, *As We Forgive Our Debtors*. But there was so much more we wanted to learn. The thick and intrusive bankruptcy files we'd studied were extremely detailed, but there were still a million unanswered questions about who these people were and why they had landed in the bankruptcy courts. So the three of us put together a questionnaire, a single page asking the people who filed for personal bankruptcy to answer some questions and tell us about themselves. The questionnaire covered a lot of basic information that was not in the files:

age, marital status, number of children at home, education level, and, yes, race. At the bottom of the questionnaire we asked the bankrupt debtor to turn the paper over and tell us in their own words what had gone wrong.

For our second dive into the data, we picked sixteen judicial districts around the country to study, a sample that we thought would capture variations but also be manageable. There was no law saying we couldn't show up at any of these public courthouses and ask people to help us. But we weren't stupid. If the bankruptcy judge made clear to the lawyers that he—and back then all the judges we dealt with were men—didn't want these pesky researchers in his courtroom, the lawyers and their clients would freeze us out.

That's where persistence came in.

By now it was 1990, and I was teaching at the University of Pennsylvania. So here I was in my office, telephone in hand, pacing as far as the cord would permit me, trying to cajole a bankruptcy judge halfway across the country into agreeing that next year some researchers he didn't know could hand out questionnaires to people who were waiting for their court hearings.

Some judges welcomed us. ("Great! How can I help?") Others were more neutral. ("Okay. But don't get in the way.") No one raised any objections to the questionnaire itself—except for the question on race. That was the only stumbling block.

All sixteen judges seemed genuinely interested in learning more about why so many families were landing in bankruptcy courts each year. In fact, they didn't need even the briefest sales pitch for the project overall. They wanted to know the same thing we did: What was going wrong in America?

Our hope was that the information we'd be collecting would give us some important clues about whether the economy was working better for some people than others. By learning more about gender and children, for example, we might discover that women with children were far more likely to end up in bankruptcy than men. (That's exactly what we discovered.) Or by collecting information about age, we might uncover growing economic vulnerability among seniors. (We found this, too.)

Or by looking at education, we might learn that going to college insulated people from ending up in bankruptcy. (It turned out to be more complicated.)

The judges were good with all of that. But the race question raised flags—big red ones. One judge said it could make people uncomfortable. Another thought it was intrusive. A third said flatly that there was no reason to ask.

One judge I called took a lecturing tone. The law is neutral, he said; anyone can file for bankruptcy, regardless of race. Search all you want—nothing in the law will say "African American" or "Hispanic." So there's nothing to ask about. And surely I wasn't suggesting that he personally was treating Black families any differently from white families?

Persistence.

I explained to this judge—and to all the judges I called—that it was entirely possible that we would find no significant differences among families of different races who ended up in bankruptcy. Maybe there would be no difference in how they were treated in the bankruptcy system. But we wouldn't know if we didn't ask. So no, we didn't want to take the question about race off the questionnaire.

For most judges, that was good enough. But for others, there were pauses and uncomfortable silences. Some judges wanted time to think about the issue and get back to us. A few judges asked a second and third time if we'd consider dropping the question about race.

In the end, every judge in our targeted districts agreed to let us ask the question. The following year, we collected the information, and as we began to analyze it I learned things about race I'd never even considered.

When we first started digging into the data in the questionnaires, I had no idea what we would find. I meant what I'd said to the judges: maybe we'd discover that race had nothing to do with whether someone ended up in bankruptcy, and nothing to do with what happened to them after they filed. And when the first data runs suggested that there *were* significant racial divides, I wasn't sure how to interpret this finding—or even how to talk about it. Bankruptcy carried (and still carries) significant stigma, and

I worried that any discussion of race could feel like an accusation against those who turn to bankruptcy for help.

To make the challenge even tougher, embedding the bankruptcy story in the larger story about the economic pressures on African Americans and Latinos would force me to learn about ideas and master data that were far beyond the territory I was familiar with. Besides, Terry, Jay, and I knew the data sets weren't perfect. For example, our study did not include a sufficient number of Asian Americans or Native Americans to provide a reliable statistical analysis. So there were plenty of reasons to direct the focus of our work elsewhere and quietly push the race issues aside.

But we could not ignore what we had learned. The racial disparities practically jumped off the page. Every review of our data, every subsequent analysis or study by other scholars, revealed more about the exceptional financial risks facing people of color. Over time, our studies developed some powerful insights and opened up new avenues of research for another generation of researchers. These were some of the discoveries:

- Latino homeowners were nearly twice as likely to end up in bankruptcy as white homeowners, and Black homeowners were more than three times as likely to end up in bankruptcy. (This finding eventually led to a lot of work that exposed discrimination in lending and foreclosure practices, long before the 2008 housing crash.)
- A college diploma made it more likely that white graduates would be insulated from the kind of financial devastation that landed people in bankruptcy, but a college diploma did not offer the same protection to Black and Latino graduates. (Later, this finding led to a lot of work about race and student loans.)
- White debtors were much more likely than Black or Hispanic debtors to get their debts discharged in bankruptcy. They were also more likely to leave bankruptcy in far better financial shape. (This finding ultimately led to a lot of work about the bias of lawyers, judges, and the two-chapter bankruptcy system.)

Each of these findings led to more studies, and each continues to have important implications that ought to inform policies in a number of areas. But the most significant thing about our work was a lesson that I carry with me to this day: You can't fix a problem you can't see. Simply saying that the laws (or the economy, or the rules that govern policing, or anything else) are racially blind doesn't mean that reality is racially blind. To attack problems head-on—to be anti-racist—begins with asking questions about race.

These questions can be difficult. They can be uncomfortable. They can be irritating. But for a learner, these questions are necessary.

## LIFE AND DEATH THROUGH THE LENS OF RACE

Nearly thirty years later, I was still learning about race, but I also sometimes felt like I wanted to bang my head against a brick wall. Shouldn't it be clear by now that if you want to understand any large social or economic problem, you have to at least look for racial disparities? But no, not in 2020. Not on the threshold of a pandemic.

In early March 2020, I ended my race for president. Within days, the coronavirus pandemic gripped the world. I had put together medical and economic response plans starting back in January, and now I jumped headfirst into an effort to help our country cope with the rapidly expanding crisis. America was woefully underprepared. Masks, gowns, and ventilators were in short supply. Tests were rationed so tightly that just about the only people that could get tested were those already showing symptoms of the virus—and even then, we were running out of tests. No high fever? No test. No dry cough? No test. No confirmed exposure? No test.

On March 6, Donald Trump declared, "Anyone who wants a test can get a test." PolitiFact rated this a "Pants on Fire" lie.

If very little testing is being done, it's virtually impossible to track the spread of a disease. In the middle of the worst pandemic in a century, we were flying blind—and the nation's president had no plan for how to ramp up testing and get the information we needed.

But there was a second issue lurking in the fog. Yes, most people found it very difficult to get tested for the virus. But *some* people were getting tested, and I wondered who these people were. While doctors in a number of cities couldn't round up tests for critically ill patients, movie stars, professional athletes, agents, and media moguls in those same cities were getting tested—and getting their results back within hours. Friends of the president also went to the front of the line. Obviously tests were in very short supply, but I started to wonder if people in communities of color were getting equal access to testing. Three decades after I'd first asked the question about bankruptcy, I asked the same question about the pandemic: Did race matter?

My next thought was that I needed to talk with Ayanna Pressley, the congresswoman who represents Massachusetts's only majority-minority district. A fighter to her core, Ayanna is principled, outspoken, and fiercely determined to raise up the voices of those who are rarely heard from in the halls of Congress. She was cochair of my presidential campaign, generously giving her time and her passion to the cause, for which I will forever be grateful. Hearing Ayanna say "Policy is my love language, and Elizabeth Warren speaks it fluently" always made me laugh, but it also gave me chills. Ayanna was only in her first term, but she was a warrior and she was ready for action.

I called Ayanna about the testing question. What did she know? What had she heard? Who had access to the tests and who didn't?

The more we talked, the more concerned we both became. Who was getting tested? Gender and age—that information was being collected systematically. But other information, like race and ethnicity, was either very spotty or not collected at all, especially at the federal level. And this could be important. If, for example, white communities had plenty of tests available and Black and Brown communities did not, there would be no way to know.

Ayanna and I got busy. We fired off a letter to the Department of Health and Human Services (HHS) and requested that they collect racial and ethnic data. We raised the issue in the press and called our colleagues in the House and the Senate. We pointed out that there are many underlying health disparities based on race—African Americans are more likely to have asthma and diabetes, for example—and those disparities could make people of color more vulnerable to bad coronavirus outcomes. People of color are also less likely to have health insurance, and their communities are less likely to have enough health-care providers. There are economic factors at play as well: people of color are less likely to be able to work from home, have access to paid time off, and live in safe and affordable housing with enough space to isolate from family members, if necessary—all of which put them at higher risk of being exposed to the virus.

But no one would have a clue about possible racial disparities unless our government carefully and continuously collected information about race, and then made that information publicly available. In March, we put in a formal request to HHS for the data. When we got no response, we tried another approach. Teaming up with our Massachusetts colleague Senator Ed Markey, we asked the Centers for Medicare and Medicaid Services—which is part of HHS—to release the racial and ethnic data on Medicare claims for COVID-19. The Trump administration resisted these efforts as well (no surprise). But we still didn't give up (no surprise).

We turned up the heat by introducing a bill that would require HHS to report this data, along with other important demographic information like age, sex, and primary language. Finally they began to crack. Soon after that, Ayanna and I—with the support of a number of colleagues—got the data collection requirement included in a COVID relief package, which was quickly signed into law. From then on, the government mandated that race and ethnicity data be collected and reported.

Once the information started rolling in, a picture emerged that was worse than most people suspected. African Americans were more than twice as likely to die from COVID-19 as whites, and they were dying at younger ages.

African Americans were not the only ones hit hard. The data showed that Asian Americans were nearly twice as likely to die from COVID-19. Native Americans and Latinos also experienced higher rates of infection and higher death rates. By early spring, disease and death were sweeping through the Navajo Nation, affecting both young and old and creating one of the worst outbreaks in the entire country.

With better data, some things changed. New Orleans, for example, realized that their drive-through testing protocols were missing large numbers of African Americans who did not have cars. They shifted to mobile testing vans, which gave health officials a better chance of stopping the virus's spread and saving lives. Johns Hopkins responded to racial disparity data by building a public/private response targeting affected communities in Baltimore. The California Department of Health changed its allocation of resources throughout the state. Someone—an aunt, a cousin, a friend—is alive today because public health officials collected information and acted on it. In fact, better information saved the lives of a lot of someones.

As reports emerged about racial disparities involving COVID-19, the press gave much greater attention to broader health disparities. Many Americans—white Americans—heard for the first time about how much worse health outcomes are for people of color. That focused new attention on the problem, which in turn ratcheted up pressure for more funding for community health centers, better medical education, and expanded health-care coverage.

With the pandemic raging, lots of people picked up on these issues—local public health officials, journalists, researchers. Even if Ayanna and I had done nothing, I have no doubt that eventually details about racial disparities and the coronavirus would have come to light. But COVID-19 offers a haunting lesson about how racism can literally be a life-and-death matter—and how necessary it is to have good information.

Information can sometimes be disruptive or damaging, which is why people are often reluctant to offer it up. Even after Ayanna and I got reporting requirements added to the relief bill, and even after the press ran a bazillion stories about race and COVID-19, there was an ongoing, behind-the-scenes fight over access to the data. Some states dragged their feet; others were simply overwhelmed and couldn't keep up with basic reporting. By January 2021, race and ethnicity data were still only available for half the reported cases.

The part that drove me crazy about these delays was that every one of them represented a lost chance to improve the system. Even if they had all the data, not every state or county or city would have raced to fix the disparities—shoot, a lot of them still haven't fixed them. But even if they couldn't—or wouldn't—fix everything, a lot of state and local governments could have done so much more. Yet as long as there was no publicly available data on race and ethnicity, it was easier for them to slide on by. No one had to learn what was happening, no one had to change anything, and no one had to take any responsibility for the people who died.

The COVID-19 crisis taught me another lesson about how powerful information can be—and how resistant some people are to giving it up, especially when issues involving race are on the table. But once again, pushing back mattered. We dug out at least some of the racial disparity information, and it helped change the discussion about both the pandemic and health care generally. And once again, collecting the right information mattered.

The old truth still held: You can't fix what you can't see.

## GETTING IT WRONG

I am not a person of color. I am not a citizen of a tribal nation. I have never experienced the injuries of bigotry, large or small. All I can do is try to understand the world, listen to those who have experienced prejudice, find ways to attack the ugliness head-on, and try to be a helpful ally. I am far from perfect, and even though I fall short, I keep trying.

An early lesson in how far short I can fall became apparent during my first campaign to be elected senator from Massachusetts. Questions about my family's heritage first surfaced in the spring of 2012, just as my Senate race was beginning to gain steam. At first, I didn't think much of it. Everybody had family stories, and I was as proud of my family as anyone. I grew up in Oklahoma and, like a lot of people, my older brothers and I learned about our family background from our mom and dad.

They told us family stories about Native American connections on our mother's side, and we believed them.

My family has always mattered to me, and, based on those stories, decades ago I sometimes identified as Native American. This became the focus of the attack from the incumbent senator I was challenging, who insisted I had gotten my teaching jobs by claiming to be someone I was not.

That was flatly untrue, and years later an in-depth investigation by the *Boston Globe* proved it. The *Globe* reached out to every living member of the Harvard faculty and to members of every faculty who hired me in earlier years. They reviewed every document they could locate and read every contemporaneous news report they could find. Their conclusion: "Warren was viewed as a white woman by the hiring committees at every institution that employed her."

Still, I should never have identified as Native American. I've never been a citizen of a tribal nation. Tribal nations—and only tribal nations—determine who their citizens are.

I had made a bad mistake, and as 2012 went on and the campaign heated up, the Republicans turned that mistake into a weapon. They aired every bigoted slur and joke they could think of. They erected a huge billboard with my face on it under a giant photoshopped headdress. Under the guise of bare-knuckle politics, the Republicans tried to turn anti-Native sentiment dating back to the earliest years of our nation into a twisted form of entertainment. Their attacks demeaned an entire people; their assaults made a joke out of a dark history. Yet their slurs went largely unremarked by both my opponent and the mainstream media.

All of this was on me, and I didn't know how to make it stop.

When the 2012 election was over and I'd beaten my opponent, the billboards disappeared and the bigoted jokes quieted down. At first, I thought silence was the right answer. Just let the attacks go, I told myself. Don't stir them up.

In my first few years in the Senate, I supported legislation and went to events that were important to tribal nations, but I tried to avoid public attention while doing so. I invited tribal leaders, both from Massachusetts and from across the country, to sit down with me and talk. Many dropped by my Senate office, and I was glad for the opportunity to discuss a range of issues affecting Indian Country.

That ongoing work might have been the soft close to the story, but then along came Donald Trump.

In early 2016, as Trump was knocking off one opponent after another during the Republican primaries, I decided to call out his bullying. In March, I called him a "loser" and chronicled his various scams. Later, as some Republicans grew increasingly uncomfortable with his rallies and the white supremacists flocking to his campaign, I tweeted: "There's more enthusiasm for @realDonaldTrump among leaders of the KKK than leaders of the political party he now controls." The result was that he turned his sights on me, calling me "Pocahontas" and thereby insulting Native Americans across the country.

Native activists and leaders demanded that he stop, but he wallowed in the attention and ratcheted up the attacks. In fact, he was so drawn to the slur that he kept it up in tweets and at rallies even after he was elected. On November 17, 2017, at a White House ceremony honoring Navajo code talkers of World War II, he abandoned his prepared script about these revered war heroes, and instead took the opportunity to perform an impromptu riff during which he again called me Pocahontas.

In February 2018, the president of the National Congress of American Indians invited me to speak at their annual meeting in Washington. I was glad to show my support, and I used the event as a chance to talk about the real Pocahontas—not the fictional character that most Americans know from the movies, but the Native woman whose real journey was far more remarkable, and far darker, than the myth admits. I committed to fighting for real change in Indian Country, such as stopping giant corporations from stealing Native resources, protecting historic monuments and land, and working to empower tribal governments. And in front of hundreds of tribal leaders, I made a promise: when detractors brought up my family's story, I would use it as an opportunity to lift up the story of Native families and communities.

I decided that from then on, I would not be cowed by bigots. Yes,

I had made mistakes, but I would keep trying to learn. And no matter what, I would keep working on Native issues.

I set up more meetings with Native leaders and visited tribal nations. I studied more. Frontline workers taught me about the chronic under-funding of the Indian Health Service and the challenges of tribal hous-ing. Activists, entrepreneurs, and community leaders met with me for long conversations about economic opportunity, discussing everything from fishing rights to the wide variety of roles that gaming plays for different tribal nations. A step at a time, I came to a deeper understand-ing of these issues, and I began making a concerted effort to move our federal government toward meeting its trust and treaty obligations to tribal nations—obligations that America has so long ignored.

Later that year, I thought I might help put the issue to rest and fend off Trump's ongoing attacks if I took a DNA test. So in October 2018, I took the test and released the results. But I was wrong to take the test, and I apologized for my mistake. The following summer, at a Native American forum for presidential candidates, I talked about the confusion my actions had caused around tribal sovereignty and citizenship, and the harm that they'd done to Native communities. I told the panelists and the audience, "I have listened, and I have learned. A lot." A number of Native leaders welcomed my apology and my promise to do better. Trump, of course, kept right on going.

When I ran for president, I wanted to make Native issues an impor-tant part of my campaign. With help from many Native leaders, I devel-oped detailed, robust plans that were designed to reset our federal government's relationship with Native nations. I worked with my cam-paign cochair, Representative Deb Haaland, one of the first two Native women in Congress, to develop a comprehensive proposal to fully fund federal programs for Native Americans.

The challenges facing Native communities are enormous. Our fed-eral government has made solemn promises to tribal nations, but we have broken them time and again. As a result, the need for urgent action in Indian Country spans the entire universe of policy areas: health care, education, public safety, housing, economic development, and many others. In 2016, for example, there were 5,712 reports of missing Native women and girls, but only 116 of them were in the federal missing persons database. The epidemic of missing and murdered Indigenous women and girls is raging out of control, so during my campaign we worked on a plan to give tribal nations the resources and legal authority to combat this emergency directly. We also looked hard at a misguided Supreme Court decision from decades ago that denied tribal governments jurisdiction to prosecute non-Natives for crimes they commit on tribal lands, and I became the first presidential candidate to recommend a legislative fix. We focused on broadband issues, too: despite the critical importance of the internet, 1.5 million people on reservations currently can't get basic wireless service, so I put together a plan to dramatically increase access.

Suicide in Indian Country is a particularly tough and heartbreaking issue, with suicide rates higher among Native communities than any other group in the United States. Over the years, I've talked with many Native people who have lost beloved family members and friends to this tragedy. These heartbreaking conversations spurred me to introduce the Native American Suicide Prevention Act in the Senate, and to make it part of my campaign plan. The 2020 end-of-year omnibus budget included my suicide prevention bill—a bit of progress in memory of those who were lost.

No one makes change alone. Tribal leaders and advocates from coast to coast have generously given their time to speak with me, sometimes traveling many hours so we could meet face-to-face. And yes, there are a huge number of problems to tackle, but I felt good about using my presidential campaign and my seat in the Senate to lift up these issues.

I will continue my efforts, and I'll keep on learning. As I think about my own role, I'm reminded that although tribal nations need good partners in Washington, ultimately the federal government's work that affects Indian Country must be guided and informed by Native leaders. The people whose voices should be heard are those who have the lived experience of being Native American, the people whose lives will be touched by federal policies. And those of us who are part of the nation's government have an obligation to ensure that the United States honors its promises.

I have gotten it wrong in the past, but I will keep doing my best to learn, and to fulfill my role as a supporting partner.

## HOT BUTTONS

Ted Kennedy spent nearly forty-seven years as a senator from Massachusetts. During his long tenure, he was the primary author of more than three hundred bills that were enacted into law. His living memorial is the Kennedy Institute in Boston, which includes a full-scale replica of the U.S. Senate that often serves as a unique venue for programs.

After I'd been in the Senate awhile, the director of the Institute called to ask if I would give a speech there. "After all," she said, "you have the Senator's seat." For her, "the Senator" would always be Ted Kennedy.

I said I'd be glad to speak, and we set up a date for the fall of 2015. The director assumed I'd want to talk about bank regulation or consumer protection, and that was fine with her. "But the decision is up to you," she said. "You talk about whatever you want."

For a lot of people in Massachusetts, this speech was a big deal. What would the woman who now held the seat that had been occupied for decades by Ted Kennedy have to say for herself?

By the summer of 2015, the Black Lives Matter movement had challenged America's perceptions of criminal justice. As I began thinking about what I wanted to focus on in the speech, the deaths of Eric Garner, Michael Brown, Sandra Bland, and so many other Black men and women were very much on my mind. I decided to talk about race.

When the day arrived, the weather was glorious, evoking the best kind of travel-brochure photograph of New England in the fall. The Kennedy Institute's re-creation of the Senate includes the carpeting with fancy medallions, the spaced-out desks—one for each senator—and the Senate chamber's sloping amphitheater down to a well. When I walked in, I saw that each seat was filled. I stood in the well, looked up and smiled, then dived right in.

I began by tying my talk to Ted Kennedy's first speech as a senator. It was 1963, and his brother, President John F. Kennedy, had just been assassinated. Undaunted, the young senator used his inaugural speech to argue for passage of the Civil Rights Act.

Using that memorable speech as my starting point, I launched into a discussion of the ongoing fight for racial justice and all that remained undone. I talked about three goals—putting an end to state-sponsored violence against African Americans, ensuring power in the democratic process through access to the vote, and creating more economic opportunity for a people that had faced government-sponsored discrimination throughout the nation's entire history. At one point in the speech, I made a point of echoing the language of the current movement and said, "Black lives matter. Black citizens matter. Black families matter."

When my talk was over, I felt deeply satisfied. I knew there was a lot more that I hadn't covered and there were probably things I'd gotten wrong, but at least this speech hit racial justice problems head-on—no dancing around. I knew some people might not like it, but I looked out at the audience, smiled, and said exactly what I was thinking: "That's a speech I really wanted to give."

The speech received some excellent reviews; the *Washington Post*, for example, said it was the speech that Black activists had been waiting for. But not everyone loved the speech, including a policeman named Patrick Rose. Officer Rose was the president of the Boston Police Patrolmen's Association at the time, and he was furious. Within days of the speech, he called to demand a meeting. Demand—that was his word.

I was willing to talk with him, but I was a little taken aback by his aggressiveness. I had a solid working relationship with the Boston police—in fact, with most police in Massachusetts. But Officer Rose was clearly determined to set me straight about my responsibilities as the Commonwealth's senator.

In 2013, following the death of Trayvon Martin, three women—Patrisse Cullors, Alicia Garza, and Opal Tometi—began the rallying cry "Black lives matter" and founded a movement. As more videos emerged of African Americans injured or dying at the hands of the police, BLM became a louder, more insistent voice demanding change. By 2015, when I spoke, some Democratic politicians were still hanging back, while others stood in solidarity with those protesting the deaths of Black men and women during encounters with the police.

Sensing racial divisions that they could exploit, Republicans launched an all-out attack on the BLM movement. At the time I spoke at the Kennedy Institute, Republican presidential candidates Ted Cruz and Scott Walker declared that BLM was putting police officers' lives in danger. Candidate Chris Christie said BLM was "calling for the murder of police officers." Mike Huckabee claimed to know that Dr. Martin Luther King Jr. would be "appalled" by BLM. Other candidates denounced BLM as dishonest for not focusing on Black-on-Black violence. The attacks were as incendiary as they were relentless.

On the appointed day, Officer Rose strode into my Boston office with his head back, chest out, and a scowl firmly in place. He seemed intent on inflicting some pain.

After taking his seat, Officer Rose leaned forward, tense and angry. He skipped the pleasantries and got straight to the point. According to Officer Rose, when I'd uttered the words "Black Lives Matter" in my speech at the Kennedy Institute, I had disrespected the police. After all, BLM—according to him—was a terrorist group that was full of radicals and anarchists. He told me that police put their lives on the line for "people like me" and said I should be "more grateful."

Officer Rose could barely contain his fury. As he leaned toward me, pushing closer and closer, he ramped up his attack. Soon he was lecturing me about ethics, what it means to be a leader, and the importance of a personal code of honor.

When he was finished, I was stunned, but not because his attack was so personal. I sat there quietly for a moment, thinking, *Really? That's it? Not one word about Michael Brown or Eric Garner? Not one word about the videos that showed one African American man after another dying during an assault by the police? Not even a passing acknowledgment that maybe there was a problem and that something needed to change?*

It's frequently argued that plenty of good people work in criminal justice. That's true, but it's also beside the point. Racist policing isn't a problem caused by one bad apple or even a dozen bad apples. It's a structural problem. It's a problem that begins with the persistent racism in our country, which in turn feeds the way we approach criminal justice. It's a broken system, and eliminating a few bad apples won't fix it.

Good people often work right alongside bad people. Over the years, some of these good people have reached out to me and others to say that racism is a problem in their police departments or their prisons or their courtrooms—and they want to see change. They understand that when it comes to racism, you are either part of the problem or part of the solution, and they want to be part of the solution.

But Boston's police union president didn't come see me to talk about a broken system. Officer Rose had a very specific target in his sights: Black Lives Matter. Under his leadership, his union had already published multiple articles about BLM in its bimonthly magazine, and now I was a target as well. The sub-headline of one article read, "Sen. Warren Embraces Radical, Cop-Hating Anarchists, Denounces Police." Using its own magazine, the union made plain its belief that the police were the victims and that they should not be questioned. As the magazine put it, the police officer who shot Michael Brown "did his job" and "did what he needed to do"—end of story.

After delivering his rant, Officer Rose clearly thought I would back down and apologize. He was wrong. When it became apparent that he couldn't bully me, he didn't stay for conversation. Instead, he stormed out.

But my run-ins with bullies weren't over. In August 2018, I visited Dillard University, a historically Black college located in New Orleans. Cedric Richmond—then a congressman who was the chairman of the Congressional Black Caucus—and I had a discussion onstage; afterward, we took questions from the audience. Someone asked about the criminal justice system, and I said that it was time to recognize "the hard truth about our criminal justice system: it's racist . . . front to back."

That comment was far from casual. The failures in our criminal justice system are evident in every phase of its operations, from the front—including the laws we pass that determine what is treated as illegal and what punishment each crime carries—to the back—including how formerly incarcerated people are denied access to public housing and shut out of many employment opportunities. The examples are everywhere. Take the disproportionate arrest of Black people on minor drug possession charges: no one can be arrested for something the legislature didn't criminalize in the first place. Or the overloaded public defender system: when poor people can't get lawyers, justice is a sham. Or marijuana criminalization: numerous laws provide an excuse for probable cause for pretty much any kind of search or harassment imaginable. Or felony disenfranchisement: several state laws ensure that even after a convicted felon has completed their sentence, they will never again have power in the voting booth. The data show that every one of these issues—and many more—are signs of ingrained, institutionalized racism.

My appearance at Dillard received a lot of press coverage, and the pushback was immediate. Some local police chiefs denounced me, with at least one calling my discussion about race "inflammatory." I was up for reelection that year, so the criticism immediately turned political. Republicans repeatedly called on me to apologize.

So there it was. To talk about how racism is embedded in our judicial system was the cardinal sin. Meanwhile, every unjustified shooting and every death should be treated as a one-off—a terrible accident, a freak set of circumstances, a bad apple in an otherwise good barrel using poor judgment. And none—none—of our criminal justice problems should ever be viewed through the lens of systemic racism.

My response during that campaign was to say pretty much the same thing over and over: if we're to have any hope of building a fairer system, we need to attack racism head-on. We can't do that if we don't first acknowledge what is wrong. I pointed out that many men and women go into policing to help people, and that police officers themselves were calling for reforms. I partnered with the family of Sergeant Sean Gannon—who served the people of Yarmouth, Massachusetts, and died in the line of duty—to advocate for police-supported gun reforms to help protect the lives of other police officers. I advanced reforms that Black police officers supported. But the police unions in Boston and elsewhere were having none of it. They endorsed my opponent, declaring that I could not be trusted.

In all the back-and-forth, I learned a lesson about the limits of facts and statistics. No matter how hard I tried, I could not persuade Officer Rose and a number of other police officials to engage with some rock-solid information. Study after study shows that for *exactly the same crimes*, African Americans are more likely than whites to be arrested, detained, taken to trial, wrongfully convicted, and given longer sentences. I don't know any way to explain this damning truth except to say that racism pervades our criminal justice system—so that's what I said. And yet, instead of prompting a useful discussion about the changes we need to make, my comments provoked sharp rebukes. I was repeatedly told that not every single police officer was racist and that any discussion of these issues would put police officers at risk.

When I ran for president, the issue of reforming our criminal justice system was front and center. In August 2019, I laid out a plan to rework every part of the system, from what we choose to criminalize; to how law enforcement and prosecutors engage with communities and the accused; to how long we keep people behind bars, how we treat them when they're there, and how we reintegrate them when they return. This plan was about criminal law, policing, courts, prisons, voting rights. To say it simply, it was about reform from front to back.

Our criminal justice plan got a good reception. Activist Brittany Packnett Cunningham wrote, "I really appreciate that @ewarren's approach to the issue of criminal justice is both comprehensive and *begins* with a systemic reimagining of public safety." I met with advocacy groups and people who had been incarcerated to learn more about what else we could do and how we could work together to get it done. I took on a wide range of issues during my campaign, but here was another great reason to run hard: if we made it to the White House, we could make big, structural change in our system of justice.

I didn't win the presidency, of course. But two and a half months after I dropped out of the race, the issue of police violence was thrust back into the headlines when a Minneapolis police officer knelt on the neck of George Floyd until he died, causing an enormous outcry. Within days, national attention focused on the death of Breonna Taylor two months earlier, when police had entered her home and shot her in her bed. Then came Ahmaud Arbery's death at the hands of two armed white men who pursued him while he was out jogging.

Protests erupted nationwide. In Washington, and later back in Cambridge, Bruce and I joined the marchers, adding our voices to the millions of Americans who were calling for reform. I believed then—and I believe today—that systemic racism and white supremacy underlie these tragic events. Sadly, we found ourselves calling for justice for George, Breonna, Ahmaud, and so many others *after* they had been killed, instead of providing justice to them before the unthinkable happened.

The summer of 2020—a summer darkened by a raging pandemic and roiling protests against racism—was a time for serious soul-searching, a time to acknowledge unacceptable racial disparities in wealth, education, employment, housing, education, and health care. More than ever, it is painfully obvious that it's time to reform our criminal justice system. We must rethink how the law is written and enforced at both the state and federal level. We need accountability for law enforcement and accountability at every stage of our criminal justice system. Any decent person who brings integrity and compassion to their work in the criminal justice system should welcome that kind of accountability. In fact, they should demand it.

Whether in Washington or Massachusetts, I marched because I believe that communities of color cannot be left to fight the scourge of racism alone. I marched because I want to learn more about my own responsibilities as a white American. And as I marched and listened, I came to understand that it is not enough to stand as an ally. We must go further and be anti-racist.

Claims such as "I'm not racist" or "so-and-so is not a racist" may sound harmless to some, but to many they cut deep. Familiar denials like these so often seem to be the justification for a second, unspoken part to that sentence: "and therefore I don't have to do anything about racism." And that's the part that is just plain wrong.

Our moral obligation goes well beyond a belief that we aren't part of the problem. Our moral obligation is to recognize the problem, face it head-on, and fix it. And that's true regardless of whether we're white, Black, Latino, Native American, Asian American, or any conceivable mix of races or ethnicities or cultures or identities. We are all humans and we all have a responsibility to each other.

Nobody gets off the hook. Nobody.

## RACE-NEUTRAL VERSUS RACIAL REALITY

Back when I was studying the bankruptcy system, I had seen how a supposedly race-neutral attitude can hide a multitude of sins. There had been whispers about whether the bankruptcy system was working differently for Black and white debtors, but no one had followed up with a serious investigation. If no one asked about racial disparities, then no racial problems existed. Whether the "don't ask" policy was inadvertent or deliberate, the impact was the same—devastating racial differences were covered up.

The infamous Supreme Court decision in *Plessy v. Ferguson* enshrined the idea of separate-but-equal, promoting a comfortable (for whites) notion that no one was getting hurt by Jim Crow laws that legalized segregation. According to the Supreme Court, segregated schools, segregated workplaces, segregated restaurants, segregated theaters, and segregated swimming pools were just a matter of personal choice—all built on the absurd assumption that African Americans and whites in every corner of America could choose from a similar range of good schools, good workplaces, good restaurants, good theaters, and good swimming pools.

*Brown v. Board of Education* demolished that comfortable assumption, decreeing that the law must recognize the reality that separate is not equal. A decade later, Congress followed up with the long-overdue Civil Rights Acts, which protected access to the vote, banned segregation in housing and education, and outlawed employment discrimination.

But conservative lawyers and judges did not yield. They fought back for decades, undermining both *Brown* and the civil rights legislation. Despite the overwhelming evidence of the impact of racism, today the fundamental idea of race neutrality continues to claim an elevated status in law. The consequence, Professor Ibram Kendi observes, is that these legal battles "ended up principally outlawing 'intention to discriminate'" so that "[i]ntent—not outcome—became the preferred proof of discrimination."

Kendi argues that the focus on state of mind (intent to discriminate) rather than the effect of specific actions (discriminatory impact) undermines the push for equality. He notes that the emphasis on intent "ignored the white head-start, presumed discrimination had been eliminated, assumed equal opportunity had taken over, and figured that since blacks were still losing the race, the racial disparities must be their own fault." As conservative lawyers and pundits urged them on, many courts ignored racial realities, shifting the conversation instead to so-called reverse discrimination and labeling affirmative action as a corrective that they argued was "entirely unnecessary in America's 'colorblind'—and now 'post-racial'—society."

These complex issues were very much on my mind in the fall of 2018 when I began thinking more seriously about running for president. I thought long and hard about how to present one of my central arguments: racism is a tool of corruption. The corruption I wanted to speak about is rooted in the struggle for power—who has it and who doesn't. For too much of our history, those who have power have used it to stir racism and divide those who don't.

When I spoke at the 2016 Democratic National Convention, I made exactly this point. In a prime-time speech on the first night of the convention, I argued that the powerful have long used fear and hate to pit Americans against each other. Whites against Black and Latino people. Christians against Muslims and Jews. Straight people against gay and trans people. Everyone against immigrants. "Divide-and-conquer is an old story in America," I said that night. "Dr. Martin Luther King knew it. After his march from Selma to Montgomery, he spoke of how segregation was created to keep people divided. Instead of higher wages for workers,

Dr. King described how poor whites in the South were fed Jim Crow, which told a poor white worker that 'No matter how bad off he was, at least he was a white man, better than the Black man.' Racial hatred was part of keeping the powerful on top."

Two years later, I knew that race would be an important part of any presidential race I ran. Long before I made the final decision to run or considered making a trip to Iowa, I started thinking about how I—a white woman—could talk about race as a presidential candidate. Silence was not an option.

Instead, I would talk about racism as part of a corrupt system. And I would do my best to walk the walk, examining problems through a racial lens and proposing meaningful solutions—racially conscious solutions—so that we could do more than just talk. With a lot of hard work, I believed we could start to make real change.

As the fall went on and the stakes became ever higher, I finally made up my mind: I would run.

I announced my decision on New Year's Eve, then headed off to Iowa the following weekend. We were a full year out from the Iowa caucuses—the first opportunity in the nation for voters to declare their preference—and this was a big debut.

That weekend, Iowa had a chance to look at me, and I had a chance to look at Iowa. It didn't come as a surprise, but those early crowds were white. *Really* white.

I knew from my Senate campaigns that having a good stump speech matters a lot. It provides one of the best opportunities to tell voters about the human being who is asking for their support. As I started preparing for the race, I knew the issues I wanted to talk about, but turning those ideas into a short, punchy speech that would allow me to introduce myself to possible voters and volunteers would be hard. I figured I shouldn't talk any longer than fifteen minutes, and I had a lot I wanted to cover. Even so, I thought it was important to speak about racial injustice right from the beginning, so I did. I talked about the Black/white wealth gap. About housing discrimination. About educational opportunities and student loan debt. As my campaign went on,

I spoke about a wide range of issues, but I felt strongly that unless we consistently addressed racial inequities, we couldn't build an America that truly worked for everyone—and that meant it was important for me to talk about it every chance I got.

As I saw it, my first task was to call out the problem, and my second was to work out a series of plans to deal with it. Well before that first trip to Iowa, I had to decide whether I was going to follow the path of so many before me and simply argue for laws and policies that would help people generally and thus, presumably, help people of color. Up to a point, this approach can work pretty well. But the problems of systemic racism run deep, and I didn't believe that this approach was rigorous enough to deal with the world as it exists. I was convinced that the best way to fight racism was to hit racial issues head-on. So I built plans— lots of plans—that dealt explicitly with race.

My housing plan was just one example. Building 3.2 million new homes and apartments would help millions of families—Black, Latino, Native American, Asian American, and white. And because Black and Latino families have been disproportionately squeezed by the cost of housing relative to income, the relief provided by my plan would be felt more by Black and Latino families. A robust housing plan would make life better for a lot of people, but it would give a particularly big boost to people of color.

So far so good, but we could do more. If we added another feature to the plan, we could provide home-buying assistance to people living in formerly redlined neighborhoods. We could also help people who lost their homes during the economic collapse of 2008. More broadly, a significant portion of this assistance would be targeted to the Black and Latino communities, and to the people who had disproportionately borne the brunt of racial discrimination. In the end I proposed both—a big housing plan for everyone and a targeted housing plan for those who had been hit hardest by racial discrimination.

Or consider higher education. Black students borrow more money than white students to go to college and have a harder time paying it back after they graduate. And the impact of having to climb this steeper hill marks a whole life. Twenty years after graduating, the average white borrower has only 6 percent of their original loan left to pay off; the end is in sight. But the average Black student still owes 95 percent of the original loan amount. A home, a business, saving for retirement— every major financial investment is still years into the future for nearly all Black borrowers.

What's the best way to end this inequity? Here's a good starting place: implement a debt forgiveness plan that considers our current state of racial inequality. By canceling $50,000 of student loan debt and limiting the benefit of debt cancellation to people earning less than $100,000, relief would be widespread. About three out of every four borrowers would see their entire debt load wiped out, and most of the remainder would see a substantial reduction. But the effect on the Black/white and Latino/white wealth gap would be stunning, reducing both by about 25 points. That shift would be historic.

But here, too, we could do more. Education is about building opportunities, and systemic discrimination has undercut opportunities for far too many minority students. Making public technical schools, two-year colleges, and four-year colleges tuition-free would open doors for millions of young people—especially people of color, who are more likely to cite cost as a reason not to continue their educations. Expanding Pell Grants for low-income students would open the doors even wider—again, particularly for students of color. And there's also a place for racially explicit policies. Direct support for both Historically Black Colleges and Universities and Minority Serving Institutions would acknowledge that an additional pathway for students who have faced racial discrimination is a critical step in creating real—not imaginary— equality of opportunity.

For me, the lesson is obvious. Every policy, not just those involving housing or higher education, should be examined in terms of the current racial realities. Every policy tool, including racially explicit tools, should be examined to see how it might help end racial inequities. And that's what I tried to do during my campaign. Every time I drew up a new plan for addressing one of the items on the long list of problems we face—from climate change to closing the pay gap for women—I made sure to find out everything I could about how racial inequities figured into the problem and then think about my plan in terms of race. To my mind, that's how a race-conscious approach to policy ought to work.

I don't pretend that I got it all. Even after decades of work and study in universities, eight years in the Senate, and fourteen months running for president, I continue to learn about areas where racial injustice runs deep and where thoughtful policy responses could make a real difference. I continue to ask for help from leaders and scholars and people whose lived experiences expose the need for real change. I try to lift up the voices of people who have a deep understanding of racism and whose policy solutions are informed by their own lives. I also think constantly about which parts of my plans will work and which parts need to be revised. But I am absolutely certain that if we don't start with hard questions about how policies directly affect—and are affected by—race, we will never build what the Constitution called "a more perfect union."

## REPRESENTATION MATTERS

The smiles flashed—the sort of 10,000-watt *Am I really here?* smiles that lit up every face in the crowd. Beautiful little boys who were four or five, dressed in their Sunday best, their dark hair slicked down and their faces scrubbed clean. Older boys, proudly imitating the poses of their fathers and grandfathers. Teenage boys trying to hide their excitement as they kept rearranging their way-too-cool expressions.

It was a selfie line. And the boys—and their moms and dads and sisters and grandparents and aunties and cousins and friends—had been standing in line for hours to get their picture taken with rock star Julián Castro.

It was January 2020, and we were in Kings Theatre, a gorgeous 1920s movie palace in Brooklyn. Earlier, every one of the 3,690 seats had been filled, and the crowd outside still packed a courtyard and stretched down the block. It had been raining all evening, but that didn't seem to dampen anyone's spirits.

Before our event started, Julián and I had gone outside to speak to the people who were turned away once the building reached capacity. I'd held the umbrella over Julián while he spoke, then he did the same for me. We thanked people for coming, apologized that there was no more room, and then made the fateful promise that if they came back later, we'd do selfies.

Now, with the speeches over, I stood off to one side of the stage, watching as Julián took time to have a word with each family waiting in the selfie line. Bantering in Spanish or English, he smiled back at every child. As they snapped photos with their phones, I thought about how many of those pictures would end up framed on someone's wall. For each of those boys—and their sisters—the photographs would be a powerful reminder about what is possible in America.

Watching the crowd, two words kept echoing in my mind: "Representation matters." In 2008, when Barack Obama ran for president and won, that mattered. In 2020, when Julián Castro ran for president, that mattered.

Now we were somewhere in our third hour of selfies—pictures with Julián, pictures with me, pictures with both of us—and I still couldn't see the end of the line. I watched as Julián lifted one foot and gave it a little shake, then did the same with his other foot. I knew that move. Standing in one place for hours can get really tiring. After a while, your feet can go numb or cramps can set in. But Julián kept smiling, and so did I.

I had first met Julián in 2014 when I was still a fairly new senator. I had a seat on the Banking Committee, which has jurisdiction over Housing and Urban Development (HUD), and Julián was President Obama's brand-new HUD secretary. Not long after his appointment, I'd talked to him on the phone a couple of times, and then I'd invited him to the Senate Dining Room for lunch. I thought it would be good for us to get to know each other.

Much later, while introducing me on the campaign trail in early 2020, he would tell the story of this lunch. He said he remembered thinking how nice it would be to have lunch, that we'd begin with some polite small talk, then maybe chat about politics or the people we knew in

Washington. A pleasant, leisurely lunch. "Boy, was I in for a rude awakening. She wasn't there for small talk." And then he laughed, a gentle, indulgent laugh, because of course he'd been as eager as I was to dig in on a wide range of issues.

I don't recall exactly how we began our lunch that day, but Julián's account was probably right. He had inherited HUD at a time when the mortgage crisis was entering a new phase. Mortgage lenders had forced millions of people out of their homes, particularly in Black and Latino communities. The lenders had then turned around and, for the houses carrying mortgages that were guaranteed through the Federal Housing Authority, dumped the properties on the federal government. Now those houses were being sold off, and Wall Street raptors were snapping them up and turning them into rental properties. Over time, the consequence would be to drain even more wealth out of communities of color, and thus keep homeownership rates low for people of color for decades to come.

We had only a limited number of tools to stop or at least slow down this predatory practice, and we were running out of time. So, yeah, I probably skipped the small talk and dived right in with an action plan for HUD—after all, that's why the two of us were meeting. Before the iced tea arrived, Julián and I were deep in conversation about FHA guarantees and bundling rules for sales of foreclosed properties. We hashed through lots of technical details, but we also traded stories about families who had been cheated and then wiped out by the crash of 2008.

An hour into our lunch, we were both still talking a mile a minute when each of us had to leave for our next appointments. I left that meeting deeply impressed. Here was a man with a good heart and a lot of political courage. He wasn't looking for headlines. He knew how the banks had laid waste to one community after another, and he was committed to repairing as much of the damage as he could.

Over the next couple of years, Julián and I talked by phone or grabbed lunch whenever we could find the time. We continued our conversation about predatory lenders, but we also talked about the Fair Housing Act and how to rebuild communities devastated by natural disasters. We tried out ideas on each other, looking for ways to put our federal government a little more firmly on the side of hardworking people.

In 2016, rumor had it that Hillary was considering Julián for her running mate. I was on the list for VP, too, but instead Hillary chose Tim Kaine, the senator from Virginia and former Democratic National Committee chairman. The 2016 presidential campaign came and went, and somehow Donald Trump ended up in the White House. Julián and I were determined to do everything possible to limit the damage Trump could do, so we both found ourselves working harder than ever.

In December 2018, Julián announced a presidential exploratory committee, and in February 2019, he declared his candidacy for president. That made us competitors in the race for the Democratic nomination, at least in theory. But it never really felt that way. There were so many people running for the nomination—first ten, then fifteen, then twenty, eventually more than two dozen major candidates. My competition with Julián never had anything like the cage-match intensity of a two-person race.

Julián and I didn't agree on everything, but he was running on big ideas and significant reform and major change. He was committed to public service. I respected his campaign as much as I respected him.

For a year, a large number of candidates spent a lot of time together waiting backstage before speaking at this or that event. I was always glad to see Julián, and each time the two of us found ourselves waiting in the wings, we talked about the things our nation could—and should—do. We still talked about housing, but we also talked about education, health care, and climate. Some of our ideas were great, and some were, well, not quite fully formed.

As the race heated up, Julián was the first candidate to roll out a fully developed immigration plan, and it was excellent. He dug into how an antiquated law from the 1920s championed by a segregationist senator was now being exploited by the Trump administration to separate families at the border, and he proposed a change that would help more immigrant families reunite. I agreed and said so.

Later, when Julián proposed a creative new disability inclusion plan, he helped change the national conversation. This plan too was excellent; just as important, it was a powerful statement that the issue of inclusion really mattered. Julián's universal pre-K commitment also broke new ground. Making a national commitment to educate all our children and to fund pre-K education at the federal level would improve the lives of millions of little kids and their parents and teachers. As I've already admitted, I borrowed shamelessly from Julián's plans—and always gave him full credit.

Latinos in the United States face multiple challenges, and I try to keep learning as much as I can about those challenges. While studying bankruptcy in the 1980s and 1990s, I discovered a double problem: both African Americans and Latinos faced high barriers. Latino students were more likely to borrow money to go to college, more likely to pay more for their loans, and more likely to have a harder time paying off their debts after college than white students. Latino business owners had more trouble accessing capital to support their small companies. Latinas were often trapped in low-paying jobs with no access to childcare or health insurance. Over the years, my research taught me that any effort to be race-conscious must include a better understanding of the bigotry and limited opportunities facing Latino communities.

I've had many conversations in recent years with Latinos, and invariably they've led to more questions about complex economic and social issues. Do Hispanics in America see themselves as a racially distinct group? Do first-generation young people from Central America face the same issues as third-generation young people whose grandparents immigrated from Cuba? What about Puerto Ricans—both those still in Puerto Rico and the Boricuas who have put down roots in New York, Massachusetts, Florida, or elsewhere? How can a president best represent all their interests? None of these questions has easy answers, but treating all people who trace their origins to Spanish-speaking countries as if they were a monolithic group is obviously wrong. I struggle, but I remind myself that learners often struggle. It's the only way to get better.

When Julián dropped out of the race on January 2, 2020, he said, *"¡Ganaremos un día!"* which translates to "One day we'll win!" Just five days later, he was in Brooklyn trying to help me get elected, while I was watching children who will one day see a president who looks like Julián.

And now, with Kamala Harris sworn in as the vice president of the United States, Deb Haaland named secretary of the interior, and many other historic nominations to President Biden's cabinet, more Black children, more immigrant children, more South Asian children, more Native American children, and more little girls and boys all across America will see leaders who look like themselves.

Representation matters.

## MAKING CHANGE

Commitment to change—bone-deep, never-say-die commitment—also matters. In April 2019, only a few months into the presidential campaign, the candidates were invited to attend a forum called She the People. It would be held at Texas Southern University, not far down the road from the University of Houston, where I'd gone to college.

I knew this event was important. Black women are the backbone of our party. In 2017, Black women delivered a win for Democratic Senate candidate Doug Jones in Alabama, and then followed up by helping to score crucial wins in the 2018 midterms, including a hard fight to get Stacey Abrams elected governor of Georgia. The latter effort officially failed by the slimmest of margins, most likely because of aggressive voter suppression by her opponent, but the race changed the landscape of electoral politics in Georgia. Black women leaders were demanding their rightful place at the decision-making table.

That's what She the People was all about. It was the first-ever presidential forum organized by women of color for women of color. The group's website said it all: "Our network will continue to grow and live well beyond any one election and ensure that women of color will never be taken for granted again in elections."

I arrived at the event early. As our car pulled up, a young woman met us at the door to the auditorium and hustled us into a small room to wait. There was lots of activity in the hallways, with candidates and their traveling teams and event organizers all buzzing back and forth.

I felt a twist of anxiety stir in my gut. Here I was at an event sponsored by Black women, appearing on the same stage as several other candidates, including Kamala Harris, Cory Booker, and Julián Castro. Each of them might have a more natural connection with the audience than a seventy-year-old white woman. Would the audience dismiss me? Did I have anything to say that would connect with the people in this room? Would I get a chance to say it?

As we sat in the cramped room, I started getting restless. I stepped out to look for a bathroom and ran smack into two other candidates. I went back to our room, asked my team how much longer until I was called, and was told that it would be a while. I was going dead last.

Aargh. I hate long programs. And I really hate long programs when I'm appearing last. People get tired of sitting. They get hungry and irritable. During the second hour, people start wandering out. And I was now scheduled to appear in the *third* hour.

I could feel it: I was going to be a disaster.

Finally I was told that I was on deck. The format would be Q&A, so I didn't have to mentally rehearse much. Instead, I tried to stay loose by doing a few deep knee bends. As I fidgeted backstage, the stage manager came over and said that things were running late, and they really, really needed to wrap up. So, sorry, but would I please make my answers short?

From the wings, I listened to MSNBC's Joy Reid and She the People founder Aimee Allison put Bernie Sanders through a series of tough questions. When he wrapped up, it was my turn.

I heard my name and stepped forward—and stubbed my toe on some kind of cable on the floor. Great start.

But I knew I didn't have any time to waste, so I waved, hugged the hosts, and took my seat as quickly as possible. With the first question, we dived right in.

First up was a woman from the audience with a question about maternal mortality. She had all the data: The United States is one of only thirteen countries in the world in which maternal deaths are higher now than twenty-five years ago, and the risk of pregnancy-related death for Black women is three to four times higher than for white women. Race differences exist even when education and income are taken into account. She didn't want to hear a general health-care-for-all answer. She wanted to hear whether I had a real, honest-to-goodness plan that would address a problem that clearly has a life-or-death racial connection.

I laid out my plan. There was nothing general about it, and I got right into some specific ideas about how to track hospitals and health-care providers in order to identify racial disparities, and then use resources where they were most needed to improve outcomes. Enough of "raising awareness" and passing the buck: I talked about how we could make real change. By now I'd been onstage for only about two minutes, but we were already deep into race-specific policies.

The Q&A that followed covered a lot of ground: criminal justice, housing, redlining, tribal sovereignty. All of the questions were razor-sharp. I felt really good about some of my answers; others could have been better. But I took a swing at all of them, happy for the chance to talk about policy and race and meaningful change.

I could feel the energy in the room. This wasn't a lecture. It wasn't a performance. It was a serious, grown-up conversation. The women in this room were smart and powerful, and they wanted specific plans to confront pressing problems. They wanted plans that we could mobilize around. They wanted plans with enough details so that leaders could be measured by yardsticks and held accountable if they failed to deliver. As the session went on, the crowd got excited. People shouted and called out. It was intense and demanding—and I loved every minute of it.

As we neared the end, Joy Reid turned to me and said: "We are at She the People, this wonderful organization that is empowering women and women of color, but when I talk with women of color in my own life, they'll say, 'Wow, that Elizabeth Warren has great plans. She's got specific plans. She's got great ideas.'"

For just a moment, I thought, *This is going even better than I hoped.* But Joy hadn't come to her question yet.

She continued. "But there's a fear in a lot of people of color and a lot of women of color that say, after the experience of 2016, they don't have the confidence in the electorate of this country to elect a woman president. They want to vote one way, but their fear says that they may need to flee to the safety of a white male candidate. How do you address—"

My brain finished her question: *the urge to flee to the safety of a white male candidate.* I looked out at the audience.

Aimee caught my look and called out: "I think that's called side-eye." The audience laughed and cheered. Aimee nodded and said, "That's side-eye."

Joy continued. "They're not confident the country is willing to elect a woman. How do you address people who may be interested in voting for you but may be afraid?"

That was a big bucket of cold water. Here we had just had this serious, thoughtful, hopeful conversation celebrating the power of the women in this room, and a woman named Joy brought us all back to earth. Fear: yup, we all knew the fear she was talking about. Could we—should we—support a woman? And as I was acutely aware, she was asking a *white* woman this question.

I paused, then I dived in. "Confidence. . . . This is the heart of it. It's 'How are we going to fight?' Not just individually, but how are we going to fight together? Are we going to fight because we are afraid? Are we going to show up for people that we don't actually believe in because we were too afraid to do anything else? That's not who we are."

Someone shouted, "That's right!"

I looked out at all the Black women, Latinas, and Native women in the audience. These were tough, intelligent women, women who could change the world. Speaking directly to them, I pushed on.

"We've got a room full of people here who weren't given anything."

Shouts of agreement in the crowd.

"We've got a room full of people here who had to fight for what they believe in."

Tell it!

"We have a room full of people here who had to reach down deep, and no matter how hard it was, no matter how scary it looked . . ."

Yes!

". . . they found what they needed to find and they brought it up and they took care of the people they loved."

Yes! Yes! Yes!

I loved these women and I loved this moment. She the People had given each of us—onstage and off—the chance to call out racism and bigotry, and then to share a moment of hope and courage. And perhaps best of all, we also shared the vulnerability of knowing that we sometimes get into fights without knowing whether we can win—and we take on these fights anyway.

I learned a great deal from these women. And during the long, challenging, exhilarating months of campaigning that followed this event, I learned and grew alongside so many people who joined a hard fight with an uncertain outcome. No one knew whether we could win, but tens of thousands of people got in the fight anyway.

When I dropped out of the presidential race nearly a year after that extraordinary day in Texas, I thought back to the room full of women who weren't given anything but who had made fighting for change a big part of their lives. I thought about fear and courage. I thought about failure and success. I hadn't won my fight, but I nourished the hope that they would win theirs.

# SIX

# A Woman

"What are you going to do about her mouth?"

Aunt Lucy looked at me with the kind of skepticism a knowledgeable farm woman might display as she regarded a pig too scrawny to be a good investment.

Aunt Lucy and Uncle Travis lived in Wewoka, and they didn't see us as often as the other aunts and uncles. They were staying with us in Oklahoma City while my uncle went to the doctor, and Aunt Lucy, famous for her lack of tact, was bearing down on a pressing question.

I was eleven, and I knew full well what it meant when someone complained about "a mouth on that kid." I was sure Aunt Lucy was referring to my manners—or lack thereof. I hadn't really said anything, at least not in front of her, so I had no idea what had set her off. Even so, I knew the answer couldn't be good.

My mother looked off. "I don't think there's much we can do."

Now I was even more confused. If I was mouthing off, there was *a lot* my mother could do. I knew that for a rock-solid fact.

Aunt Lucy pressed on. "It's bad. You and Don ought to do something."

"Hmmmm."

They both looked at me. "Open your mouth," Aunt Lucy commanded.

I did, and Aunt Lucy said, "*See?* Look at those teeth." She lifted her heavily painted black eyebrows and shook her dyed-black head of curls. Whatever she was upset about, it was apparently so awful that she didn't want to say it out loud.

And that's how I found out that I had crooked teeth. Teeth so crooked that Aunt Lucy could spot them from across the room. Teeth so crooked that my future was obviously in jeopardy.

I'd seen other kids in the seventh grade with braces on their teeth, but I'd never thought much about it. My parents had never said anything about my teeth; besides, I knew we couldn't possibly afford anything as extravagant as braces.

But what Aunt Lucy said stuck with me. I learned to smile with my lips closed. Then I learned to show just some of my top teeth and keep my lips over my bottom teeth, which were much worse. It wasn't so bad. I got used to my crooked teeth the same way I got used to a lot of other things.

When I was twenty-five years old, I still had my cover-the-bottom-teeth smile. That summer, between my second and third years of law school, I had a job as an intern at a Wall Street law firm. The firm repeatedly referred to itself as "very open-minded." Translation: they had two—count 'em, two!—female interns working there that summer. Our internships were meant to be a sign of major progress: this was during a period when a bunch of Wall Street firms got sued for discriminating against women in hiring and promotions.

At the end of the summer, the firm made lots of job offers to interns, but no offers were made to either my female colleague or me. I wasn't surprised. The summer had been a jungle marathon, a blur of trips for coffee and sandwiches for the firm's partners, crosshatched with assignments to write a fifth mortgage for a ship or figure out what to do when someone tangled up the date on a futures contract for pork bellies. (Really.)

No job offer, but the money I'd made that summer was terrific. It paid the tuition for my upcoming final year at Rutgers Law, a truly wonderful state school. In fact, I made so much money that summer that, even after tuition, there was still enough money for something I'd kept tucked away in a secret part of my brain for more than half my life: a chance to get my teeth straightened.

By the end of October, four teeth had been pulled and I was now sporting an amazing architecture of wires and rubber bands and wax blobs. It hurt like the devil, but whenever I walked by a mirror, I admired the ingenious construction job in my mouth. I was on my way to a big, beautiful smile.

I was now in my final year of law school, and every two weeks I sat in an orthodontist's waiting room with a bunch of junior high kids. We all did our homework while we waited for our turns to get our wires tightened, snipped, expanded, or realigned. And that's how I ended up one afternoon in the treatment chair with a law book in my lap.

The orthodontist walked in. A nice-looking guy, probably in his mid-thirties. Cheerful. Friendly. Either he or his partner had now seen me several times, and they might have remembered me because I seemed to be their only patient with a driver's license.

He glanced at the book in my lap and asked what it was. I said, "Tax law."

He asked why I was reading a tax law book. With a quick grin I said, "I'm in law school."

He tilted his head and gave me a quizzical look. "Law school? Is your husband a lawyer?"

I tilted my head back at him. "No," I said. "Is your wife an orthodontist?"

Now he was really confused. "No. Why would you think that?"

"I don't know," I said. "Why would you think my husband is a lawyer?"

Loooong pause. "Oh."

In the 1970s, nobody had to tell me outright that women don't become lawyers. My orthodontist was just one of the never-ending stream of people who delivered that message loud and clear every day.

## EXPECTATIONS 2.0

A couple of years later, I was a real, full-fledged, member-of-the-bar lawyer. Okay, maybe I wasn't quite the go-getter that description implies.
More accurately, I was a mom with two little ones. I remember this period
as the Endless Diapers Era. But I wasn't giving up on being a lawyer. I
had hung out a shingle and was practicing law out of my living room.
Just before a client came over, I would turn off the washing machine,
straighten up the living room, and say a quick prayer asking for the kids
to be quiet. My work was in no way fancy, but I had a few cases. I set up
a couple of small businesses, managed a few bankruptcies. Wrote some
wills. Handled an adoption. My clients were mostly neighbors, my business mostly word-of-mouth.

In the late spring of 1977, two of my neighbors, Mr. and Mrs. Holt,
came to see me. They lived in the house on the corner, barn-red with
bright white trim. Jim Holt had been in a car accident. No one was hurt,
but their car had been banged up pretty badly. They were quite sure that
the other guy was at fault, but he—or, more accurately, his insurance
company—wouldn't pay. After telling me their story, Mrs. Holt asked if
I could "do something."

I tried calling. Nothing. I sent a letter. Nothing. I sent another letter.
Nothing. So I filed a lawsuit in state court. A date was set for late sum-
mer. When the day came, I parked the kids with another neighbor while
Mr. and Mrs. Holt and I trekked off to the courthouse in Elizabeth, New
Jersey.

I'd never actually been in a courtroom before. Some people might be
shocked to learn that in many parts of the country a person can graduate from law school, pass the bar, hang out a shingle, take clients, file
a lawsuit—and never see the inside of a courtroom. It shocked me. But
here I was.

Here I was, and I was rapidly rethinking this whole "I'm going to be
a lawyer" thing. I had no idea what I was doing. I had tried to prepare,
but I was completely on my own. I had no senior lawyer to guide me, no
cocounsel to hold my hand, no older friend to make a few suggestions.

I was lost, and whatever confidence I had felt when I'd sent those law-yer letters and made those lawyer phone calls began draining away the moment I walked into the courthouse.

Worse yet, I guessed why the Holts had hired me: I was the only lawyer they knew. (Well, that, and I was cheap.) My work for them had started with a couple of pretty standard legal letters, and no one—certainly not me—thought the case would actually end up in court. But there was no turning back now. Mr. Holt had taken the day off from work, and they were both dressed for church. They kept asking me ques-tions about what would happen. I didn't have a clue, and the growing look of concern on their faces was making me even more anxious.

I had done what I could to get ready. I'd found the courthouse on a map. I'd read a bar journal article about the etiquette of appearing in court. And—most important!—I had dressed the part. Off-white suit. Brown polka-dot blouse. Bow at the neck. Stockings. Heels. Spiffy little briefcase. Surely that would get me through. Surely.

The three of us arrived early, a tight little clutch. We sat down in the churchlike pews and glanced around, taking in the proceedings.

At first blush, the process seemed fairly straightforward. The clerk of the court would stand up and, in a loud voice, call a case—"Smith versus Jones!" Then two men would shuffle to their feet. One would call out, "Ready for the defendant!" and the other would yell, "Ready for the plaintiff!" The judge would glance at the men, look at his papers, then motion them to the front where they would sort out how to proceed—maybe a trial, maybe a motion to delay, whatever.

I thought to myself, *This isn't so bad.* My heart was hammering, but I kept repeating the lines in my head: *I can do this. I can do this.*

After about half an hour, our case was called. A big guy wearing mismatched suit pants and a baggy suit jacket lumbered to his feet. I jumped up as well.

"Ready for the defendant," he boomed out.

"Ready for the plaintiff," I chirped back.

The judge glanced at each of us and looked down at his papers. Then he looked back up at me, seeming to appraise my spiffy suit and the perky little bow at my neck. "Mrs. Holt," he said, "couldn't you get a lawyer?"

Everything stopped.

The other lawyer rolled his head my way. Mr. and Mrs. Holt stared up at me. People in the courtroom looked over at me. I was dumbstruck.

I glanced again at Mr. and Mrs. Holt, just in time to see them look at each other with "I told you she couldn't handle this" written all over their faces. I felt sick.

I looked back at the judge. After a long pause, I lifted my chin a bit and said as calmly as I could muster, "I *am* the lawyer, Your Honor."

Now it was the judge's turn to look dumbstruck. He was clearly confused. The silence in the courtroom stretched out.

Finally the judge repeated the word, as if it had never been heard in this room, rolling it around in his mouth like an unfamiliar foreign object, perhaps a large marble or a small toy. "Lawyer . . . Lawyer . . . Oh, the lawyer."

A longer pause followed while he stared at me and considered what to do next. "We just never, uh, never had a, um, never . . ." He trailed off.

My hands were shaking. Mr. and Mrs. Holt had now progressed to staring at me like I was a bizarre creature from outer space who had passed itself off as a lawyer. The thought seemed to have dawned on them that their misguided decision to hire me was going to cost them any chance of getting the damage to their car repaired. They shrank away from me, as if distance might give them a second chance to have their case considered.

By this point my best-case scenario was either an earthquake or a raging fire—something big that would require immediate evacuation. Maybe I could get lost in the chaos.

But no such act of God occurred. Instead, the judge recovered enough to call the defendant's lawyer and me forward. He asked if either of us wanted a trial, and I said that my clients did.

The other lawyer and I took our places, and the trial began. The facts of the case were pretty straightforward, and I stumbled through them, asking Mr. Holt questions just as we'd practiced. At the trial's conclusion, the judge ordered the insurance company to pay Mr. and Mrs. Holt.

There was no great thrill of victory. Still, the insurance company paid up. The Holts got all their money. But neither the Holts nor any other close neighbor ever asked me for legal help again.


## EXPECTATIONS 3.0

Of course, that was the 1970s. Before millions of women had gone to law school. Before millions of women had started their own businesses or farmed their own land. Before millions of women had earned their electrician's license or run the local gas station. Before women had been shot into space and landed on the Supreme Court. Before so many women had blazed their own trails.

That was a long time ago. A long, long time ago.

I remember a morning not so long ago. March 2018. I'd taken my shower, gotten dressed, and gone downstairs for breakfast. Bruce was already in the kitchen, making oatmeal with nuts and apples and blueberries—one of his specialties. Newspapers were spread out on the table. Bruce is old school, so we still get two papers delivered every day, plus a local paper every week and a couple more online.

A headline in one of the papers caught my eye. "Draw a Leader. What's She Like? Trick Question!"

By this point, I was beginning to think about running for president, so I read the story with sharpened attention. The article drew on both the experiences of business seminar leaders and academic studies that asked people to draw a picture of an effective leader.

Before I read another word, I glanced at the illustrations, which were drawings of a leader. There was a guy in a suit. Another guy in a suit. A guy in a tie. Winston Churchill chomping a cigar. The message, both from in-the-field experience and from careful research, was the same: women can do all sorts of things, but no one thinks of them as leaders. The experts patiently explained that when it comes to leaders, people believe it's a men-only club.

Sigh.

Yes, I get the message. And, yes, I also know that more than a dozen countries around the world have women leaders—good for them. But if I jumped in the race, I wouldn't be running to be president of those countries. I would be running to be president of the United States, so the question I had to face was whether our country would pick a woman leader.

I didn't want to run for president to make a point. I wasn't carefully measuring how hard to hit a glass ceiling. I didn't need to be heralded as the First Something. I just wanted a chance to fight for the things I cared about—economic opportunity, racial justice, halting climate change, combating Washington corruption, improving our education system. I had been talking about these issues for a long time.

All during my many years as a law professor, I swam in the boys' end of the pool. I specialized in corporate and commercial law, bankruptcy, and finance. I took on Wall Street. By the time I won my first race for the Senate in 2012, I wasn't exactly an exotic novelty, but I soon discovered that women in the Senate were still few enough in number that there were women-only dinners and let's-find-a-woman-to-be-in-the-picture scrambles for press conferences. I'd been in the Senate for about two years when one of my Republican colleagues mistook me for Wisconsin Senator Tammy Baldwin and another thought I was a real senator's wife. Sigh.

I became accustomed years ago to working in male-dominated areas, but that didn't mean I saw the world the same way the boys did. And it sure didn't mean I fought the same fights they did. So as I began thinking about jumping into the race, I thought about how, if I ran for president, I could fight the battles I believed were important—and maybe even win them.

## DISCRIMINATION THAT LASTS A LIFETIME

It isn't just women who run for public office or women who join the space program who run smack into discrimination. It's millions of women all across this country for whom cramped opportunities have been so much a part of their lives that it colors everything they experience. These are women in white-collar jobs, blue-collar jobs, no-collar jobs—every kind of job. Women like the other female intern who worked for that Wall Street firm the summer I was twenty-five. Women like an elementary school teacher named Kristie, a never-say-die woman I met while working on a book. In fact, in a parallel universe, I could have been Kristie.

In the early 2000s, Amelia had her first baby, a gorgeous little person she and her husband Sushil named Octavia. Amelia had been working at a start-up she'd launched with a few partners, but with the new baby, she wasn't sure she could manage the long commute and the long hours and the struggle to find infant care. So now she was home with a new baby. I headed out to California to visit Octavia—and Amelia and Sushil, of course.

Octavia was beautiful, but she was a prickly baby who always seemed to be a few seconds away from a loud wail. She could be soothed, however, if someone would rock her or take her for long walks in her stroller. That gave Amelia and me hours and hours to fill with conversation.

Amelia is a bit of a data nerd (yeah, this apple didn't fall far from the tree), so we spent lots of time talking about the data that my academic partners and I had been collecting as part of what we now called the Consumer Bankruptcy Project. By this point, the other professors and I had spent years gathering information about the people who filed for bankruptcy. And in the course of those studies, we'd noticed a twist in the numbers: women were filing bankruptcy in higher and higher numbers.

While I walked the floor jostling the baby, Amelia loaded up our data on her computer and tried to tease new information out of the pile of numbers. Her creative slicing of the data brought a key finding to the surface: the single best predictor of going broke in America was to be a woman with a child. Not a woman alone. Not a couple with no kids. Not elderly or African American or Latina. One kid. Two kids. It didn't matter. The *strongest* predictor was to be a woman with at least one child.

The data didn't tell a story about poor, young, unwed mothers. These were largely middle-class moms who'd had a fair number of advantages—decent educations, good jobs, nice homes. They were urban and rural. Coastal and midland. Black, Latina, and white. What united these women was that their financial lives were upside down, and now they were mamas in desperately bad financial shape.

Amelia and I ended up writing a book about what had gone wrong for them. Some of the stories started with a divorce or an absent father who didn't pay child support. Some stories were about women with partners, but then a job loss or serious medical problem had ripped through their lives. Some had been cheated by mortgage lenders or credit card companies. We covered all that, but the book was about the larger forces that were bearing down on America's families—and fell particularly hard on women.

In 2001, when Terry, Jay, and I launched our third round of collecting bankruptcy data, we got the chance to interview several hundred of the people who were going through bankruptcy. Kristie was one of those people. She was a delight. Short, with bright blue eyes, she called herself a redhead-by-choice, and her brilliant hair suited her well. She had the kind of high energy that everyone noticed and wanted to be near.

Kristie told her story quickly, though occasionally she slowed down to savor the taste of the best parts. She had met her husband, Leo, at the University of Illinois. She explained that she was "a good Midwestern girl," and he was "Italian on his mother's side." They married straight out of college. She had no trouble finding a job as a teacher, and she taught second grade for a year, then got pregnant. Her beginning teacher's salary barely covered infant care, so after a frustrating few months, she and Leo decided she should stay home. Leo changed companies and they moved to another state, where Kristie's provisional teaching license wasn't valid. But that didn't worry them: with a second baby on the way, it seemed easier for Kristie to stay home a while longer. They bought a house and a second car. As Leo got promoted, his pay went up slowly but steadily.

Their third pregnancy went badly wrong. The baby was born early, and even after insurance, the bills from the hospital put Kristie and Leo in a big hole. Before he was a month old, the infant had used up his lifetime cap on insurance (these were the days before the Affordable Care Act banned lifetime caps). This meant that from that moment forward, every time this little boy got a bad cold or had an accident requiring stitches, his family would go deeper into debt. And in his early years the baby needed extra help—speech therapy and coaching to deal with dyslexia—all of which Kristie and Leo had to pay for.

Kristie told us her life was a constant balancing act. Keeping the family afloat when her three kids were young proved to be a full-time job; before she knew it, Kristie had been home eleven years. Just when she was finally ready to go back to work, her dad had a heart attack and her mom needed help. She moved her parents so they could be near her, and they had almost settled in when her mom got sick. Then her dad developed Alzheimer's. After she'd been home fourteen years, Kristie decided to take a part-time job as a teacher's aide, still caring for her kids and her parents. It was a stretch, but she managed. Four years later, she was ready to work full-time, but the world had moved on, and she needed new courses and a new certification before she could get a job as an entry-level teacher.

In the meantime, Leo's company had folded. He'd jumped into a start-up, but it never got off the ground. Then a couple of other jobs didn't work out. Eventually, Kristie and Leo's marriage fell apart, and before long Leo moved in with his new girlfriend. Kristie borrowed money so she could go back to school to get certified as a teacher.

Twenty years after originally graduating from college, Kristie at last got another job, this time as an entry-level teacher at a nearby elementary school. She was on her own now, but her paycheck plus Leo's hit-or-miss child support wasn't nearly enough to cover the mortgage, her student loan debt, and the ongoing medical bills and expenses for three growing kids. She borrowed a little, then a little more, then a little more. Here she was in her mid-forties, her three kids now teenagers, and it had all come apart.

That's how Kristie ended up in bankruptcy. A couple of especially hard hits—a preemie and a divorce—piled on an already-fragile budget.

Going bankrupt was embarrassing and painful, but Kristie said she didn't regret one minute of the time she spent with her kids or with her mom and dad before they died. She teared up and laughed at the same time. "I loved it all," she told me. I believed her.

But take a close look at the lifelong consequences of Kristie's choices and decisions. Across the twenty-two years of her marriage to Leo, she had worked outside the home only at the beginning and the end, while Leo had worked full-time for all those years. In her forties, she earned an entry-level salary in a profession that didn't pay well. Over the years, Kristie had made less money than Leo, a lot less.

But here comes the hard kick in the shins: Because Kristie worked outside the home for only a few years and also earned a lower salary, she will face retirement with far less savings and a much smaller Social Security check than her ex-husband and her worked-for-forty-years male counterparts. In other words, even as Kristie was struggling through a bankruptcy, it was already clear that she would suffer from financial problems all her life.

Caregiving is wonderful and fulfilling and important. It is also very costly for the caregiver. And this is a big part of the reason our bankruptcy study found so many mothers—mothers who had busted their tails for years, but who got squeezed by lower salaries and fewer working years and ultimately found themselves tangled up in the kind of debts that landed them in bankruptcy. And for every mother we studied who ended up filing for bankruptcy, I knew there were many, many more mothers scraping together just enough money to make it month to month, constantly wobbling on the verge of bankruptcy and facing down a bleak financial future.

When we met her, Kristie was just one of countless bankrupt single mothers. Even today, the very ordinariness of her story thrums through millions of families and hundreds of thousands of bankruptcy files. The details vary, but the high cost of the caregiving role that so many women take on is real.

## FIGHTING FOR WOMEN

In the months after I saw that story about leadership, I thought a lot about what a woman running for president would be up against. But I also thought about what it would mean for a presidential candidate to run *for* women. I knew that if I decided to run, a big part of my fight would be about women. I knew I'd want to fight for childcare, pre-K and public school, and eldercare (partly so the elderly's caregivers—most commonly their daughters and nieces and daughters-in-law—could keep working). But I was also eager to fight for another plan that would round out what it means to promote true equality of opportunity for women: I wanted to adjust Social Security so that it would account for caregiving years.

Here's a simple explanation of the problem. Social Security retirement benefits are calculated by taking the average monthly wage of the highest-earning thirty-five years of an individual's work history. Most men work thirty-five years and most men earn more than most women. They won't retire rich on Social Security, but they will do okay. The system was designed to work for them—and that's what it does.

But women are still earning only about eighty-two cents for every dollar earned by a man, so the woman who earns less during all her working years won't do nearly as well as a man. And mothers get hit especially hard. For a mom who keeps working full-time after the baby arrives, her income stalls out. She may work fewer hours, pass up the tougher assignments, travel less—whatever. Meanwhile, dad keeps charging ahead. Over time the impact is crushing: a working mom earns only seventy-one cents for every dollar earned by a working dad.

And that's just the start. Any woman who stayed out of the workforce for a number of years to care for her family will get hit even harder. She will likely fall short of thirty-five years of work, so when her Social Security retirement benefits are calculated, she'll receive a zero for each year of missing income. Basic math really bites here: those zero years badly hurt her average earnings. Even if she works part-time while raising children, she gets slammed because her part-time work is likely to yield a much lower income during those years—and those lower-income years are swept into her average.

After a lifetime of lower wages and fewer working years, these caregiving women will retire with a far smaller Social Security stipend. It's so small, in fact, that women over sixty-five are much more likely to be poor than men—regardless of their race, their education, or their marital status. They will be poor because they are women.

As I thought about running for president, I really dug into this issue. I got excited, and I found myself thinking: Let's fix this. Sure, let's fight for equal pay for equal work, and let's make a special push for equal pay for mamas. But that's a damn slow road. At the current rate of improvement, the gender pay gap for people working full-time will finally close—in thirty-eight years. And the special gap for mothers, that seventy-one cents on the dollar and the Social Security penalty for caregiving years? So far, I can't find anyone who has estimated how many eons it will take for that gap to disappear.

I'm not interested in waiting four decades for the day when women don't pay a penalty for being women. I'm not interested in waiting who-knows-how-long for the day when mamas don't pay an even bigger penalty for being mamas. One way to fix part of this immediately is to readjust Social Security payments so that they'll lift more older women out of poverty. We should build a payment floor so that no one has to live in poverty—no one. And we should create Social Security credits for years taken off work to care for families, credits that would boost a woman's payout in the retirement years. These two changes would improve millions of lives.

And yes, of course this plan should also include caregiving fathers and sons and nephews. But let's be clear: it's still mostly women who leave the workforce to deal with caregiving for children or elderly relatives, and it's still mostly women who earn less, save less, and face retirement with less money.

But let's not stop with help for caregivers. Let's also boost Social Security benefits across the board. A small change that resulted in a $200-a-month increase in Social Security benefits would lift an estimated five million people out of poverty. For tens of millions more, that extra couple of hundred dollars could be the money that makes it possible to repair a damaged roof or buy new tires for their car. It could be the money that covers a co-pay on prescriptions or prevents the utilities from getting shut off.

I often pitched the idea of a modest increase in Social Security benefits during my presidential campaign. But some people didn't see the point. In December 2019, I spoke in a middle school gym in Iowa—no stage, about two hundred people. An older woman who had a ticket for a question explained that she was trying to take care of her retired husband, her adult daughter on disability, and her grandchildren. Her family members were dealing with several medical problems, and she said that although they had good insurance, they were living "one small hiccup away from homelessness." She wanted to know how I could help.

I talked about my plan to increase Social Security payments by $200 a month. A man in the crowd yelled out, "How will $200 a month help her?" She shot back, "It will help me buy toilet paper at the end of the month." It was one of those laugh-or-cry moments. She was stretched *so* thin that she was counting her pennies to figure out whether she could afford to buy toilet paper, but she didn't know the meaning of quit. She was still in the fight.

After a speech like that one, or after a town hall or a selfie line, I sometimes thought about the "draw a leader" exercise. I knew that reworking Social Security calculations or boosting basic Social Security benefits might not inspire someone to draw a picture of a skinny lady in her seventies who wears glasses and sneakers. But that was the kind of leader I wanted to be, and that was the kind of change I wanted to deliver. I wanted it enough that in the end I decided to jump into the crazy, all-consuming tornado of running for president.

## RUNNING IN THE SHADOW

In 2012, I wasn't the first woman to run for the Senate from Massachusetts. In 2020, I wasn't the first woman to run for president of the United

States. In both elections, I ran for office in the immediate wake of two women who'd been expected to win right up until they didn't. In 2012, I ran in Martha Coakley's wake; in 2020, I ran in Hillary Clinton's. Both were talented, very well qualified, fundamentally decent people who had spent much of their lives in public service.

In both races, I was eager to talk about what was broken in America and how my plans would fix our problems. But at the start, I couldn't run against incumbent Republican senator Scott Brown or incumbent president Donald Trump. I couldn't even run against other Democrats in a primary. Before I could do anything else, I had to run against the shadows of Martha and Hillary.

Here's just one example.

One of the ways to kick-start a political campaign is to call people you don't know and tell them you're thinking about running for office. Many of them will offer advice and, if they like what they hear, some of them will agree to help. If enough people offer to help, a potential campaign begins to generate a little momentum.

These phone calls are just as embarrassing as they sound. It's more than a little awkward to cold-call strangers to see if they will volunteer some of their time and credibility and energy to a campaign that doesn't yet exist—and might not ever exist.

The calls aren't random. As a campaign begins to form, experienced operatives draw up a long list of politically active people whose support could be really important. The candidate's job is to start at the top of the list and just keep working through it.

In 2011, I'd never done anything like this, but I was determined to give it everything I could. A few weeks before formally announcing my run for Senate, I sat on a barstool in my kitchen, holding the list I'd been given. I stared at it for a couple of minutes, and then put on my headset, took three long breaths, and started punching numbers into my phone. Before hearing even one full ring I was off my stool and pacing—I was too nervous to sit still.

The first call was to a longtime Democratic activist in Massachusetts, a woman known for her ability to organize volunteers and build energy all across the state. Here was someone who had been called many times through the years, a political powerhouse who'd been called for all kinds of races from mayor to president. The notes on my sheet said she was smart, savvy, and potentially a great ally. Heart thumping hard, I introduced myself and explained why I was calling.

There was a long pause, and then she said: "Martha lost."

Oof.

And just in case I'd missed it, she listed Martha's many fine qualities, her excellent connections, and her deep experience. The woman then drew the obvious conclusion. If, in the last race, Martha couldn't beat her opponent—the same guy I'd be running against, in fact—neither could I or any other woman. She wasn't going to bust her tail and put her credibility on the line for another woman who couldn't win.

Nine years later, my decision to run for president wasn't like flipping a light on. It was more like slowly pushing up a dimmer switch. In early 2018, my desire to run was fairly faint. But I kept trying out the idea and thinking about the plans I could lift up, and my desire to run got brighter. By early fall, I was taking a hard look at running; after Thanksgiving, I was getting really close to making a decision. So I did the same thing I'd done when I first ran for the Senate—I sat down in the kitchen and started making cold calls. People who knew about such things had drawn up a list of potential supporters in Iowa, New Hampshire, Nevada, and South Carolina for me to contact.

This time around, I knew the drill, but that only made it worse, because I knew how hard it was to sell myself in just a few minutes. And it didn't help that the recipients of my calls were probably getting calls from lots of other candidates as well.

And there was one more twist: this time I was calling about a race for president of the United States. Wow—president? Sometimes the enormity of this undertaking would hit me. I'd flash back to the wobbly thirteen-year-old trying out for the debate team in Oklahoma, and my heart rate would jump. Now, decades later, I was pacing around my kitchen while talking to influential people about why I wanted to lead our nation.

The first call on my list was to a woman who had been organizing people in advance of the Iowa caucuses for as long as anyone could remember. In the lingo favored by political operatives, she was a high-value target. I introduced myself and explained why I was calling.

Long pause. Then: "Hillary lost."

Oof.

She followed up with a list of Hillary's fine qualities, her connections, and her experience. Then she stated the apparently obvious conclusion that if Hillary couldn't beat Trump, neither could I or any other woman.

And so it went. On that first day of cold-calling, about half the people I spoke to pointed out that the last woman who ran for president had lost.

As I fell into bed that first night, I wondered whether anyone said to Bernie Sanders when he asked for their support, "Gore lost, so how can you win?" I wondered whether anyone said to Joe Biden, "Kerry lost, so clearly America just isn't ready for a man to be president."

I tried to laugh, but the joke didn't seem very funny.


## THE IMPOSSIBLE WOMAN

In fact, by 2018, nothing about sexism seemed funny. The president of the United States—the man who two years earlier had won the vote of about sixty-three million Americans—called women "fat," "slob," "pig," "dog," "disgusting animals," and more. Dozens of women credibly accused him of assault or unwanted sexual contact. He joked about having sex with girls under seventeen. He defended himself against more than one of the accusations of rape by claiming that the woman just wasn't attractive enough for him to have any interest in raping her. And yet he had been elected president. Maybe it wasn't all that surprising that some people—including me—were a little uneasy about exactly how American voters felt about women.

During the course of the presidential campaign, the question that came up repeatedly during my first day of cold-calling kept resurfacing: Could a woman win? Polls asked the question over and over. Would you be comfortable with a woman as president? *Sure*, said many of those polled. *Absolutely*, said 74 percent of Democrats and independents polled.

When I heard that number, I thought, *Wait, what?* 74 percent? Of Democrats and independents? So one in four Democrats and independents would *not* be comfortable with a woman as president? Good Lord.

That was a little terrifying, but then the research got worse. One in-depth study probed people's sexist attitudes, asking them whether they agreed with fairly blunt statements like: "Most women fail to appreciate fully all that men do for them," and "Women are too easily offended." Once they got respondents sorted out and asked about political preferences, the researchers concluded that a quarter of likely Democratic primary voters were *more* sexist than the population generally.

Does this sexism have an impact at the ballot box? It sure does, at least according to an article in the *Washington Post* by the researchers summarizing their polling. When they queried the most sexist likely voters in the Democratic primaries, Kamala Harris and I lost about two-thirds of our support.

The scary poll numbers kept on coming. When Democratic and independent voters were asked, in effect, "We know *you* are a wonderfully open-minded and fair person, but how about your neighbors? Would *they* be comfortable with a woman as president?" Now even the yes-of-course-I-would-vote-for-a-woman crowd began to backpedal. Only 33 percent of Democrats and independents thought *other* people would be comfortable with a woman president.

And the bad news *still* wasn't over. Across the summer of 2019, as the presidential primary heated up, more and more people said they would be comfortable with a woman president themselves—but, at the same time, more and more people said that a woman would have a harder time than a man running against Trump. Evidently it's one thing to get caught up in the early stages of dreaming about change or hoping to make history, but when it comes time to sober up and pick a leader to win, a woman starts to look like a risky bet.

That's the really tricky part about "what will you do" versus "what will your neighbors do." The former says it's up to you to make an informed decision and be morally responsible for it. And in that case three out of four Democrats and independents said, *Yes, I'd be okay with a woman president.* But "what will your neighbors do" takes voters down a very different path, one that accommodates and strengthens prejudice—*No way a woman should be president!*—while removing any personal stigma because, *Hey, that's just my* neighbors' *prejudice.* That was exactly the argument used against John Kennedy—*a Catholic can't win!* The same argument was resurrected against Barack Obama—*an African American can't win!* The difference, of course, was that once they got the nomination, they both won.

The question of whether a woman could win in 2020 was complicated by how desperately Democrats (and some independents and Republicans) wanted to pry Donald Trump out of the White House. People proclaimed that they would vote for anyone—anyone!—if that meant getting rid of Trump. ANYONE BUT TRUMP 2020 was a hugely popular bumper sticker, along with LITERALLY ANYONE ELSE 2020 and ANY FUNCTIONING ADULT 2020. But as anxiety about whether Trump could really be defeated rose ever higher, the question was infused with a trickle of fear: *Was this really the time to take a chance on a woman? Wouldn't a man be safer?*

Late in the campaign, when it leaked that Bernie had told me that a woman couldn't win, the news caused a stir. But the question of whether a woman could win the presidency was clearly on voters' minds, and it would come up in debates and town halls. When asked, I always told an upbeat story about why I believed success was within our grasp, but I was under no illusion—I knew that winning would be an uphill battle.

I once heard from a campaign insider that when Hillary ran for president in 2008, she was told to run "like a man," meaning that she needed to reassure voters that she could be as tough and unemotional as a man. Voters needed to know whether she—whether *any* woman—could be trusted to make really hard decisions, such as using nuclear weapons or negotiating with ruthless foreign dictators. But during that same campaign, she got slammed for being too unemotional and too guarded, for not showing enough of her authentic self, for not being *likable*. She was criticized, in other words, for not living up to the classic stereotype of the ideal woman. Throughout the campaign, Hillary was simultaneously told to reject this stereotype and to embrace it. She needed to be Woman and Not-Woman. Sure, she could definitely win—she just needed to be the Impossible Woman, the one human being on earth who could be two completely contradictory things at the same moment.

It's easy to dismiss the classic stereotype of a woman as absurdly old-fashioned, but it still packs a punch—especially when people draw a mental picture of a leader, and particularly when that leader has *always* been a man. The sharp contrast between deep-seated images of the ideal woman and portraits of the ideal leader creates cross-currents and doubts. The disconnect between the two images heightens discomfort and scrutiny. And for any woman running for president of the United States, it pulls even a highly qualified candidate in two opposite directions, demanding that she be two contradictory things at once. And then, even more remarkably, she must pretend that no contradiction exists.

The Impossible Woman trap echoed in my head for years.

In 2016, Hillary Clinton, an extremely accomplished and immensely qualified public servant, was once again caught in the trap. In 2020, the fact that half a dozen women ran for president was greeted with great fanfare. Yay! But the trap lay just below the surface, and I wasn't the only one caught in it. Just one example: Kamala Harris, Kirsten Gillibrand, Amy Klobuchar, and I all had better campaign win-loss records than any of the leading men. But the question was never whether a man could be elected. Despite our stronger records, it was always, "Can a woman win?"

Consider the question that regularly got tossed at us from voters and reporters: Are you treated differently as a presidential candidate because you're a woman? The two possible answers expose the trap. First answer: "Yes, I'm treated differently." A woman responding that way would immediately hear a swarming mass of people whisper, "Whiner," or "Weakling," or "Complainer." Next would come the inevitable accusation that she'd just "played the gender card," as well as the predictable comment that she was "just not tough enough." Now try out the opposite answer: "No, of course not." That will get a laugh, because at least half the population will wonder what planet she's living on.

So far as I know, no one ever asked the men in the 2020 race if they felt they were treated differently because they were men. And if that sounds like whining, please reread the preceding paragraph.

When I began thinking seriously about running for president, I knew I didn't have some magic power that would allow me to succeed where other women had failed. I also knew that, regardless of my gender, I would face plenty of other problems and challenges if I decided to run. But that didn't mean I would give up. It just meant that I needed to be realistic—and I needed a plan.

By late 2018 I had made up my mind. I would run, and I would run the same way I'd run for the Senate in 2012: I would throw body and soul into it. I would set my sights high and work as hard and as smart as I possibly could. I would build a great team, support grassroots organizing, and be generous to other Democratic candidates. I would talk about the ideas and issues I deep-down cared about. I would lay out every plan that I truly believed could make a difference.

And I would do more. I would put my unflinching determination on display, sounding the call for a fight against some of the most powerful people and corporations in our nation. I would also put my full heart on display, telling stories that only a woman could tell. I would do pinkie promises with little girls and give hugs to their mothers and grandmothers. I would fill up every space with ideas and energy and optimism. I would hope that my being a woman wouldn't matter so much.

And—please, please, please—I would show everyone that a woman could win.

## THE THINGS WOMEN WHISPER

Several months after starting my run, I traveled to the Recreational Vehicle Hall of Fame in Elkhart, Indiana, to hold a town hall. Elkhart is in a heavily Republican area, but the crowd was pumped up on that June morning in 2019. I laid out my plan to develop a real industrial policy in the United States. I showed how we could begin to attack the climate crisis by investing in carbon capture and green energy, and, if we did it right, we could create about 1.2 million new manufacturing jobs along the way. It was wonky, but it was a really good plan and it was fun to roll it out for the first time in the industrial Midwest.

When we'd finished the Q&A, people lined up for selfies. One of the first was a woman in her late thirties—hair tied back, brightly colored sneakers, big dimples. She leaned in close for her picture, our arms around each other's waists. After the shot, she hugged me tight and whispered, "Please protect *Roe*. My fourteen-year-old was raped by her coach. Getting an abortion was a nightmare."

For an instant, we stood perfectly still. The hug was frozen as that plea left her heart and lodged in mine.

Then we stepped apart. Her eyes were filled with tears. I could feel myself starting to tear up, too. I wanted to say something more, but she dropped her eyes and shook her head no. She turned and was gone.

And I turned to smile for the next selfie—a group of teenage girls who were sooooo excited to be here!

We finished up the selfie lines, took a look at the RVs, then headed on to Fort Wayne.

That night, by myself in my room at the Holiday Inn, I looked up Indiana's abortion laws.

*Roe v. Wade* has been the law of the land since 1973, when the Supreme Court affirmed a pregnant person's right to have an abortion without undue government interference. But the constant chip-chip-chip at *Roe* has thrown up barriers that in some states make terminating a pregnancy very difficult. Indiana is one of those states.

Indiana Right to Life proudly proclaims on its website that the rule of *Roe* "has changed substantially since 1973, thanks to the hard work of a lot of individuals and elected officials." Hard work indeed. By 2017, 96 percent of counties in Indiana had no clinics providing abortion services. Instead of state-supported counseling to help a young girl recover from rape, the law required state-mandated counseling to show her that her choice to terminate the resulting pregnancy would be wrong. And there were a host of other barriers, all of them adding up to delays in care, financial burdens, unnecessary medical procedures, and more.

I sat in my room, in the dark, thinking about the woman in the selfie line and her doubly traumatized daughter. Thinking, too, about another encounter that had stopped me in my tracks.

Months earlier, at my very first town hall back in freezing cold Iowa, a woman asked me about abortion. In one of those bizarre coincidences that make me wonder about cosmic influences, the woman whose ticket had been drawn from hundreds in the ticket bucket was one of my first law students; later, she was my research assistant, and she was now the mother of four children. Catherine and I had exchanged Christmas cards for years. I had hosted her daughter's Girl Scout troop's trip to Boston a few years earlier and sent small gifts when her babies were born. When she wrote me to say that her youngest son had passed away after a long bout with cancer, I cried over her letter. Now she had driven from her home in Nebraska to see my debut as a presidential candidate.

There she stood, bundled up against the cold in the drafty warehouse, ready to ask her question. As soon as I saw her face, I knew what she would ask. Over the years, Catherine had become active in the pro-life movement, and she had often asked me to reconsider my pro-choice position. I knew that her advocacy came from a good place in her heart, and I respected her for it. But I couldn't agree. So Catherine had come to Iowa to ask me again, now with a big audience and national press coverage.

Catherine started her question by mentioning all the issues on which she agreed with me—health care, antitrust policy, consumer protection. But then she said that whenever I talked about reproductive rights, people heard "murdering babies" and couldn't hear anything else I said. Would I please change my mind?

The crowd got very quiet. Talking about abortion can be like touching a hot iron—instantly painful.

I could have mushed around, but I thought that would be disrespectful both to Catherine and to the people in the room. I didn't talk about whether abortion is right or wrong. Instead, I talked about the question that faces us as nation: What role should the law play when the decision about whether to get an abortion is being made? This is how I answered her question:

> I know that these are very hard personal family decisions. I think the role of government here is to back out. I think a woman makes a decision with her family, her priest, her doctor—the people the woman chooses—and I think that's what respects all of us the most.

I was reasonably satisfied with the answer I gave Catherine that day, but nothing about this issue is easy. Questions about abortion and reproductive rights came up over and over during my campaign, and every time they did, I struggled to find the right words when responding.

I don't think any woman makes the decision to terminate a pregnancy lightly. For some, the answer may be nearly automatic, as it clearly was for the mother I met in Indiana whose daughter had been raped. For others, the choice may be agonizing. And for nearly every woman, the decision whether to end a pregnancy or go forward has a potentially life-altering impact.

Women who seek abortions are as varied as all of us. I heard the stories everywhere—in my faculty office, my Senate office, on the campaign trail. Riding in cars, waiting in lines. I talked with a woman with three children who could not support a fourth. A woman whose partner had left her. A woman about to accept her commission into the Army. A woman battling addiction. A woman with a severely damaged fetus.

Whatever goes into any individual woman's decision, I can't know. But I don't need to know. I believe in that woman's ability to make the choice, no matter how difficult. To me, this is about respect: it is not my place or anyone's to tell a woman what choice she should make. It's also true that I cannot imagine forcing a woman to carry a pregnancy against her will. And by the way, I cannot imagine that men—male judges and legislators, male governors and presidents—would permit women to pass laws that would determine something very specific about men's bodies.

In the days before *Roe*, abortion was illegal—and women still terminated pregnancies. Some made it through the experience with their lives and their health intact; others didn't. But somehow they found ways.

If the Supreme Court overturns *Roe v. Wade*, the impact will be immediate. Ten states have already passed "trigger laws" that will automatically ban abortions if *Roe* is overturned. Meanwhile, other states such as New York, California, and Massachusetts have headed in the opposite direction, using state law to expand protection of a woman's right to choose. The boundaries between the states that support abortion and those that don't would be sharp.

Even if *Roe* were overturned, women in large parts of the United States could still get abortions. And for those living in states where abortion had been banned, abortion would still be available for women who could afford to travel. These women could visit a friend who lived in a pro-choice state, cross the border to some parts of Mexico, or travel to one of the many countries where abortion is legal.

But that's the part about overturning *Roe* that really makes the bile rise in my throat—it's deeply unfair that these rules would fall hardest on those who have the fewest options. A law replacing *Roe* might be neutral on its face, but the only people who would effectively be denied abortions would be those who didn't have the resources to travel to a place where abortion is legal. Poor women, teenagers, girls who have been raped but have nowhere to turn for help—these and others would suffer terribly. I can't support a law that will make life miserable for the most vulnerable among us.

*Roe* has already been hollowed out, and now at least five Supreme Court justices have expressed outright hostility to a woman's right to choose. We've reached a crossroads—and I, for one, am not willing to rely on the Supreme Court to protect a woman's right to choose any longer.

I propose a different plan: Take abortion out of the courts and put it in the hands of Congress. In the same way that Congress passed laws to provide access to health care—think Medicare and Medicaid—Congress should pass a law to protect nationwide access to abortion. And while Congress is protecting a woman's right to choose, we should also outlaw the many barriers to abortions that have been thrown up over the years. Even now, women in Indiana and other states are forced to travel elsewhere for abortions—except, of course, for the poor, the young, and the vulnerable, who have no choice but to carry pregnancies they may desperately want to terminate.

Some people may think, *Congress? You mean we should ask Congress to do something that may be politically hard because a relatively small, intense minority doesn't like it?*

Yeah, that's exactly what I mean, because that's Congress's job. About 70 percent of the people in this country want *Roe* to remain the law of the land. That's 70 percent of *all* Americans, including Democrats and Republicans, religious and nonreligious people, women and men.

And Congress should pass the necessary law now. That fourteen-year-old in Indiana—and thousands of other teenagers like her—needs Congress on her side *today*.

## YOUNG AND VULNERABLE

It was Christmas break 1972. I was in my early twenties, married with a baby, and now living in New Jersey. We had made the long drive home to Oklahoma City to celebrate the holidays. Several of the kids I'd gone to high school with were also in town, so we all got together at someone's house to have a few drinks and tell funny stories.

Late in the evening, the topic turned to working under stress. Each storyteller outdid the last—finishing homework on the front lawn after the house had caught on fire, showing up at work with a broken leg and not going to the hospital until some project was completed, and so on.

Finally, Jack bested everyone else. He'd spent a year in Vietnam, the last few months as a company clerk. "I'm cool under pressure," he announced. "I could type fifty-five words a minute while our HQ was being shelled."

Without missing a beat, I topped him. "Yeah? Well, I could type sixty words a minute while a creepy old guy reached under the table and patted my knee."

Everyone laughed. So did I, but the memory still stung.

Actually, it wasn't one memory—it was a whole filing cabinet of memories. During high school and my first year of college, I'd spent three summers working in a big insurance office, and multiple creepy guys patted my knees, stroked my butt, squeezed my arms, and hugged my shoulders. Oh, and let's give a special mention to the other creepy guys who asked about my boyfriends, told dirty stories, and wanted to know what I thought about sex. But I was still young during those years, and like millions of other girls, part of my teenage education was learning to bob and weave. Besides, I felt damn lucky to have a summer job, and I knew that if I complained, I'd be gone by the end of the day.

By the late 1970s, I was a brand-new professor at the University of Houston law school. I was beyond excited. I had a real, honest-to-goodness, tenure-track teaching job. By now I was on my own with two little children. And I'd found my calling: I loved loved loved teaching. I scrambled to manage babies and childcare and laundry and dinners, and I worked late into the night to prepare my classes and deliver my committee assignments. I loved my job, and I desperately wanted to keep it.

Tenure is an amazing thing: it's a promise that a faculty member has a teaching job pretty much forever. Sure, someone can be fired for really bad behavior, but basically tenure is about getting an invitation to join a small band of people who will devote their lives to teaching and scholarship. For a young professor, tenure is the Holy Grail.

When a university grants tenure it makes a very big commitment—in my case, it would mean telling a twenty-nine-year-old that she can count on having her job into her seventies or eighties. It's no surprise that the process is demanding. The university's administration has to be willing to bind itself to this person for the long haul, but the biggest hurdle, at least in most law schools, is the faculty. The tenured faculty evaluate a young professor for a few years, then vote on whether to invite the person to join their elevated ranks. In most places, if the supplicant doesn't get at least two-thirds or three-quarters of the possible yes votes, out he or she goes. Many then leave teaching altogether; being denied tenure is often the academic equivalent of the death penalty.

When evaluating someone for tenure, the tenured faculty sit like high priests. They look at teaching evaluations and written work, but there is no set formula that guarantees a successful outcome. Votes are secret and the high priests can use whatever criteria they wish. When I was a young law professor, I knew that when faculty members discussed tenure over lunch or at dinner parties, words like "likable," "fits in," and "our kind of guy" regularly made it into the conversation. Since there was only one other woman on the faculty, I worried about whether someone like me "fit in."

A long-tenured faculty member named Gene had led the committee at the University of Houston that made me an initial job offer, the standard, short-term, hoping-for-tenure teaching contract. Everyone at the law school knew Gene; he had a sort of gravitational force. Adult-onset polio had left him with a twisted spine, a bad limp, and floppy hands. But anyone who was thinking of pitying him was in for a bad surprise—the kind of surprise someone might get when trying to pet a piranha. Gene was razor-sharp and aggressive. He had a finely tuned radar for everyone else's vulnerabilities, and he was quick to openly ridicule and embarrass anyone who crossed him. His wicked laugh reinforced his nickname: Mean Gene.

At UH, tenure evaluations started in the first semester. Was the candidate a good teacher? Did the candidate's scholarship show promise? The idea was that the tenure committee would spend a few years building a file, then vote up or down.

The year I started teaching, Gene shifted from recruiting faculty to heading up the tenure committee. To a baby law professor like me, Gene was a terrifying figure. He regularly asked me about my scholarship and visited my classes, and I knew he would be the principal filter for how most of the rest of the faculty saw me. His opinion would matter enormously, and I tried my hardest to do a good job. But his early comments about my teaching were brutal. I dreaded every time he showed up unannounced in my class.

One afternoon he called me into his office. As I came in, he told me to close the door. Gene already had a bottle of something—scotch? bourbon?—on his desk. He raised his glass and offered me a drink. I said no thanks. I didn't drink hard liquor, but I worried whether turning him down would make me look like I didn't "fit in." *Oh Lord*, I thought, *just get me out of here.*

We talked for a bit. He sat on one side of the desk; I sat on the other. After a few minutes, he made several sexual remarks. I didn't want to admit what was happening. I kept deflecting him, but I was quickly moving from uneasy to sweaty. I knew our conversation was going nowhere good, but I couldn't afford to offend him.

Suddenly he got up and started to come around the desk. I jumped up from my chair, and as I moved away from him, I said in a low voice that was much steadier than I felt, "You don't want to do this. You don't want to do this. Please don't do this." For a minute or two, I felt like I'd stepped into a bad cartoon. He came around the desk. I moved to the other side. He faked one way and I faked the other. I was trying to keep the desk between us while I kept repeating, "You don't want to do this. You don't want to do this."

Finally, I saw my opening and ran for the door. He made a last lunge just as I wrenched it open and escaped. I ran past the secretaries' desks, down a flight of stairs, and into my office. I sat there by myself for a long time, trying to stop shaking and steady my breathing.

I kept thinking, *My God, what just happened?* And now that it had happened, what comes next? Will he come back? Will he try to grab me again? And then the magnitude of the encounter began to wash over me. Gene's power wasn't physical; it was far stronger. In those days, very few women were teaching in law schools anywhere, and getting this job had been hard—it was my only offer, in fact. Now that I'd bolted from his office, would he tell people that I was a terrible teacher or that I just didn't "fit in"? Would I be forced to leave? Worst of all, if I left with a bad recommendation, I knew I would likely be shut out of teaching law forever.

I felt sick. I couldn't eat. I couldn't sleep. I dreaded going in to school. What would he do? What would he say?

In fact, Gene never said anything. He saw me the next day, and it was as if nothing had ever happened.

I quietly spoke to another senior member of the faculty, John Mixon, about what Gene had done. I don't remember much about our conversation, but years later John recalled that his advice had been, "Say nothing." After all, I was brand-new in the business, and I couldn't survive if I earned a reputation as a troublemaker.

But I really didn't need any advice about how to respond. This kind of behavior was part of the air I'd breathed and the water I'd drunk since I was a little girl, and I knew what I was supposed to do: say nothing; do nothing. And for years, that's what I did. I didn't report the incident to the dean. I didn't call Human Resources. I didn't hire a lawyer. Instead, I stayed watchful and quiet—and I kept smiling.

I also did something millions of other women have done: I asked myself over and over what part I'd played in making Gene think that crossing the line would be okay. Were my cute little skirts and blouses too sexy? While trying to fit in, had I laughed too much at his dirty jokes? What had I done wrong?

Gene didn't drop out of my life. For the rest of my time at UH, he visited my classes and gave me good teaching evaluations. And when I was under consideration for teaching jobs at the University of Texas and the University of Pennsylvania, he gave me favorable recommendations. Years later, when Harvard made me an offer, someone on the faculty specifically mentioned that Gene had spoken very highly of me. It was an unintentional but not-so-subtle reminder that everyone knows everyone, and that good or bad recommendations trail you forever. Hearing that comment made me believe I'd been right to keep my mouth shut.

Gene also kept calling me. Every month or two, my office phone would ring. I'd pick up the receiver with my usual "Elizabeth Warren." Speaking in his low, gravelly voice, he always started with "Hey, She-Wolf. What are you doing?"

For years, that opening line would flood me with adrenaline. My throat would tighten and I'd stop breathing. But I would never hang up. I would talk to him for a while about teaching or listen while he shared some piece of academic gossip. Years passed, and little by little my fear eased up.

Nearly twenty years after he had chased me around the desk, Gene called to say he was dying. He was his usual blunt self, almost daring me to be sympathetic. When I said I was sorry, he snarled back at me, saying that I shouldn't be sorry, because he was old, sick, and in pain. Laughing, he said: "And I've had a hell of a run."

Then he told me there was something he wanted me to do: speak at his funeral.

I said no.

He insisted.

I said that if I spoke at his funeral, I would tell the story about what had happened that day in his office. Neither of us had ever mentioned the incident, and I held my breath after I said it, wondering where the knife I'd just thrown would land.

Gene laughed again, almost as if I'd delivered the punch line he'd been waiting for. He told me that telling the story was exactly what he wanted me to do.

So I did. Two decades after he chased me around his desk, I stood up at his funeral and told the story. I made it funny and oh-so-Gene. And my heart did not race and my hands did not shake. Gene had no more power over me.

Once Gene was gone and his funeral was behind me, I rarely thought about the incident. But then, after almost twenty more years had passed, the Me Too movement splashed into the open. And I told the story about Gene again.

I lived this story when I was young and vulnerable. I told the story nearly twenty years later to prove to myself and everyone who had known me back then that I had survived Gene just fine, thank you. And I told the story twenty years after that in the hope that I might make it a little easier for the next woman who gets chased around a desk somewhere.

I was lucky—really lucky. By the time I spoke at Gene's funeral about that awful day, I was a full professor with tenure at Harvard. I had done just fine. Moreover, Gene hadn't been a vengeful boss or a nasty coworker. He hadn't harassed me for weeks or months or made my life a living hell. Lots of other women (and some men) are not nearly so fortunate.

## WHO DO YOU BELIEVE?

Gene and my years as a vulnerable young professor are in a long-buried past, but once in a while something happens that causes those memories to push back to the surface. A night in late February 2020 was one of those times. I had just come off the debate stage in Charleston, South Carolina, and was about to enter the spin room—the nickname for the giant circus of post-debate candidates, surrogates, and interviewers. I knew I was in for some intense questioning, because I had once again gone after Michael Bloomberg.

By then, Bloomberg was falling in the polls. But it appeared he could still grab the nomination, and I still thought this was a terrible idea. So during the debate, I had again argued that his long history of crude and sexist comments to women made him the wrong person to be the Democratic nominee. I reminded the audience that one of Bloomberg's former employees had said that when she told him she was pregnant, he had said, "Kill it." She had made the claim public and sued him. The case had been settled, and now she was yet another woman covered by a Bloomberg nondisclosure agreement. At one point during the debate, I'd turned to Bloomberg and said that if he wanted to be the Democratic nominee for president, he needed to release this woman and all the others from the NDAs and let them tell their stories.

Shortly after entering the spin room, I sat down with Chris Matthews, then the host of one of MSNBC's most popular evening news shows. He immediately went on the attack. "Do you believe that the former mayor of New York said that to a pregnant employee?"

I replied, "Well, the pregnant employee sure said that he did."

We were off and running. Six times in just over a minute, Matthews wanted to know why I would believe her instead of Bloomberg. Forget the corroboration. Forget Bloomberg's reputation. Forget all those NDAs he paid women to sign. The unspoken—and unshakable—assumption of this interview was that the man simply wouldn't lie.

"Why would he lie?" Matthews asked me. "Just to protect himself?"

"Yeah," I replied. "And why would *she* lie?"

For a moment, Matthews was speechless, stunned to have his own question thrown back in his face. His mouth hung open. He shook his head. He looked like a man who had just seen the world turn upside down.

And there I was, four decades after Gene had chased me around the desk and I had kept my mouth shut. Now a candidate for the highest office in the land, I was listening to Chris Matthews remind every woman watching his program why it's dangerous to call out powerful men for bad behavior.

Sure, not every story about sexual harassment and assault is true. Not every story is about men going after women, either; sometimes the aggression goes in other directions. And not all claims should be accepted at face value; every claim should be carefully examined. But no dispute about a claim should start with the assumption that powerful men never lie and less powerful women are just trying to make trouble. No one should automatically believe men.

I think of it this way. It takes a lot of guts for a woman to come forward and accuse a man of harassing or assaulting her—especially a man who has power over her. When she does, she's likely to encounter a lot of pain. Mostly, she will stand by herself; mostly, the injury she initially suffered will be made much worse by the experience of going public with her story. But if no one comes forward, nothing changes. I believe that anyone considering a woman's claim of harassment or assault should start by giving her the benefit of the doubt. And in the specific case under discussion during the debate, I thought that Bloomberg's refusal to release the woman from an NDA and let her tell her story was a powerful piece of information about who was and who wasn't telling the truth.

Matthews's determination to put me on the spot because I believed the pregnant woman rather than her billionaire boss crossed a line for many women. In fact, Matthews had crossed that line a lot of times—my exchange with him was just the latest. But by this point, post–Me Too and in the middle of a presidential primary, the world had shifted. In the days that followed, more women spoke up about their encounters with Matthews, and finally the network told him it was over. On March 2, Matthews announced his resignation.

And then, on March 4, after spending over a billion dollars and failing to win a single state on Super Tuesday, Mike Bloomberg dropped out of the primary.

Change is hard, often way too hard. Change is slow, usually way too slow. But the lesson is clear: we have power—and we *can* make change.

## LIFTING UP THE WOMEN WHO LIFTED US UP

A presidential campaign often has two starts. The first is the day a candidate announces an exploratory committee. For me, that was New Year's Eve 2018, when I released a video and drank a beer. A formal announcement usually comes a little later. For me, that was February 9, 2019, when I put on my coat and scarf, hugged Bruce, our kids, and our grandkids, and climbed up on a built-for-the-occasion outdoor stage in Lawrence, Massachusetts. Standing in front of one of the city's old brick mills on a below-freezing morning, I told a cheering crowd that I was running for president.

I made my announcement at the Everett Mills, site of the famous 1912 Bread and Roses Strike. I picked this place because I wanted to tell a story about the women who had stood on the same cobblestones we were standing on, the women who had looked out the windows of the same factory buildings that surrounded us, the women who had endured the same bitter cold that buffeted us on this morning. More than a century earlier, these women taught America a lesson about power.

The story of the Bread and Roses Strike has always given me goose bumps. In the early 1900s, the mills in Lawrence employed tens of thousands of people, mostly women and children, mostly immigrants from dozens of countries. These mills were wildly profitable for the owners, but workers were paid so little that many lived on beans and scraps of bread. Multiple families often crowded together in a single tenement apartment. Workers, including young children, lost hands, arms, legs, and even their lives while operating dangerous equipment. In January 1912, when the mill owners decided to boost profits by cutting wages, these women—who didn't even share a common language—found a way to say, "Enough is enough." They walked out.

The winter that year was bitterly cold. People were hungry, and food was scarce. Mothers worried about their little ones freezing to death. The strike seemed doomed to fail.

The mill owners had long controlled town government. First the police, then the militia were called out. Strikers were beaten, and some died. But the women held on. Nine long weeks later, the owners conceded. They agreed to raise wages and improve conditions. Soon after, more than a quarter of a million mill workers across New England also got pay raises, and the Massachusetts legislature passed America's first minimum wage law.

I loved telling that story. In fact, one of my favorite things about my campaign was that it gave me an opportunity to tell stories about women who worked hard for their families, fought hard for what they believed in, and ultimately changed the world.

Seven months after that day in Lawrence, I had a chance to tell another story, this time in New York City. The day broke clear and cool—perfect September weather. The morning began on a terrifically hopeful note when the Working Families Party announced that they were endorsing me for president. WFP is a stalwart progressive organization, a political party with chapters in New York and fourteen other states. WFP often supports Democratic candidates but also sometimes runs its own candidates. It has strong support from a number of unions and activist groups—exactly the kind of partner I was hoping for as I tried to build a movement that would make our government work, not just for the rich and powerful but for everyone. Their endorsement was a big deal. In progressive circles, in fact, it was a Really Big Deal.

The day was full of excitement and buzz, culminating in a huge evening event in Washington Square Park in lower Manhattan. The park's giant stone arch, in all its classic grandeur, was brilliantly lit up, and an enormous American flag had been suspended in the middle of the arch. More than twenty thousand people crammed into the park, the crowd spilling onto the streets in all directions. People in many of the surrounding apartment buildings opened their windows and joined us. Maurice Mitchell, the activist leader of WFP, was there with a big WFP contingent. It was an electric and celebratory moment: lots of cheering, hollering, and waving signs. It felt like we were about to make history—good history.

Washington Square Park is just a block away from the site of the infamous Triangle Shirtwaist Factory fire in March 1911, and that night I told the story of the fire. The workers in the factory were once again mostly immigrant women, including girls as young as fourteen, and they worked long hours to feed themselves and their families. Worried that the women might steal leftover scraps of material, the owners had blocked the building's fire escapes. When a fire broke out, many of the women were trapped on the top floors of the building. In eighteen minutes, 146 people died.

Despite this devastating loss of life, the factory owners had enough influence in government to ensure that no new safety regulations were put in place. And the fire might have been forgotten, but for a young woman who ran across the park while the factory was burning and saw several of the women jump to their death, some of them holding hands and jumping together. She saw, and she committed to make change.

At a time when women didn't even have the vote, that young woman—Frances Perkins—got a job at the capitol in Albany, then worked from inside New York's state government to help pass new fire regulations and other worker protection laws. Later, when Franklin Roosevelt became president, Frances became his secretary of labor, the first woman ever to serve in a president's cabinet. And from that perch, she helped push through Social Security, the prohibition on child labor, the right to join a union, unemployment insurance, and a federal minimum wage.

As I told that story, I drew connections to corruption in today's America—different in detail but very much the same in intent as that of a century ago—and laid out my plans to beat back the influence of giant corporations and billionaires. I talked about how, if we succeeded, we could open more doors by passing a wealth tax, attacking climate change, and investing in education. I argued that, like Frances Perkins, one very persistent woman backed up by millions of people across the country could create big, structural change.

In November I traveled to Atlanta for another debate and stayed an extra day to speak at Clark Atlanta University. It was a special event because I had just been endorsed by Black Womxn For, a group of hundreds of Black women from across the country, led by the dynamic Angela Peoples. In the speech, I reached back to 1881, just sixteen years after the end of slavery, to tell the story of the many Black women and girls in Atlanta who had scratched out the barest living by laundering clothes for white people. The work was backbreaking and the pay pitifully low—and like so many before them, these workers realized that they were on their own if they wanted to make real change. So they banded together, and twenty courageous women led a strike that soon swelled to thousands.

Their employers hit back hard, persuading the police to arrest the strikers. But the women persisted, and they eventually won pay increases. As word of their success spread, Black cooks, Black maids, and Black nurses fought for better pay as well.

The story took another turn as another form of racism reared its ugly head. After Reconstruction, white supremacists used threats and violence to oppress Black people across the country—including the women in Atlanta. Jim Crow laws were ferociously enforced to strip these women of power, but their spark didn't die. Two generations later, in 1924, a little girl was born to an Atlanta washerwoman. The little girl grew up to be Dorothy Bolden, who worked alongside Dr. Martin Luther King Jr. in the 1960s civil rights struggles and who helped launch the National Domestic Workers Alliance. Dorothy reminded us that the fight for justice is never over.

In the months that followed, I told other stories about inspiring women. On New Year's Eve 2019—exactly one year after I'd stepped outside my house with Bruce and Bailey to start this presidential race—I spoke at the Old South Meeting House in Boston about an enslaved young woman, Phillis Wheatley, who wrote poetry so powerful that George Washington asked to meet with her on the eve of the American Revolution. And in March 2020, on the eve of Super Tuesday, I visited the East Los Angeles neighborhood that was home to the Latina janitors who fought to form a union and in April 1990 marched proudly while carrying the banner JUSTICE FOR JANITORS.

I told some of my own stories, too. I talked about my mother's grit when my daddy had a heart attack and we were on the edge of losing our home. I talked about my Aunt Bee, who carried me home from the hospital and rescued me more than once when life had dished out more than I could handle. I talked about Mrs. Lee, my second-grade teacher who whispered in my ear when I was seven years old that I could be a teacher—and who set my entire life off in a direction that I am grateful for every day. These three women made my run for president possible. So did the women whose stories I told. None of them expected to lead a movement. None were famous. But they saw a job that needed doing and showed the courage and leadership and willingness to fight that made change a reality. I carry these women with me every day—walking into classrooms or Senate hearings, campaigning for elected office, or carrying my own grandbabies home from the hospital.

I spoke about these women to show my gratitude for all they made possible. I also talked about them so that other women would be reminded of their own power. I told the stories of these women so that little girls and little boys would come to see women's leadership as an ordinary and unremarkable part of the world they live in.

## I LOVE YOU, BUT

In the early months of 2019, I could feel our campaign take shape. As the year went on, it began to radiate its own energy. I traveled back and forth to Iowa, New Hampshire, Nevada, and South Carolina. I also went to not-so-typical places for a Democratic primary candidate—West Virginia and Mississippi, Arizona and Utah. Eventually, I held rallies and town halls in thirty states and Puerto Rico. Red states and blue states, urban and rural locales, rich and poor neighborhoods. Many different places and many different people.

At every stop I talked about the same interconnected issues—about childcare and student loan debt, about expanding Social Security and investing in housing. I talked about racial justice, economic justice, the wealth tax, and rooting out corruption in Washington. And we ended every event with a selfie line so that I could meet as many people as possible.

The crowds kept growing, and the enthusiasm grew with them. Polling isn't always terribly accurate, but it did tell one part of the story of the 2020 presidential race. Two months into our campaign, polls had me at about 6 percent among Democratic voters—way behind Beto O'Rourke (11 percent), Kamala Harris (12 percent), Bernie Sanders (20 percent), and Joe Biden (28 percent). By midsummer, I had nearly tripled my numbers to about 15 percent—now I was way ahead of Beto (2 percent), tied with Bernie, and still trailing Biden (25 percent). By early fall, most polls had me ahead of Bernie, and some of them had me a little ahead of Biden.

As my poll numbers kept climbing, news outlets started carrying stories saying that since I was now among the leaders, I actually had a chance to capture the Democratic nomination. The *New York Daily News*, for instance, published a story under the headline "Why Warren's the One to Watch." In mid-September, the *Des Moines Register* ran a story touting the fact that for the first time I was leading the paper's highly respected poll, besting both Biden and Bernie. Leading in Iowa? Wow—this campaign had wings.

One night around this time, Bruce and I stopped into a bar at about eleven. We'd just finished a town hall, followed by a long, long selfie line. After months and months on the road, I wasn't quite sure where we were—but the few people left in the place were friendly and the beer was cold. Once I'd finished a campaign event, I needed time to shake off the adrenaline. Burger-and-beer had become my go-to remedy.

Bruce—and everyone else around me—knew I didn't read the polls. A lot of candidates pretended not to look at their numbers, but I made a really deliberate effort to stay away from polls because I didn't want them in my head. My job was to give every town hall and every television interview everything I had, not to worry about whether I was up two points or down two points from yesterday. But it was impossible to stay completely insulated from the polls. Reporters asked questions about them, people in selfie lines mentioned them, and sometimes I'd see a headline or read a reference to a poll in a story I was reading. So, like it or not, I knew generally what the polls looked like.

I was on my second beer, and so was Bruce. We'd eaten our burgers and fries, and the empty plates were still in front of us. Bruce was holding my hand across the table, and I was leaning my head back against the booth.

We were both quiet for a long time, and then he said, "Babe, you could actually do this. You could be president."

He didn't smile. He didn't wink. He just looked directly at me, waiting.

We never talked like this. I jerked upright, my defenses instantly on high alert. *Don't go there.*

But it was late and I was tired and I was on my second beer, so I took a couple of breaths and leaned back again and just let the idea wash over me. The town halls were going great. People loved the plans. I was doing a good job in the debates. We had tons of volunteers. I hadn't made any big gaffes in the press.

Sitting there, late at night after another long town hall, the first image that came to mind was from a trip about eighteen months earlier to McAllen, a small American town on the Mexico-Texas border. That's where I'd seen the cages—cage after cage, packed with children. I'd never forgotten the sad faces and slumped shoulders, the way these children stared off with the kind of deeply exhausted resignation that I'd never seen on a child's face. *No more,* I thought. *Never again. If I become president we will stop this nightmare. We will be a nation that treats people with decency. No more breaking up families. No more threatening Dreamers. No more treating people around the world as if we are the only human beings on this planet who matter.*

Once I started, I couldn't stop. All the discipline of taking the race a day at a time, all the months of holding a tight grip on my heart—it all started to melt away. A stream of images started to click through my brain. Childcare centers, bright and cheerful with well-paid teachers. Hardworking people getting letters saying that their student loan debts had been canceled. People smiling over bigger Social Security checks. Policing reforms. New housing. Closing the wealth gap between Black and white families. Full funding for the Indian Health Service. An end to drilling on our national lands. Gun safety. Voting rights. Wind energy. Enforcing the antitrust laws. A wealth tax.

More and more images streamed past, almost like a high-speed slideshow. Everything I'd talked about for months and months. Every plan I'd worked on. I stretched my legs under the table and closed my eyes and let the thoughts flash through my brain. *My Lord, the things we could do!*

Suddenly I sat upright again. "Pinkie promises!"

Bruce laughed. It was late and I was bone-tired, but now—this moment—I wanted to make one more plan. On Inauguration Day, we could set up a line for pinkie promises for little girls and their families. I started to think about how we could make that work. Instead of spending time at fancy dress balls that night, could we spend the time on a selfie line for children?

My eyes filled with tears. I started to cry and laugh at the same time. Who might be in that line? What little girls or little boys would tell their own grandchildren about a long-ago pinkie promise made with an American president?

Bruce held my hand while each of us finished our beer.

I looked at Bruce and let out a deep breath. "God, I really want to do this."

Bruce's smile had disappeared, and now I saw a shadow of worry on his face. I think he understood that I could get my heart broken. We'd come such a long way. We'd put so much into this. And now I could see it—I could almost taste and touch and smell the ways we could make this nation work better for tens of millions of people. The change felt so close. Losing would be incredibly painful.

Within days of that delicious late-night moment, an undercurrent of different stories began taking hold. Sure, Democrats could nominate me, but could I win? Was I really and truly electable? Could I beat Trump? As I kept rising in the polls, the electability drumbeat in the press got louder and louder. The headlines told the story:

"How Electable Is Elizabeth Warren, Anyway?" (*New York Magazine*)

"Elizabeth Warren Is Surging. This One Big Question Looms over Her." (*Washington Post*)

"Elizabeth Warren's Latest Hurdle to the Presidency: Democrats' Belief Women Face Tougher Fight Against Trump" (*USA Today*)

"Biden Allies Attack Warren's Electability" (*Politico*)

And it wasn't just the press. By late September, my improving poll numbers caught the attention of the other candidates in the race. At a debate on October 15, they ripped into me, mostly for not yet having nailed down the details of how I would pay for Medicare for All. Almost immediately, my numbers started falling, and soon I was far behind both Bernie and Biden. I never came close again.

I'm sure that plenty of people would be happy to provide their own explanations for the reversal. I'm definitely not the most objective observer, but it's not hard to figure out some of what happened. Bernie had built an army of loyal supporters during his 2016 bid, and many of them were there for him this time around, too. He was fearless and determined, and he promised a full-on revolution to turn us into a better America. Biden had plenty of strengths as well. He had been Obama's faithful second-in-command. He brought years of experience to the table and was clearly a steady, decent man who could deliver us from the nightmare world of Donald Trump and govern with compassion. Each of them had captured a large portion of the Democratic Party, and there wasn't much space left for me.

Rational explanations, every one. And I'm sure that dozens of self-styled pundits would be happy to offer their own theories. But there's always another possibility, a much more painful one: in this moment, against this president, in this field of candidates, maybe I just wasn't good enough to reassure the voters, to bring along the doubters, to embolden the hopeful.

## PERSISTENCE

Ayanna Pressley grew up in a world of activists. Her mother, Sandy, carried her along to tenants' rights meetings and bounced baby Ayanna on her hip as she rallied voters. In 2009, when she was thirty-five, Ayanna ran for Boston City Council, her first elective office. Sandy was right there, her daughter's not-so-secret weapon. When Ayanna won, Sandy adopted the whole city council as family. A year into Ayanna's first term, when Sandy lost her long battle with leukemia, the mayor and the entire council turned out for her funeral. Today when Ayanna stands up to speak, she often talks about her mother and the power she draws from her.

Ayanna is rooted in strength. The strength of her mother, the strength of her faith, the strength of purpose she brings to every fight. She is strong down to her toes.

In 2018, Ayanna decided that change couldn't wait. She challenged a well-established, well-liked, ten-term incumbent Massachusetts congressman. Many people wrote off her effort as hopeless, but they didn't know Ayanna's strength. Her powerful message—that people closest to the pain should be closest to the power—caught fire. Despite a big deficit in the polls and a Democratic establishment that endorsed her opponent, she won by a breathtaking 17 points and became the state's first Black woman in Congress.

When Ayanna went to Washington, she instantly became a rock star. She was part of The Squad, a group of four newly arrived members of the House. These young women of color were an inspiration for a diverse generation of activists. They were also targets of constant attacks by President Trump. Ayanna wasn't the least bit intimidated; she leaned in, calling herself and her sisters "Donald Trump's worst nightmare." She worked tirelessly, crafting plans on criminal justice reform, income inequality, maternal health, immigration and ICE, and the decriminalization of sex work. And from her first day, she was outspoken on behalf of people who too often don't have a voice in Washington.

Ayanna was one of three women who cochaired my campaign for president; the other two were Deb Haaland and Katie Porter. They were a remarkable crew. Working together and separately, they traveled to a number of states, talking with people about plans but also talking about power—the power to make change. Ayanna made a point of saying that she was proud to support a candidate who talked about the racial wealth gap to white audiences, about childcare to seniors, about Social Security to college students. She often said she was proud to support a candidate who talked about Black people not only in the context of pain and crime and poverty but also in the context of opportunity, entrepreneurship, investment in education, and the power of community. I was proud to have these three women—all of them gifted leaders—help me run for president.

Ayanna, Deb, and Katie care deeply about policy, and they know that it's always personal. Policy touches our lives in profound ways, changing who we are as individuals and who we are as a country. But for all of us who fight for change, no single policy defines us. And none of us can be limited to just one fight, because no single fight defines us, either. Yes, I'm a mother, and I fight for changes that I believe will improve the lives of millions of mothers. But I'm also a teacher and a planner. And a fighter, a learner, and a woman. I'm all these things and more, and I'll keep fighting for the changes that I believe will make our government work for everyone. Ayanna, too, is many things, as are Deb and Katie. And they, too, will bring every part of who they are to the fight to make our country better.

One gorgeous summer afternoon in 2019, I spoke to a crowd of about twelve thousand people in a big green field in St. Paul, Minnesota. Some families came early and picnicked on the grass. The selfie line included an Elizabeth Warren look-alike, right down to her glasses and cheerfully colored sweater. In fact, my double was so convincing that some people took a look at the three-hour line and decided to get a picture with her instead.

As always, there were many pinkie promises. One was with a lively and impatient little girl of about eight or nine. She had been waiting a long time, and when she and her daddy got to the front of the line, she hopped on one foot and then the other. She wanted her own picture—not just a shot with her father. And she had her pinkie out, ready to go.

With our pinkies locked, I said to her the same thing I'd said a zillion times before: "My name is Elizabeth, and I'm running for president because that's what girls do."

Big smiles, good photos, another pinkie promise to remember. Next.

The girl started to walk away, and then she seemed to think about what I'd said—and it just wasn't enough. She abruptly turned around. "And they win!"

I laughed and said, "Yes—and they win!"

Her father tried to hustle her off, but she was having none of it. She clearly had more she more she wanted to say. She didn't move on, and I didn't turn to the next person in line. For just an instant, it was just this little girl and me, standing in a beautiful, sun-drenched field, with lots of laughing and talking in the background. She planted her feet, put her hands on her narrow hips, and looked straight into my eyes. In her dead-serious, I'm-warning-you tone, she said, "You better win. I've been waiting for a girl president since . . . since . . . since *kindergarten!*"

Yes, I get it. Waiting is hard.

And no, I didn't win. But in the middle of the night, I don't think about losing. I don't think about waiting. Instead, I think about the plans. I think about the fights ahead that can make those plans real. I think about all the fights we need to win, and all the people who can help us win even if they don't look like leaders. I think about righteous fights and the extraordinary opportunities packed into this moment in history.

I think about that morning in March 2020 when I walked out my kitchen door and saw a message written in big chalk letters on the sidewalk:

PERSIST

# NOTES

## PROLOGUE

4 *I'd issued a plan:* Elizabeth Warren, "Preventing, Containing, and Treating Infectious Disease Outbreaks at Home and Abroad," Team Warren, Medium, January 28, 2020, https://medium.com/@teamwarren/preventing-containing-and-treating-infectious-disease-outbreaks-at-home-and-abroad-3336e1e80a88.

4 *I followed it soon after:* Elizabeth Warren, "Protecting Our People and Our Economy from Coronavirus," Team Warren, Medium, March 2, 2020, https://medium.com/@teamwarren/protecting-our-people-and-our-economy-from-coronavirus-481b79dd0089; Elizabeth Warren, "My Updated Plan to Address the Coronavirus Crisis," Team Warren, Medium, March 12, 2020, https://medium.com/@teamwarren/my-updated-plan-to-address-the-coronavirus-crisis-64303a3a6fed.

7 *more than 2.2 million consumer complaints:* Consumer Financial Protection Bureau, "Consumer Financial Protection Bureau Issues Consumer Complaint Bulletin," press release, May 21, 2020, https://www.consumerfinance.gov/about-us/newsroom/cfpb-issues-consumer-complaint-bulletin/.

8 *Two-thirds of America's eligible population:* James M. Lindsay, "The 2020 Election by the Numbers," Water's Edge blog, Council on Foreign Relations, December 15, 2020, https://www.cfr.org/blog/2020-election-numbers.

8 *more than double the number:* Nathaniel Rakich, Geoffrey Skelley, Laura Bronner, and Julia Wolfe, "How Democrats Won the Georgia Runoffs," FiveThirtyEight, January 7, 2021, https://fivethirtyeight.com/features/how-democrats-won-the-georgia-runoffs/.

9 *more votes than any presidential ticket in the history of the republic:* Domenico Montanaro, "President-Elect Joe Biden Hits 80 Million Votes in Year of Record Turnout," NPR, November 25, 2020, https://www.npr.org/2020/11/25/937248659/president-elect-biden-hits-80-million-votes-in-year-of-record-turnout.

10  *Florida voted to raise the minimum wage to $15:* Lawrence Mower, Sara DiNatale, and Carlos Frias, "Florida Voters Passed a Minimum Wage Increase. What Does That Mean?," *Tampa Bay Times,* November 4, 2020, https://www.tampabay.com/news/florida-politics/elections/2020/11/04/florida-voters-passed-a-minimum-wage-increase-what-does-that-mean/.

10  *Arizona voted to increase taxes on wealthy people:* Lily Altavena, "Arizona Voters Approve Prop. 208, Education Tax on State's Highest Earners," *Arizona Republic,* November 6, 2020, https://www.azcentral.com/story/news/politics/arizona-education/2020/11/03/proposition-208-invest-education-act-election-results-raise-taxes-high-earners/6041668002/.

10  *Colorado voted for twelve weeks of paid family leave:* Joe Rubino, "Colorado Prop 118: Paid Family and Medical Leave Passes," *Denver Post,* November 3, 2020, https://www.denverpost.com/2020/11/03/colorado-prop-118-results-paid-family-leave/.

## CHAPTER 1

20  *The Civil Rights Act of 1964 had banned:* Public Law 88–352, Sec. 703(a).

20  *In 1976, the Supreme Court ruled:* General Electric Co. v. Gilbert, 429 U.S. 125 (1976).

20  *For some, the anger:* Elizabeth Warren, October 9, 2019, https://twitter.com/ewarren/status/1181782923231531008.

21  *if ratified by thirty-eight states:* The Equal Rights Amendment has now been ratified by thirty-eight states. Congress will have to remove the original deadline for ratification.

21  *many insurance companies could say:* Louise Norris, "How Obamacare Changed Maternity Coverage," HealthInsurance.org, November 1, 2020, https://www.healthinsurance.org/obamacare/how-obamacare-changed-maternity-coverage/. Even then, the coverage isn't complete. An insurance plan is required to cover an adult child until age twenty-six, but it need not cover maternity care for that adult child. Megan Leonhardt, "This 24-Year-Old Mistakenly Thought Her Health Insurance Covered Her Pregnancy—and 4.2 Million Others Like Her May Be at Risk," CNBC Make It, November 26, 2019, https://www.cnbc.com/2019/11/26/when-your-insurer-does-not-cover-your-maternity-costs.html.

21  *A study of more than thirty-five hundred individual insurance plans:* National Women's Law Center, *Still Nowhere to Turn: Insurance Companies Treat Women Like a Pre-Existing Condition* (2009): 18–19, https://nwlc.org/wp-content/uploads/2015/08/stillnowheretoturn.pdf.

21  *And not until 2015:* Young v. UPS, 575 U.S. __ (2015); Liz Morris, Cynthia Thomas Calvert, and Joan C. Williams, "What Young vs. UPS Means for Pregnant Workers and Their Bosses," *Harvard Business Review,* March 26, 2015, https://hbr.org/2015/03/what-young-vs-ups-means-for-pregnant-workers-and-their-bosses.

22  *"Hell, I'm young and personally know":* CC, October 8, 2019, https://twitter.com/CCoceans311/status/1181561465767186433.

22  *When asked about pregnancy discrimination by a reporter:* Dee-Ann Durbin, "Pregnancy Discrimination Continues, 41 Years After US Ban," Associated Press, October

12, 2019, https://abcnews.go.com/Business/wireStory/pregnancy-discrimination -continues-41-years-us-ban-66230140.

22  *In 2018, the* New York Times *completed:* Natalie Kitroeff and Jessica Silver-Greenberg, "Pregnancy Discrimination Is Rampant Inside America's Biggest Companies," *New York Times,* February 8, 2019, https://www.nytimes.com/interactive /2018/06/15/business/pregnancy-discrimination.html.

22  *Black women are three to four times more likely:* U.S. Centers for Disease Control and Prevention, "Pregnancy-Related Deaths," February 26, 2019, https://www.cdc .gov/reproductivehealth/maternalinfanthealth/pregnancy-relatedmortality.htm; U.S. Centers for Disease Control and Prevention, "Racial and Ethnic Disparities Continue in Pregnancy-Related Deaths," press release, September 5, 2019, https:// www.cdc.gov/media/releases/2019/p0905-racial-ethnic-disparities-pregnancy -deaths.html.

23  *About six million women get pregnant:* Lawrence B. Finer and Mia Zolna, "Declines in Unintended Pregnancy in the United States, 2008–2011," *New England Journal of Medicine* 374, no. 9 (March 3, 2016): 843–52, https://www.nejm.org/doi/full/10 .1056/nejmsa1506575.

23  *there are about twenty million children:* Mark Zandi and Sophia Koropeckyj, *Universal Child Care and Early Learning Act: Helping Families and the Economy,* Economy.com/Moody's Analytics, February 2019, 2, https://www.economy.com/mark -zandi/documents/2019-02-18-Child-Care-Act.pdf.

23  *And there are another thirty million or so:* National Center for Education Statistics, *Digest of Education Statistics,* December 2019, Table 203.10, https://nces.ed.gov/ programs/digest/d19/tables/dt19_203.10.asp?current=yes.

23  *So we have all these provisions:* Ryan Abbott and Bret Bogenschneider, "Should Robots Pay Taxes? Tax Policy in the Age of Automation," *Harvard Law & Policy Review* 12 (2018): 145–75, https://robotic.legal/wp-content/uploads/2018/06/ Should-Robots-Pay-Taxes.pdf; Robert Green, "How to Fix the Tax Code So It Doesn't Favor Robots over Humans," *Forbes,* May 30, 2017, https://www.forbes .com/sites/greatspeculations/2017/05/30/how-to-fix-tax-reform-so-it-doesnt -favor-robots-over-humans/?sh=3696c3ac2d09.

24  *The study found that if not for the thirty-eight million:* Joanna Barsh and Lareina Yee, *Unlocking the Full Potential of Women in the U.S. Economy,* April 1, 2011, https:// www.mckinsey.com/business-functions/organization/our-insights/unlocking-the -full-potential-of-women.

24  *But in 1999, women hit their peak participation:* U.S. Bureau of Labor Statistics, *Women in the Labor Force: A Databook,* December 2019, 8–16, Table 2, https:// www.bls.gov/opub/reports/womens-databook/2019/pdf/home.pdf.

24  *Standard and Poor's estimates that if the United States:* S&P Global, "Women at Work: The Key to Global Growth," 2019, https://www.spglobal.com/en/research -insights/featured/women-at-work-the-key-to-global-growth.

25  *Among 37 of the highest-income countries:* Sarah A. Donovan, *Paid Family Leave in the United States,* Congressional Research Service, May 29, 2019, https://fas.org /sgp/crs/misc/R44835.pdf.

25  *In fact, 184 nations offer:* Catalyst, "Women in the Workforce—Global: Quick Take," January 30, 2020, https://www.catalyst.org/research/women-in-the-workforce

-global/; World Bank, "Women, Business and the Law: Parenthood," https://wbl
.worldbank.org/en/data/exploretopics/wbl_hc.

30   *More than 80 percent of parents with children under five struggle:* Rasheed Malik,
Katie Hamm, Leila Schochet, Cristina Novoa, Simon Workman, and Steven Jessen-
Howard, *America's Child Care Deserts in 2018,* Center for American Progress, December 6, 2018, https://www.americanprogress.org/issues/early-childhood/reports/2018
/12/06/461643/americas-child-care-deserts-2018/.

30   *The average cost of childcare:* Economic Policy Institute, "Child Care Costs in the
United States," https://www.epi.org/child-care-costs-in-the-united-states/.

30   *Infant care is even more challenging:* Child Care Aware of America, *The US and the
High Cost of Child Care,* 2018, https://cdn2.hubspot.net/hubfs/3957809/COCre
port2018_1.pdf.

32   *when I arrived at the auditorium and found it filled:* Natalie Martinez, "Senator Elizabeth Warren Draws Crowds to Annie's List 15th Anniversary Celebration," FOX
7 Austin, February 2, 2018, https://www.fox7austin.com/news/senator-elizabeth
-warren-draws-crowds-to-annies-list-15th-anniversary-celebration.

34   *about one-third of the workforce:* Audrey Kearney and Cailey Muñana, "Taking
Stock of Essential Workers," Kaiser Family Foundation, May 1, 2020, https://www
.kff.org/policy-watch/taking-stock-of-essential-workers/.

35   *Boston and Worcester . . . turned their convention centers:* Angus Chen, "Convention
Centers Fill with Beds for COVID-19, Including 500 for Boston's Homeless," WBUR,
April 9, 2020, https://www.wbur.org/commonhealth/2020/04/09/convention-centers
-transform-into-field-hospitals-in-boston-and-worcester; Angus Chen and Jack
Mitchell, "Worcester's DCU Center Will Become 250-Bed Field Hospital for Stable
COVID-19 Patients," WBUR, April 1, 2020, https://www.wbur.org/commonhealth
/2020/03/31/dcu-arena-covid-19-field-hospital.

35   *But one in five of those who couldn't work:* Misty L. Heggeness and Jason M.
Fields, "Working Moms Bear Brunt of Home Schooling While Working During
COVID-19," U.S. Census Bureau, August 18, 2020, https://www.census.gov/library
/stories/2020/08/parents-juggle-work-and-child-care-during-pandemic.html.

36   *working parents found that the increased demands:* Matt Krentz, Emily Kos, Anna
Green, and Jennifer Garcia-Alonso, "Easing the COVID-19 Burden on Working
Parents," May 21, 2020, https://www.bcg.com/publications/2020/helping-working
-parents-ease-the-burden-of-covid-19.

36   *And who did most of this childcare and schooling burden fall on?:* Heggeness and
Fields, "Working Moms Bear Brunt of Home Schooling While Working During
COVID-19."

36   *Research showed that before COVID-19, even among dual-earning couples:* Sarah
Schoppe-Sullivan, "Dads Are More Involved in Parenting, Yes, But Moms Still Put
In More Work," The Conversation, February 2, 2017, https://theconversation.com
/dads-are-more-involved-in-parenting-yes-but-moms-still-put-in-more-work
-72026.

36   *mothers' share of the work actually increased:* Meghan McCarty Carino, "Mothers
Overwhelmingly Supervise Remote Learning, Poll Finds," Marketplace, October 15,
2020, https://www.marketplace.org/2020/10/15/mothers-overwhelmingly-supervise
-remote-learning-poll-finds/.

37   *Experts speculate that without sufficient childcare infrastructure:* Patricia Cohen

and Tiffany Hsu, "Pandemic Could Scar a Generation of Working Mothers," *New York Times*, June 3, 2020, https://www.nytimes.com/2020/06/03/business/economy/coronavirus-working-women.html; Julie Kashen, Sarah Jane Glynn, and Amanda Novello, "How COVID-19 Sent Women's Workforce Progress Backward," Center for American Progress, October 30, 2020, https://www.americanprogress.org/issues/women/reports/2020/10/30/492582/covid-19-sent-womens-workforce-progress-backward/.

37 *From 1970 through 2019:* The total increase is 12.7 percent. That works out, across the forty-nine years, to about one-quarter of one percent a year. U.S. Census Bureau, "Historical Income Tables: People," Table P-5, https://www.census.gov/data/tables/time-series/demo/income-poverty/historical-income-people.html.

37 *Housing costs are up over 60 percent:* Bureau of Labor Statistics, "Consumer Expenditure Survey, 1972–73," Table 2: Selected Family Characteristics, Annual Expenditures, and Sources of Income Classified by Family Size, United States, https://www.bls.gov/cex/1973/Standard/cusize.pdf. Data inflation-adjusted (CPI).

37 *health insurance expenses have more than tripled:* "Consumer Expenditure Survey, 1972–73," Table 2.

37 *the price of a college degree has increased:* College Choice, "The Rising Cost of College," October 26, 2020, https://www.collegechoice.net/the-rising-cost-of-college/.

37 *the cost of childcare went up:* Sabino Kornrich, "Inequalities in Parental Spending on Young Children: 1972 to 2010," *AERA Open* 2, no. 2 (April–June 2016): 1–12; Sabino Kornrich and Frank Furstenberg, "Investing in Children: Changes in Parental Spending on Children, 1972–2007," *Demography* 50 (2013): 1–23; additional calculations by Kornrich.

37 *In nearly half of all states, childcare costs:* Claire Zillman, "Childcare Costs More Than College Tuition in 28 U.S. States," *Fortune*, October 22, 2018, https://fortune.com/2018/10/22/childcare-costs-per-year-us/.

37 *about two-thirds of mothers with young children have jobs:* Bureau of Labor Statistics, "Employment Characteristics of Families—2019," press release, April 21, 2020, https://www.bls.gov/news.release/pdf/famee.pdf.

38 *One study estimated that in early 2020:* Steven Jessen-Howard, Rasheed Malik, and MK Falgout, "Costly and Unavailable: America Lacks Sufficient Child Care Supply for Infants and Toddlers," August 4, 2020, Center for American Progress, https://www.americanprogress.org/issues/early-childhood/reports/2020/08/04/488642/costly-unavailable-america-lacks-sufficient-child-care-supply-infants-toddlers/.

39 *and dozens of other countries:* OECD, *Is Childcare Affordable?*, policy brief, June 2020, http://www.oecd.org/els/family/OECD-Is-Childcare-Affordable.pdf; Vassil Kirov, *Country Report: Bulgaria*, European Public Service Union, 2018, https://www.epsu.org/sites/default/files/article/files/Country%20report%20Bulgaria%20childcare.pdf; Federal Chancellery, Republic of Austria, "Child Care in Austria," https://www.women-families-youth.bka.gv.at/families/child-care-in-austria/child-care-in-austria.html.

39 *Companies' depreciation write-offs totaled:* Joint Committee on Taxation, *Estimates of Federal Tax Expenditures for Fiscal Years 2020–2024*, November 5, 2020, 28, https://www.jct.gov/publications/2020/jcx-23-20/.

40 *$70 billion:* The estimate comes from Moody's Analytics and would cover about

twelve million children of working parents. Zandi and Koropeckyj, *Universal Child Care and Early Learning Act.*

40   *Currently, childcare workers earn:* Elise Gould, *Child Care Workers Aren't Paid Enough to Make Ends Meet,* Economic Policy Institute, November 5, 2015, https://www.epi.org/publication/child-care-workers-arent-paid-enough-to-make-ends-meet/; Zandi and Koropeckyj, *Universal Child Care and Early Learning Act;* Bureau of Labor Statistics, "Occupational Employment and Wages," May 2017, https://www.bls.gov/oes/2017/may/oes399011.htm.

40   *More than 90 percent of these workers cannot meet:* Gould, *Child Care Workers Aren't Paid Enough to Make Ends Meet.*

40   *More than 93 percent of childcare workers are female:* Bureau of Labor Statistics, "Labor Force Statistics from the Current Population Survey," Table 11: Employed Persons by Detailed Occupation, Sex, Race, and Hispanic or Latino Ethnicity, January 22, 2020, https://www.bls.gov/cps/cpsaat11.htm; Christine Fernando, "Coronavirus Takes Toll on Black, Latino Child Care Providers," Associated Press, December 7, 2020, https://apnews.com/article/race-and-ethnicity-child-care-coronavirus-pandemic-a0 e9c01e7961e1d144c480e2ac5be903.

41   *the benefits of high-quality early childhood education can be measured:* Dana Charles McCoy, Hirokazu Yoshikawa et al., "Impacts of Early Childhood Education on Medium- and Long-Term Educational Outcomes," *Educational Researcher* 46, no. 8 (November 2017): 474–87, https://journals.sagepub.com/doi/full/10.3102/0013189X17737739.

41   *Studies also show that high-quality early childhood education:* James J. Heckman, "Early Childhood Education: Quality and Access Pay Off," https://heckmanequation.org/resource/early-childhood-education-quality-and-access-pay-off/.

41   *it also reduces the likelihood of arrest:* National Institute of Child Health and Human Development, "Small Investment in Children's Education Yields Big Results," press release, March 11, 2015, https://www.nichd.nih.gov/newsroom/releases/031115-podcast-reynolds.

41   *Sure, our government provides some tax breaks for childcare:* Office of Senator Elizabeth Warren, "Universal Child Care and Early Learning Act," February 2019, https://www.warren.senate.gov/imo/media/doc/Universal_Child_Care_Policy_Brief_2019.pdf.

44   *When we introduced our bill, Deb said:* Office of Senator Elizabeth Warren, "Senator Warren and Congresswoman Haaland Unveil New Legislation to Provide Universal Child Care and Early Learning to All Families," press release, June 18, 2019, https://www.warren.senate.gov/newsroom/press-releases/senator-warren-and-congresswoman-haaland-unveil-new-legislation-to-provide-universal-child-care-and-early-learning-to-all-families.

47   *The overwhelming majority of our fellow citizens:* Juliana Menasce Horowitz, "Despite Challenges at Home and Work, Most Working Moms and Dads Say Being Employed Is What's Best for Them," Pew Research Center, September 12, 2019, https://www.pewresearch.org/fact-tank/2019/09/12/despite-challenges-at-home-and-work-most-working-moms-and-dads-say-being-employed-is-whats-best-for-them/. The survey shows that about 76 percent of respondents think fathers of small children definitely should work, but only about 33 percent believe mothers of small children should hold down jobs.

47    *45 percent of fathers said they were doing most of the work:* Claire Cain Miller, "Nearly Half of Men Say They Do Most of the Home Schooling. 3 Percent of Women Agree," *New York Times,* May 8, 2020, https://www.nytimes.com/2020/05/06/upshot /pandemic-chores-homeschooling-gender.html.

## CHAPTER 2

55    *Kamala Harris, then the attorney general of California, appointed:* Office of the California Monitor, *By the Numbers: Mortgage Relief Across California,* September 24, 2013, https://oag.ca.gov/sites/all/files/agweb/pdfs/mortgage_settlement /04-report-by-the-numbers.pdf; Office of the Attorney General of California, "Attorney General Kamala D. Harris Appoints Independent Monitor to Protect Interests of Homeowners in $18 Billion California Commitment," press release, March 16, 2012, https://oag.ca.gov/news/press-releases/attorney-general-kamala -d-harris-appoints-independent-monitor-protect-interests; Abby Vesoulis, "California Rep. Katie Porter Schools Congress with a White Board," *Time,* August 6, 2020, https://time.com/5876593/katie-porter-congress/.

58    *At the federal level in 2020, American taxpayers put $72 billion:* Committee for Education Funding, FY 2020 Budget Charts, December 18, 2019, https://cef.org /wp-content/uploads/FY-2020-budget-charts-12.18.19.pdf.

58    *less than 2 percent of all federal spending:* Committee for Education Funding, FY 2020 Budget Charts.

58    *American taxpayers put $738 billion into national defense:* White House, "Remarks by President Trump at Signing Ceremony for S.1790, National Defense Authorization Act for Fiscal Year 2020," December 20, 2019, https://trumpwhitehouse .archives.gov/briefings-statements/remarks-president-trump-signing-ceremony -s-1790-national-defense-authorization-act-fiscal-year-2020/.

58    *we consistently dedicate about half of our nation's discretionary budget to defense:* Congressional Budget Office, "Discretionary Spending in 2019: An Infographic," April 15, 2020, https://www.cbo.gov/publication/56326.

60    *Nearly every homeowner in America pays a property tax:* Tax Policy Center, "The State of State (and Local) Tax Policy," 2020, https://www.taxpolicycenter.org/briefing -book/how-do-state-and-local-property-taxes-work.

60    *a big chunk of that tax is used to support local schools:* National Center for Education Statistics, "The Condition of Education 2020," https://nces.ed.gov/programs /coe/pdf/coe_cma.pdf.

60    *most of the wealth of our richest families is held in stock:* Reuven Avi-Yonah, "The Shaky Case Against Wealth Taxation," *American Prospect,* August 28, 2019, https:// prospect.org/economy/shaky-case-wealth-taxation/; Reuven S. Avi-Yonah, "Taxation and the New 'Progressives,'" April 26, 2020, https://papers.ssrn.com/sol3 /papers.cfm?abstract_id=3585596.

61    *We also planned to significantly step up IRS enforcement:* Partly this would make up for the way tax enforcement has been gutted in recent years. Paul Kiel and Jesse Eisinger, "How the IRS Was Gutted," ProPublica, December 11, 2018, https://www .propublica.org/article/how-the-irs-was-gutted; Paul Kiel, "IRS: Sorry, but It's Just Easier and Cheaper to Audit the Poor," ProPublica, October 2, 2019, https://www .propublica.org/article/irs-sorry-but-its-just-easier-and-cheaper-to-audit-the-poor.

61  *my two-cent wealth tax would produce $275 billion a year:* Letter from Emmanuel
    Saez and Gabriel Zucman to Senator Elizabeth Warren, January 18, 2019, https://
    elizabethwarren.com/wp-content/uploads/2019/01/saez-zucman-wealthtax
    -warren-v5-web.pdf.

62  *A two-cent wealth tax would allow us to pay for universal childcare:* For the major-
    ity of families, care would be free. For the rest, families would contribute a small
    payment, up to 7 percent of family income. That's it.

62  *Study after study shows that more investment in education:* See, e.g., C. Kirabo Jack-
    son, Rucker C. Johnson, and Claudia Persico, "The Effects of School Spending on
    Educational and Economic Outcomes: Evidence from School Finance Reforms,"
    *Quarterly Journal of Economics* 131, no. 1 (February 2016): 157–218, https://doi
    .org/10.1093/qje/qjv036.

62  *Rigorous studies estimate that when we invest in preschool education:* Hirokazu
    Yoshikawa, Christina Weiland et al., *Investing in Our Future: The Evidence Base on
    Preschool Education,* Society for Research in Child Development and the Foun-
    dation for Child Development, October 2013, https://www.srcd.org/sites/default
    /files/file-attachments/mb_2013_10_16_investing_in_children.pdf.

63  *the federal government has never come close to meeting that promise:* National Cen-
    ter for Learning Disabilities, "IDEA Full Funding: Why Should Congress Invest
    in Special Education?," https://www.ncld.org/news/policy-and-advocacy/idea-full
    -funding-why-should-congress-invest-in-special-education.

63  *The average public school building is forty-four years old:* Education Week, "Data:
    U.S. School Buildings: Age, Condition, and Spending," November 28, 2017,
    https://www.edweek.org/ew/section/multimedia/data-us-school-buildings-age
    -condition-and.html.

64  *oldest schools typically located in the poorest districts:* National Center for Edu-
    cation Statistics, "How Old Are America's Public Schools?," https://nces.ed.gov
    /surveys/frss/publications/1999048/.

64  *More than half the school buildings in America:* National Center for Education Sta-
    tistics, "Condition of Public School Facilities," https://nces.ed.gov/fastfacts/display
    .asp?id=94.

64  *the most commonly identified facilities problem:* Education Week, "Data: U.S. School
    Buildings: Age, Condition, and Spending."

64  *our country's nonwhite school districts get about $23 billion less every year:* EdBuild,
    "Nonwhite School Districts Get $23 Billion Less Than White Districts Despite
    Serving the Same Number of Students," https://edbuild.org/content/23-billion.

64  *Bureau of Indian Education schools are also chronically underfunded:* U.S. Com-
    mission on Civil Rights, *Broken Promises: Continuing Federal Funding Shortfall
    for Native Americans,* December 2018, 102–13, https://www.usccr.gov/pubs/2018
    /12-20-Broken-Promises.pdf; Linda Darling-Hammond, "Education and the Path
    to One Nation, Indivisible," Learning Policy Institute, February 2018, https://
    learningpolicyinstitute.org/sites/default/files/product-files/Education_Path_To
    _One_Nation_BRIEF.pdf; Denise Juneau, "The Bureau of Indian Education Is
    Broken," *Education Week,* February 6, 2018, https://www.edweek.org/leadership
    /opinion-the-bureau-of-indian-education-is-broken/2018/02.

66  *about one out of six public school teachers works:* Katherine Schaeffer, "About One-
    in-Six U.S. Teachers Work Second Jobs—and Not Just in the Summer," Pew

Research Center, July 1, 2019, https://www.pewresearch.org/fact-tank/2019
/07/01/about-one-in-six-u-s-teachers-work-second-jobs-and-not-just-in-the
-summer/.

66   *the rate is much higher:* Schaeffer, "About One-in-Six U.S. Teachers Work Second
Jobs."

66   *Asking men and women to supplement their salaries:* The Public Service Loan Forgiveness Program was touted as a way to forgive student loans for teachers and others who make our country function—firefighters, police officers, city employees, etc.
Unfortunately, the program is so complicated and mismanaged that the applications
for eventual forgiveness have a 98 percent rejection rate, leaving the teachers and
others still struggling with their debt.

66   *these teachers are making less than others with similar educations:* Earlier studies
compared women earners to women earners; later studies compare all workers to
all workers. Economic Policy Institute, "Teachers Are Paid Almost 20% Less Than
Similar Workers," press release, September 17, 2020, https://www.epi.org/press
/teachers-are-paid-almost-20-less-than-similar-workers-when-including-benefits
-teachers-still-face-a-10-2-total-compensation-penalty/.

67   *By 2018, 70 percent of America's workers were in jobs:* Goldie Blumenstyk, "The
Edge," *Chronicle of Higher Education,* January 22, 2020, https://www.chronicle
.com/article/By-2020-They-Said-2-Out-of-3/247884.

67   *And the trend line is clear: More than 90 percent:* Steve Goldstein, "Nine out of
10 New Jobs Are Going to Those with a College Degree," MarketWatch, June 5,
2018, https://www.marketwatch.com/story/nine-out-of-10-new-jobs-are-going-to
-those-with-a-college-degree-2018-06-04.

67   *a respectable accomplishment:* In 1880, 17 percent of adults were illiterate. National
Center for Education Statistics, National Assessment of Adult Literacy, "Literacy
from 1870 to 1979," https://nces.ed.gov/naal/lit_history.asp.

68   *The resulting leap in Americans' standard of living:* Robert Gordon, *The Rise and
Fall of American Growth* (Princeton, NJ: Princeton University Press, 2016).

69   *Over the past two decades, state governments that once supported:* Michael Mitchell, Michael Leachman, and Kathleen Masterson, "Funding Down, Tuition Up,"
Center on Budget and Policy Priorities, August 15, 2016, https://www.cbpp.org
/research/state-budget-and-tax/funding-down-tuition-up.

69   *tuition at state schools has increased:* Mitchell et al., "Funding Down, Tuition
Up." Arizona universities increased tuition by 90 percent, and California schools
jumped 60 percent.

70   *a whopping 40 percent of all federal student loan debt was not in repayment:* Federal
Student Aid, "Federal Student Loan Portfolio," https://studentaid.gov/data-center
/student/portfolio.

70   *Almost 40 percent of people with student loan debt never made it to graduation:* Paul
Specht, "Alma Adams: 'Almost 40% of Borrowers with Student Loan Debt Didn't
Finish Their Degree,'" PolitiFact, February 12, 2021, https://www.politifact.com
/factchecks/2021/feb/12/alma-adams/democrats-say-40-people-college-debt
-didnt-get-deg/.

70   *Today about thirty-six million people are trying to manage:* National Student Clear-
inghouse Research Center, "Some College, No Degree," October 30, 2019, https://
nscresearchcenter.org/some-college-no-degree-2019/.

70    *The government is even taking a bite:* U.S. Government Accountability Office, "Social Security Offsets: Improvements to Program Design Could Better Assist Older Student Loan Borrowers with Obtaining Permitted Relief," December 2016, https://www.gao.gov/assets/690/681722.pdf.

70    *Two out of every three college graduates now carry student loan debt:* Institute for College Access and Success, *Student Debt and the Class of 2018*, September 2019, https://ticas.org/wp-content/uploads/2019/09/classof2018.pdf.

70    *People with student loan debt are 36 percent less likely:* Scholarship America, "The Far-Reaching Impact of the Student Debt Crisis," https://scholarshipamerica.org/blog/the-far-reaching-impact-of-the-student-debt-crisis/.

70    *They are less likely to buy a car:* Scholarship America, "The Far-Reaching Impact of the Student Debt Crisis."

70    *less likely to start a small business:* Vadim Revzin and Sergei Revzin, "Student Debt Is Stopping U.S. Millennials from Becoming Entrepreneurs," *Harvard Business Review*, April 26, 2019, https://hbr.org/2019/04/student-debt-is-stopping-u-s-millennials-from-becoming-entrepreneurs.

70    *They are more likely to be living with their parents:* Scholarship America, "The Far-Reaching Impact of the Student Debt Crisis."

71    *African American and Latino students are more likely:* Ben Miller, "The Continued Student Loan Crisis for Black Borrowers," Center for American Progress, December 2, 2019, https://www.americanprogress.org/issues/education-postsecondary/reports/2019/12/02/477929/continued-student-loan-crisis-black-borrowers/.

71    *And these effects last:* Judith Scott-Clayton and Jing Li, "Black-White Disparity in Student Loan Debt More Than Triples After Graduation," Brookings Institution, October 20, 2016, https://www.brookings.edu/research/black-white-disparity-in-student-loan-debt-more-than-triples-after-graduation/.

71    *In order to build more opportunity, Congress funded:* U.S. Department of Agriculture, National Institute of Food and Agriculture, "1890 Land-Grant Institutions Programs," https://nifa.usda.gov/program/1890-land-grant-institutions-programs.

71    *HBCUs—Historically Black Colleges and Universities—have had particular success:* Julian Wyllie, "How Are Black Colleges Doing? Better Than You Think, Study Finds," *Chronicle of Higher Education*, April 13, 2018, https://www.chronicle.com/article/how-are-black-colleges-doing-better-than-you-think-study-finds/.

71    *Both public and private HBCUs have significantly more constrained budgets:* Autumn A. Arnett, "Funding at HBCUs Continues to Be Separate and Unequal," *Diverse: Issues in Higher Education*, May 31, 2015, https://diverseeducation.com/article/73463/. While the federal government makes some allocations to HBCUs, the endowments of these schools significantly trail other colleges. "HBCUs Struggle to Close the Endowment Gap," *Philanthropy News Digest*, July 19, 2017, https://philanthropynewsdigest.org/news/hbcus-struggle-to-close-the-endowment-gap.

72    *Among Black Americans with student loan debt, the gap would close by an estimated 25 points:* "Projected relative wealth gap closure and wealth gains among borrowing households only would be formidable. Among borrowing households, the relative White-Black wealth gap would be reduced by a considerable amount, from 2.5% to 27.6%, and the White-Latino wealth gap closes from 53.7% to 81.0%.

The wealth gains among Black borrowing households is projected at $15,700 and at over $27,000 for Latino households." Letter from Raphaël Charron-Chénier, Thomas Shapiro, Louise Seamster, and Laura Sullivan to Senator Elizabeth Warren, April 18, 2019, 2, https://elizabethwarren.com/wp-content/uploads/2019/04 /Experts-Letter-to-Senator-Warren-.pdf; Mark Huelsman, "These Are the Questions We Should Be Asking in the Student Debt Cancellation Debate," Demos, July 3, 2019, https://www.demos.org/blog/these-are-questions-we-should-be-asking-student-debt-cancellation-debate.

72  *In effect, those for whom a college degree hasn't paid off:* Huelsman, "These Are the Questions We Should Be Asking in the Student Debt Cancellation Debate."

74  *The next night I appeared on* All In with Chris Hayes: *All In with Chris Hayes*, May 9, 2013, https://www.nbcnews.com/id/wbna51843142.

75  *More than a dozen billionaires:* David Dawkins, "George Soros Leads Chorus of Wealthy Calling for a New Wealth Tax," *Forbes*, June 24, 2019, https://www.forbes .com/sites/daviddawkins/2019/06/24/george-soros-leads-chorus-of-billionaires -calling-for-a-new-wealth-tax/#346def4e1ce7.

75  *They thought taxing the wealthy was both fair and a good way:* "An Open Letter to the 2020 Presidential Candidates: It's Time to Tax Us More," Medium, June 24, 2019, https://medium.com/@letterforawealthtax/an-open-letter-to-the-2020 -presidential-candidates-its-time-to-tax-us-more-6eb3a548b2fe.

75  *"I hate the wealth tax":* Jessica Bursztynsky, "Billionaire Investor Ron Baron: I'm Not Opposed to Higher Taxes, but 'I Hate the Wealth Tax,'" CNBC, February 4, 2020, https://www.cnbc.com/2020/02/04/billionaire-ron-baron-is-against-wealth -tax-not-opposed-to-higher-taxes.html.

75  *called the wealth tax "mean":* Edward Helmore, "Elizabeth Warren Rips into Billionaires Who Oppose Wealth Tax in Scathing Ad," *Guardian*, November 14, 2019, https://www.theguardian.com/us-news/2019/nov/14/elizabeth-warren-wealth -tax-campaign-ad-billionaires.

75  *Lloyd Blankfein called this kind of change "cataclysmic":* Matt Egan, "Lloyd Blankfein Fears Elizabeth Warren Wants 'Cataclysmic Change' for US Economy," CNN Business, October 25, 2019, https://www.cnn.com/2019/10/24/success/lloyd -blankfein-elizabeth-warren-boss-files/index.html.

75  *Peter Thiel said he was "scared":* Cheyenne Haslett and Sasha Pezenik, "Sen. Elizabeth Warren Leverages Attacks from Millionaires and Billionaires," ABC News, November 14, 2019, https://abcnews.go.com/Politics/sen-elizabeth-warren-besieged-attacks -millionaires-billionaires-playing/story?id=66877762.

75  *a wealth tax "would ruin what we have":* Bess Levin, "Billionaire Demands Elizabeth Warren Show Some Respect for His Net Worth," *Vanity Fair*, November 14, 2019, https://www.vanityfair.com/news/2019/11/elizabeth-warren-billionaire-attack-ad; Helmore, "Elizabeth Warren Rips into Billionaires Who Oppose Wealth Tax in Scathing Ad."

75  *"I think we should applaud successful people":* Tal Axelrod, "Warren Hits Back at Jamie Dimon After He Suggests She 'Vilifies Successful People,'" *Hill*, November 5, 2019, https://thehill.com/homenews/campaign/469157-warren-hits-back -at-jamie-dimon-after-he-suggests-she-vilifies-successful.

76  *"This is the fucking American dream she is shitting on":* Ben White, "Corporate

America Freaks Out over Elizabeth Warren," *Politico*, October 23, 2019, https://www.politico.com/news/2019/10/23/elizabeth-warren-corporate-america-055142.

76  *he finally broke down and cried:* Helmore, "Elizabeth Warren Rips into Billionaires Who Oppose Wealth Tax in Scathing Ad."

76  *A slew of Republican pundits jumped in:* See, e.g., Joshua Nelson, "Elizabeth Warren's Wealth Tax Plan Torched by GOP Financier," Fox News, December 26, 2019, https://www.foxnews.com/media/elizabeth-warren-wealth-tax-dan-palmer.

76  *along with Democrats like Larry Summers:* Former Treasury secretary Larry Summers and Natasha Sarin disputed the revenue projections for the wealth tax; Professors Emmanuel Saez and Gabriel Zucman supported the revenue projections. Lawrence H. Summers and Natasha Sarin, "Be Very Skeptical About How Much Revenue Elizabeth Warren's Wealth Tax Could Generate," *Washington Post*, June 28, 2019, https://www.washingtonpost.com/opinions/2019/06/28/be-very-skeptical-about-how-much-revenue-elizabeth-warrens-wealth-tax-could-generate/; Emmanuel Saez and Gabriel Zucman, "Response to Summers and Sarin, 'A Wealth Tax Presents a Revenue Estimation Puzzle,'" June 25, 2019, http://gabriel-zucman.eu/files/saez-zucman-responseto-summers-sarin.pdf.

76  *Conservative think tanks:* Naomi Jagoda, "Conservatives Hit Back on 2020 Wealth Tax Proposals," *Hill*, January 20, 2020, https://thehill.com/policy/finance/478894-conservatives-hit-back-on-2020-wealth-tax-proposals.

76  *A wealth tax is unconstitutional:* The federal government put a tax on carriages—a wealth tax—in 1796. A unanimous Supreme Court upheld the tax. *Hylton v. United States*, 3 U.S. (3 Dall.) 171 (1796). Every member of that court had been a drafter of the Constitution. Groups of constitutional law professors drafted public letters reiterating the constitutionality of a wealth tax. Letter from Bruce Ackerman et al. to Senator Elizabeth Warren, January 24, 2019; letter from Dawn Johnson et al. to Senator Elizabeth Warren, January 24, 2019, https://www.warren.senate.gov/imo/media/doc/Constitutionality%20Letters.pdf. See also Calvin H. Johnson, "A Wealth Tax Is Constitutional," ABA Tax Times, August 8, 2019, https://www.americanbar.org/groups/taxation/publications/abataxtimes_home/19aug/19aug-pp-johnson-a-wealth-tax-is-constitutional; Bruce Ackerman, "Taxation and the Constitution," *Columbia Law Review*, January 1999, vol. 99, no. 1, 1–58, https://digitalcommons.law.yale.edu/cgi/viewcontent.cgi?article=1126&context=fss_papers; Dawn Johnsen and Walter Dellinger, "Yes, a Wealth Tax Would Be Constitutional," *Washington Post*, January 11, 2020, https://www.washingtonpost.com/opinions/yes-a-wealth-tax-would-be-constitutional/2020/01/11/ef6d3b5e-330d-11ea-91fd-82d4e04a3fac_story.html; Ari Glogower, "A Constitutional Wealth Tax," *Michigan Law Review,* March 2020, vol. 118, no. 5, 717–84, http://michiganlawreview.org/a-constitutional-wealth-tax/; David Gamage, "A Wealth Tax Is Definitely Constitutional," Medium, November 20, 2019, https://medium.com/whatever-source-derived/a-wealth-tax-is-definitely-constitutional-9742fd21819.

76  *wouldn't collect much money:* The vast majority of billionaires' wealth is in publicly traded stock, bonds, and other financial assets that are already known to the SEC and easy to track and value. As one tax expert noted, "The tax would bring in trillions even if it completely exempts art or real estate." Avi-Yonah, "The Shaky Case Against Wealth Taxation."

76  *complicated to administer:* The European countries that tried a wealth tax included

several loopholes and let citizens escape the tax by moving property outside the country. As a result, they created a cat-and-mouse game with the taxing authorities that was a mess. We can learn from the mistakes of others, so my wealth tax covers all property, wherever held. Avi-Yonah, "The Shaky Case Against Wealth Taxation"; Emmanuel Saez and Gabriel Zucman, "How Would a Progressive Wealth Tax Work? Evidence from the Economics Literature," February 5, 2019, http://gabriel-zucman .eu/files/saez-zucman-wealthtaxobjections.pdf.

76  *"morally objectionable"*: Michael R. Strain, Twitter, November 5, 2019, https://web .archive.org/web/20191105150112if_/https://twitter.com/MichaelRStrain/status /1191723136263315458.

76  *Since 1980, taxes for billionaires*: Bob Lord, "The Case for a U.S. Wealth Tax," Institute for Policy Studies, April 2020, https://inequality.org/wp-content/uploads /2020/04/WealthTax-Briefing-Paper-April9-2020.pdf.

77  *Today, the top one-tenth of one percent*: Letter from Emmanuel Saez and Gabriel Zucman to Senator Elizabeth Warren, January 18, 2019, https://elizabethwarren .com/wp-content/uploads/2019/01/saez-zucman-wealthtax-warren-v5-web.pdf.

77  *They pay taxes at a lower rate than any other group*: David Leonhardt, "The Rich Really Do Pay Lower Taxes Than You," *New York Times*, October 6, 2019, https:// www.nytimes.com/interactive/2019/10/06/opinion/income-tax-rate-wealthy.html.

77  *two cents doesn't leave billionaire Lloyd Blankfein unable*: Ian Salisbury, "Lloyd Blankfein Is Retiring from Goldman Sachs. Here's How Much Money He Made There," *Money*, March 9, 2018, https://money.com/lloyd-blankfein-net-worth/; "Goldman Sachs CEO Lloyd Blankfein Sells Sagaponack Home," *Dan's Papers*, May 20, 2016, https://www.danspapers.com/2016/05/goldman-sachs-ceo-lloyd -blankfein-sells-sagaponack-home/.

77  *Two cents doesn't leave billionaire Mark Zuckerberg searching*: Jeff Perez, "Mark Zuckerberg Allegedly Bought a Pagani Huayra," Yahoo!, July 11, 2014, https://autos .yahoo.com/s/mark-zuckerberg-allegedly-bought-pagani-huayra-123017329 .html?nf=1.

77  *Two cents doesn't leave billionaire Mark Cuban shaking out*: Tom Huddleston Jr., "Mark Cuban Partied in Vegas and Bought a Mansion When He First Became a Billionaire," CNBC, January 24, 2020, https://www.cnbc.com/2020/01/24/what -mark-cuban-bought-after-becoming-a-billionaire.html.

77  *From 2010 to 2020, the average net worth of America's billionaires increased*: Institute for Policy Studies, "New Report Finds Billionaire Wealth Still Surging Compared to Median Wealth," press release, April 23, 2020, https://www.commondreams.org /newswire/2020/04/23/new-report-finds-billionaire-wealth-still-surging-compared -median-wealth.

78  *the net worth of the non-billionaire part of America*: Institute for Policy Studies, "New Report Finds Billionaire Wealth Still Surging Compared to Median Wealth."

78  *Within a year, more than 450,000 Americans had died from the coronavirus*: "COVID-19 United States Cases by County," Johns Hopkins University and Med- icine Coronavirus Resource Center, https://coronavirus.jhu.edu/us-map.

78  *thousands of essential workers who had taken extraordinary risks*: Christina Jewett, Robert Lewis, and Melissa Bailey, "More Than 2,900 Health Care Workers Died This Year—and the Government Barely Kept Track," *PBS NewsHour*, December 29, 2020, https://www.pbs.org/newshour/health/more-than-2900-health-care-workers-died

-this-year-and-the-government-barely-kept-track; Sky Chadde, "Tracking Covid-19's Impact on Meatpacking Workers and Industry," MidWest Center for Investigative Reporting, April 16, 2020, https://investigatemidwest.org/2020/04/16/tracking -covid-19s-impact-on-meatpacking-workers-and-industry/.

78    *In 2020, more than seventy million Americans filed for unemployment benefits:* Jack Kelly, "803,000 Americans Filed for Unemployment Last Week: 70 Million Sought Unemployment Benefits Since the Pandemic," *Forbes,* December 23, 2020, https://www.forbes.com/sites/jackkelly/2020/12/23/803000-americans-filed-for -unemployment-last-week-70-million-sought-unemployment-benefits-since-the -pandemic/.

78    *more than fourteen million small business owners applied for help:* U.S. Government Accountability Office, "Small Business Administration: COVID-19 Loans Lack Controls and Are Susceptible to Fraud," testimony, October 1, 2020, p. 12, https://www.gao.gov/assets/710/709912.pdf.

78    *An estimated forty million people spent much of the year on the brink:* Jacob Passy, "Calculating America's Eviction Crisis: Up to 40 Million People Are at Risk of Being Kicked out of Their Homes," MarketWatch, August 10, 2020, https://www .marketwatch.com/story/calculating-americas-eviction-crisis-up-to-40-million -people-are-at-risk-of-being-kicked-out-of-their-homes-2020-08-07.

78    *They welcomed thirty-two new billionaires to their ranks:* Chuck Collins, "Updates: Billionaire Wealth, U.S. Job Losses and Pandemic Profiteers," December 9, 2020, https://inequality.org/great-divide/updates-billionaire-pandemic/.

78    *the 630 members of the Billionaires Club increased their total net worth:* Americans for Tax Fairness, "Net Worth of U.S. Billionaires Has Soared by $1 Trillion—to Total of $4 Trillion—Since Pandemic Began," December 8, 2020, https://americansfortaxfairness .org/issue/net-worth-u-s-billionaires-soared-1-trillion-total-4-trillion-since -pandemic-began/.

81    *Today, a kid's chance of doing better than his or her parents:* Richard V. Reeves and Katherine Guyot, "Fewer Americans Are Making More Than Their Parents Did— Especially if They Grew Up in the Middle Class," Up Front blog, Brookings Institution, July 25, 2018, https://www.brookings.edu/blog/up-front/2018/07/25/fewer -americans-are-making-more-than-their-parents-did-especially-if-they-grew-up -in-the-middle-class/.

## CHAPTER 3

85    *At thirty-nine he retired, ready to settle down:* Jess Bidgood, "Elizabeth Warren's Oldest Brother Dies of Coronavirus in Oklahoma," *Boston Globe,* April 23, 2020, https://www.bostonglobe.com/2020/04/23/nation/elizabeth-warrens-oldest -brother-dies-coronavirus-oklahoma/.

87    *"American citizens will become serfs of the state":* Media Matters for America, "Fox's Tammy Bruce on Elizabeth Warren's Plan to Expand Medicare: 'American Citizens Will Become Serfs of the State,'" November 1, 2019, https://www.mediamatters.org /stuart-varney/foxs-tammy-bruce-elizabeth-warrens-medicare-all-plan-its-absurd -dynamic-it-creates.

87    *"to have illegal aliens come across this border and kill Americans":* Media Matters for America, "Fox Business' Trish Regan Lets Corey Lewandowski Claim Bernie

Sanders and Elizabeth Warren 'Want to Have Illegal Aliens Come Across This Border and Kill Americans,'" October 1, 2019, https://www.mediamatters.org /corey-lewandowski/fox-business-trish-regan-lets-corey-lewandowski-claim -bernie-sanders-and.

87   *When I talked about breaking up Big Tech, I was on a "jihad"*: Media Matters for America, "Fox's Stuart Varney: 'Senator Warren Is on a Jihad Against Big Tech and Big Business Generally,'" March 13, 2019, https://www.mediamatters.org/stuart-varney/foxs -stuart-varney-senator-warren-jihad-against-big-tech-and-big-business-generally; Media Matters for America, "Herman Cain on Fox Business: Sen. Elizabeth Warren's Proposal to Break Up Big Tech Companies Would Fit In with Venezuela or Cuba," March 8, 2019, https://www.mediamatters.org/fox-business/herman-cain-fox -business-sen-elizabeth-warrens-proposal-break-big-tech-companies-would.

87   *"essentially a communist"*: Media Matters for America, "Fox Business Anchor: Sen. Elizabeth Warren Is 'Essentially a Communist,'" March 20, 2019, https:// www.mediamatters.org/fox-business/fox-business-anchor-sen-elizabeth-warren -essentially-communist; Media Matters for America, "Fox Business Panel Panics over Democratic Proposals to Tax the Wealthy: 'That Is Communist,'" February 1, 2019, https://www.mediamatters.org/fox-news/fox-business-panel-panics-over -democratic-proposals-tax-wealthy-communist.

87   *"as good little servants of globalized market capitalism"*: Media Matters for America, "Tucker Carlson Says Government-Sponsored Child Care Will 'No Doubt' Be Used 'to Justify More Immigration,'" February 21, 2019, https://www.mediamatters.org /tucker-carlson/tucker-carlson-says-government-sponsored-child-care-will-no -doubt-be-used-justify.

89   *More than 450,000 Americans died:* "COVID-19 United States Cases by County," Johns Hopkins University and Medicine Coronavirus Resource Center, https:// coronavirus.jhu.edu/us-map.

90   *Multiple analyses project that if the United States:* Isaac Sebenius and James K. Sebenius, "How Many Needless Covid-19 Deaths Were Caused by Delays in Responding? Most of Them," STAT, June 19, 2020, https://www.statnews.com/2020/06/19 /faster-response-prevented-most-us-covid-19-deaths/; Sen Pei, Sasikiran Kandula, and Jeffrey Shaman, "Differential Effects of Intervention Timing on COVID-19 Spread in the United States," medRxiv, May 29, 2020, https://www.medrxiv.org /content/10.1101/2020.05.15.20103655v2; Philip Bump, "How Many Coronavirus Deaths Are Truly Attributable to Trump?," *Washington Post*, October 23, 2020, https://www.washingtonpost.com/politics/2020/10/23/how-many-coronavirus -deaths-are-truly-attributable-trump/; Irwin Redlener, Jeffrey D. Sachs, Sean Hansen, and Nathaniel Hupert, *130,000–210,000 Avoidable COVID-19 Deaths— and Counting—in the U.S.*, National Center for Disaster Preparedness, October 21, 2020, https://ncdp.columbia.edu/custom-content/uploads/2020/10/Avoidable -COVID-19-Deaths-US-NCDP.pdf; Jean-Paul Renne, Guillaume Roussellet, and Gustavo Schwenkler, "Two-Thirds of COVID-19 Deaths in the US Could Have Been Prevented Through Unified State and Federal Policies," VoxEU, November 26, 2020, https://voxeu.org/article/unified-state-and-federal-policies-could-have-prevented -two-thirds-covid-19-deaths-us; Howard K. Koh, Alan C. Geller, and Tyler J. VanderWeele, "Deaths from COVID-19," *JAMA* 325, no. 2 (December 17, 2020): 133–34, https://jamanetwork.com/journals/jama/fullarticle/2774464; Steffie Woolhandler,

David U. Himmelstein et al., "Public Policy and Health in the Trump Era," *Lancet* Commissions, February 11, 2021, https://www.thelancet.com/journals/lancet /article/PIIS0140-6736(20)32545-9/fulltext.

90    *Trump said that no one could see the virus coming:* Aaron Blake, "Trump Keeps Saying 'Nobody' Could Have Foreseen Coronavirus. We Keep Finding Out About New Warning Signs," *Washington Post*, March 19, 2020, https://www .washingtonpost.com/politics/2020/03/19/trump-keeps-saying-nobody-could -have-foreseen-coronavirus-we-keep-finding-out-about-new-warning-signs/.

90    *Shortly before he was sworn in, Trump's team was briefed:* Nahal Toosi, Daniel Lippman, and Dan Diamond, "Before Trump's Inauguration, a Warning: 'The Worst Influenza Pandemic Since 1918,'" *Politico*, March 16, 2020, https://www.politico .com/news/2020/03/16/trump-inauguration-warning-scenario-pandemic-132797.

90    *but Trump went ahead with cuts that swept away any preparation:* Blake, "Trump Keeps Saying 'Nobody' Could Have Foreseen Coronavirus"; Donald G. McNeil Jr., "Scientists Were Hunting for the Next Ebola. Now the U.S. Has Cut Off Their Funding," *New York Times*, October 25, 2019, https://www.nytimes.com/2019/10 /25/health/predict-usaid-viruses.html.

90    *By January 2020, information about a dangerous new virus in China began pouring in:* World Health Organization, "Archived: WHO Timeline—COVID-19," April 27, 2020, https://www.who.int/news/item/27-04-2020-who-timeline—covid-19.

90    *In February, Trump himself told reporter Bob Woodward:* Robert Costa and Philip Rucker, "Woodward Book: Trump Says He Knew Coronavirus Was 'Deadly' and Worse Than the Flu While Intentionally Misleading Americans," *Washington Post*, September 9, 2020, https://www.washingtonpost.com/politics/bob-woodward-rage -book-trump/2020/09/09/0368fe3c-efd2-11ea-b4bc-3a2098fc73d4_story.html.

90    *urged Trump to begin making plans:* Aaron Blake, "2 Months in the Dark: The Increasingly Damning Timeline of Trump's Coronavirus Response," *Washington Post*, April 21, 2020, https://www.washingtonpost.com/politics/2020/04/07 /timeline-trumps-coronavirus-response-is-increasingly-damning/.

90    *The World Health Organization declared an international public health emergency:* World Health Organization, "Archived: WHO Timeline—COVID-19."

90    *I put out a plan to address the coronavirus:* Elizabeth Warren, "Preventing, Containing, and Treating Infectious Disease Outbreaks at Home and Abroad," Team Warren, Medium, January 28, 2020, https://medium.com/@teamwarren /preventing-containing-and-treating-infectious-disease-outbreaks-at-home-and -abroad-3336e1e80a88.

90    *Former vice president Biden was also sounding alarm bells:* Joe Biden, "Trump Is Worst Possible Leader to Deal with Coronavirus Outbreak," *USA Today*, January 27, 2020, https://www.usatoday.com/story/opinion/2020/01/27/coronavirus -donald-trump-made-us-less-prepared-joe-biden-column/4581710002/.

91    *the World Health Organization issued its own plan for dealing with the crisis:* World Health Organization, *2019 Novel Coronavirus (2019-nCoV): Strategic Preparedness and Response Plan for COVID-19*, February 3, 2020, https://www.who.int /docs/default-source/coronaviruse/srp-04022020.pdf.

91    *In January, the president reassured America:* CNBC, "President Donald Trump Sits Down with CNBC's Joe Kernen at the World Economic Forum in Davos,

Switzerland," January 22, 2020, https://www.cnbc.com/2020/01/22/cnbc-transcript-president-donald-trump-sits-down-with-cnbcs-joe-kernen-at-the-world-economic-forum-in-davos-switzerland.html.

91  *he publicly promised that it would "disappear"*: White House, "Remarks by President Trump in Meeting with African American Leaders," February 28, 2020, https://trumpwhitehouse.archives.gov/briefings-statements/remarks-president-trump-meeting-african-american-leaders/.

91  *"be open for business—very soon—a lot sooner than three or four months"*: White House, "Remarks by President Trump, Vice President Pence, and Members of the Coronavirus Task Force in Press Briefing," March 24, 2020, https://trumpwhitehouse.archives.gov/briefings-statements/remarks-president-trump-vice-president-pence-members-coronavirus-task-force-press-briefing-9/.

91  *he was aiming for it to happen "by Easter"*: William Wan, Reed Albergotti, and Joel Achenbach, "Trump Wants 'the Country Opened,' but Easing Coronavirus Restrictions Now Would Be Disastrous, Experts Say," *Washington Post*, March 24, 2020, https://www.washingtonpost.com/health/2020/03/24/coronavirus-strategy-economy-debate/.

91  *he said COVID-19 "is going to go away"*: White House, "Remarks by President Trump, Vice President Pence, and Members of the Coronavirus Task Force in Press Briefing," April 3, 2020, https://trumpwhitehouse.archives.gov/briefings-statements/remarks-president-trump-vice-president-pence-members-coronavirus-task-force-press-briefing-18/.

91  *he suggested coronavirus testing was "overrated"*: Myah Ward, "Trump: Coronavirus Testing May Be 'Overrated' and Reason for High U.S. Case Count," *Politico*, May 14, 2020, https://www.politico.com/news/2020/05/14/trump-coronavirus-testing-high-case-numbers-259524.

92  *in some parts of America "you can't use golf courses"*: White House, "Remarks by President Trump and Members of the Coronavirus Task Force in Press Briefing," April 21, 2020, https://trumpwhitehouse.archives.gov/briefings-statements/remarks-president-trump-members-coronavirus-task-force-press-briefing-3/.

94  *providing our common defense requires that we recognize the threats to our nation*: Even Alexander Hamilton explicitly mentioned "plans" as part of ensuring the common defense mentioned in the Constitution. Federalist 23.

96  *the proof was how "awkward" I was*: Media Matters for America, "Fox News Panel Attacks Elizabeth Warren for Drinking a Beer on Instagram Live: 'She's Playing the Gender Card,'" January 2, 2019, https://www.mediamatters.org/fox-news/fox-news-panel-attacks-elizabeth-warren-drinking-beer-instagram-live-shes-playing-gender.

96  *and was still talking about it a year later*: Tucker Carlson, "Forget Warren. Democrats Are Left with Only Two Options—Elderly Socialist or Elderly Shill," Fox News, January 15, 2020, https://www.foxnews.com/opinion/tucker-carlson-elizabeth-warren-is-fraud-and-liar-dems-have-reason-to-be-nervous-about-other-2020-options.

98  *We're currently on a path that could lead temperatures on Earth to rise*: Chi Xu, Timothy A. Kohler, Timothy M. Lenton, Jens-Christian Svenning, and Marten Scheffer, "Future of the Human Climate Niche," *Proceedings of the National Academy of Sciences* 117, no. 21 (May 26, 2020): 11350–55, https://www.pnas.org/content/117/21/11350.

98   *Scientists believe that in some places:* Eun-Soon Im, Jeremy S. Pal, and Elfatih
     A. B. Eltahir, "Deadly Heat Waves Projected in the Densely Populated Agricul-
     tural Regions of South Asia," *Science Advances* 3, no. 8 (August 2, 2017), https://
     advances.sciencemag.org/content/3/8/e1603322.

98   *The rise in sea levels and ocean temperatures already puts millions of people at
     risk:* National Ocean Service, "Is Sea Level Rising?," November 5, 2020, https://
     oceanservice.noaa.gov/facts/sealevel.html.

99   *Scientists predict that by 2100, sea levels:* Marlowe Hood, "Latest Estimates on Sea
     Level Rise by 2100 Are Worse Than We Thought," Agence France-Presse, May 11,
     2020, https://www.sciencealert.com/oceans-are-on-their-way-to-rising-over-a
     -meter-as-soon-as-2100.

99   *Food supplies will be disrupted, millions of people will migrate:* Abrahm Lustgarten,
     "The Great Climate Migration," *New York Times Magazine,* July 23, 2020, https://
     www.nytimes.com/interactive/2020/07/23/magazine/climate-migration.html.

100  *By the end of the decade, most Americans wanted more environmental regulation:* Riley
     E. Dunlap, "Public Opinion in the 1980s Clear Consensus, Ambiguous Commit-
     ment," *Environment: Science and Policy for Sustainable Development* 33, no. 8 (1991):
     10–37, https://www.tandfonline.com/doi/abs/10.1080/00139157.1991.9931411.

100  *During George H. W. Bush's campaign for president in 1988:* See, e.g., Bush's cam-
     paign speech on August 31, 1988, C-SPAN, https://www.c-span.org/video/?4248
     -1/bush-campaign-speech. As president, Bush signed the United Nations Frame-
     work Convention on Climate Change in 1992 and said at that summit in Rio de
     Janeiro that "the United States would lead the world on environmental protec-
     tion." He also established the U.S. Global Change Research Program in 1989, and
     Congress codified it in 1990 in the bipartisan Global Change Research Act.

100  *promising that he would counter the "greenhouse effect":* "Some White House Effect,"
     *New York Times,* April 21, 1990, https://www.nytimes.com/1990/04/21/opinion/some
     -white-house-effect.html.

101  *They spent billions of dollars:* Greenpeace, "Koch Industries: Secretly Funding
     the Climate Denial Machine," https://www.greenpeace.org/usa/global-warming
     /climate-deniers/koch-industries/; E360 Digest, "Fossil Fuel Interests Have
     Outspent Environmental Advocates 10:1 on Climate Lobbying," July 19, 2018,
     https://e360.yale.edu/digest/fossil-fuel-interests-have-outspent-environmental
     -advocates-101-on-climate-lobbying; Emily Holden, "How the Oil Industry Has
     Spent Billions to Control the Climate Change Conversation," *Guardian,* Janu-
     ary 8, 2020, https://www.theguardian.com/business/2020/jan/08/oil-companies
     -climate-crisis-pr-spending; Neela Banerjee, "How Big Oil Lost Control of Its
     Climate Misinformation Machine," Inside Climate News, December 22, 2017,
     https://insideclimatenews.org/news/22122017/big-oil-heartland-climate-science
     -misinformation-campaign-koch-api-trump-infographic.

101  *established more than a hundred loosely related organizations and think tanks:*
     Eric Roston, "Unearthing America's Deep Network of Climate Change Deniers,"
     Bloomberg, November 30, 2015, https://www.bloomberg.com/news/articles/2015
     -11-30/unearthing-america-s-deep-network-of-climate-change-deniers.

101  *They even pulled in the national Chamber of Commerce to front for them:* Senate
     Democrats' Special Committee on the Climate Crisis, *The Case for Climate Action:*

*Building a Clean Economy for the American People*, August 25, 2020, https://www
.schatz.senate.gov/imo/media/doc/SCCC_Climate_Crisis_Report.pdf.

102   *each of the dozen-plus Republican presidential candidates downplayed, questioned,*
*or outright denied climate change:* Dawn Stover, "The Republican Race: Five
Degrees of Climate Denial," *Bulletin of the Atomic Scientists*, March 9, 2016, https://
thebulletin.org/2016/03/the-republican-race-five-degrees-of-climate-denial/;
Tony Dokoupil, "Republican Candidates Score Abysmally on Climate Change: AP,"
MSNBC, http://www.msnbc.com/msnbc/gop-candidates-score-abysmally-climate
-change-ap; Emma Foehringer Merchant, "How the 2016 Presidential Candidates
View Climate Change," *New Republic*, November 29, 2015, https://newrepublic
.com/article/124381/2016-presidential-candidates-view-climate-change.

102   *Senate candidate Tommy Tuberville explained:* James Bruggers, "Senate 2020:
In Alabama, Two Very Different Views on Climate Change Give Voters a Clear
Choice," Inside Climate News, September 17, 2020, https://insideclimatenews
.org/news/16092020/senate-2020-alabama-climate-change-doug-jones-tommy
-tuberville.

102   *He won his race in Alabama by 20 points:* New York Times, "Alabama U.S. Senate Election Results," updated December 9, 2020, https://www.nytimes.com
/interactive/2020/11/03/us/elections/results-alabama-senate.html.

102   *Scientific consensus about the risks posed by climate change is now at 100 per-*
*cent:* James Powell, "Scientists Reach 100% Consensus on Anthropogenic Global
Warming," *Bulletin of Science, Technology & Society*, November 20, 2019, https://
journals.sagepub.com/doi/abs/10.1177/0270467619886266.

102   *And they are still at it today:* Even as Trump was a lame duck, his administration
rushed to advance drilling in the Arctic National Wildlife Refuge. Rachel Frazin,
"Trump Administration to Further Advance Lease Sales at Arctic Refuge: Report,"
*Hill*, November 13, 2020, https://thehill.com/policy/energy-environment/525929
-trump-administration-to-further-advance-lease-sales-at-arctic.

102   *As one report put it:* Patrick J. Egan and Megan Mullin, "Climate Change: US Public Opinion," *Annual Review of Political Science* 20 (May 2017): 209–27, https://
www.annualreviews.org/doi/full/10.1146/annurev-polisci-051215-022857.

102   *Today, about one in five Americans is a climate denier:* Brady Dennis, Steven Mufson,
and Scott Clement, "Americans Increasingly See Climate Change as a Crisis, Poll
Shows," *Washington Post*, September 13, 2019, https://www.washingtonpost.com
/climate-environment/americans-increasingly-see-climate-change-as-a-crisis
-poll-shows/2019/09/12/74234db0-cd2a-11e9-87fa-8501a456c003_story.html.

102   *the Trump administration rolled back 125 environmental regulations:* Juliet Eilperin, Brady Dennis, and John Muyskens, "Trump Rolled Back More Than 125
Environmental Safeguards. Here's How," *Washington Post*, October 30, 2020,
https://www.washingtonpost.com/graphics/2020/climate-environment/trump
-climate-environment-protections/.

103   *Today, Denmark produces almost half of its energy from wind:* Jacob Gronholt-
Pedersen, "Denmark Sources Record 47% of Power from Wind in 2019," Reuters, January 2, 2020, https://www.reuters.com/article/us-climate-change-denmark
-windpower/denmark-sources-record-47-of-power-from-wind-in-2019
-idUSKBN1Z10KE.

103   *While the United States fought over whether climate science data is fake:* Joseph E. Uscinski, Karen Douglas, and Stephan Lewandowsky, "Climate Change Conspiracy Theories," *Oxford Research Encyclopedia of Climate Science*, September 26, 2017, https://oxfordre.com/climatescience/view/10.1093/acrefore/9780190228620.001.0001/acrefore-9780190228620-e-328.

107   *Here's how he describes Amazon's extraordinary rise:* Catherine Clifford, "The Majority of Billionaires in the World Are Self-Made," CNBC Make It, May 10, 2019, https://www.cnbc.com/2019/05/10/wealthx-billionaire-census-majority-of-worlds-billionaires-self-made.html.

108   *In fact, nobody got rich on their own:* I've said that a few times before. Lucy Madison, "Elizabeth Warren: 'There Is Nobody in This Country Who Got Rich on His Own,'" CBS News, September 22, 2011, https://www.cbsnews.com/news/elizabeth-warren-there-is-nobody-in-this-country-who-got-rich-on-his-own/.

109   *were trying to pay off old medical bills:* Commonwealth Fund, "Survey: 79 Million Americans Have Problems with Medical Bills or Debt," December 2018, https://www.commonwealthfund.org/publications/newsletter-article/survey-79-million-americans-have-problems-medical-bills-or-debt.

109   *were struggling to keep up with the cost of their prescription drugs:* Thomas Goetz, "Health Insurance Aside, Americans Still Struggle to Pay for Their Medications," GoodRx, November 25, 2018, https://www.goodrx.com/blog/health-insurance-aside-americans-still-struggle-to-pay-for-their-medications/.

109   *In 2019, one out of four people failed to get the medical care they needed:* Lydia Saad, "More Americans Delaying Medical Treatment Due to Cost," Gallup, December 9, 2019, https://news.gallup.com/poll/269138/americans-delaying-medical-treatment-due-cost.aspx.

109   *more than 250,000 people turn to the website for help with medical expenses:* GoFundMe, "Get Help with Medical Fundraising," https://www.gofundme.com/start/medical-fundraising.

110   *In January 2018, almost a year before I became a presidential candidate:* Families USA, "Senator Elizabeth Warren's Speech to the Health Action 2018 Conference," January 26, 2018, https://www.familiesusa.org/resources/senator-elizabeth-warrens-speech-to-the-health-action-2018-conference/.

111   *two-thirds of all Americans relying on private insurance coverage:* Katherine Keisler-Starkey and Lisa N. Bunch, "Health Insurance Coverage in the United States: 2019," U.S. Census Bureau, September 15, 2020, https://www.census.gov/library/publications/2020/demo/p60-271.html.

111   *So I put together a three-part plan that built:* Elizabeth Warren, "Ending the Stranglehold of Health Care Costs on American Families," https://elizabethwarren.com/plans/paying-for-m4a.

111   *without raising taxes on middle-class families:* A year later, a month after the election, the Congressional Budget Office—whose conclusions about the economic impact of legislative proposals can dictate what lives and dies on Capitol Hill—released a comprehensive analysis that built on our work and affirmed my conclusion that it is possible to spend less money and save more lives through a single-payer system. Phil Swagel, "How CBO Analyzes Proposals for a Single-Payer Health Care System," Congressional Budget Office, December 10, 2020, https://www.cbo.gov/publication/56898.

113   *After a couple of minutes of casual conversation:* Eric Bradner and Arlette Saenz, "Biden Endorses Warren's Bankruptcy Plan, Calling It 'One of the Things That I Think Bernie and I Will Agree On,'" CNN Politics, March 14, 2020, https://www.cnn.com/2020/03/14/politics/joe-biden-elizabeth-warren-bankruptcy-plan/index.html.

115   *Half of independent farmers lose money every year:* Farm Bureau, "Net Farm Income Projected to Drop to 12-Year Low," Market Intel blog, February 12, 2018, https://www.fb.org/market-intel/net-farm-income-projected-to-drop-to-12-year-low.

115   *the tens of billions of dollars U.S. taxpayers spend on farm subsidies:* Anne Schechinger, "New USDA Records Show Trade Bailout and Coronavirus Payments Went to the Largest Farms," Environmental Working Group AgMag, September 22, 2020; Environmental Working Group, "Total USDA - Subsidies," https://farm.ewg.org/progdetail.php?fips=00000&page=conc&progcode=total.

115   *I put their work to good use:* Elizabeth Warren, "Addressing Discrimination and Ensuring Equity for Farmers of Color," https://elizabethwarren.com/plans/equity-farmers-of-color.

115   *Senator Cory Booker introduced a groundbreaking plan:* Tom Philpott, "Black Farmers Have Been Robbed of Land. A New Bill Would Give Them a 'Quantum Leap' Toward Justice," *Mother Jones*, November 19, 2020, https://www.motherjones.com/food/2020/11/black-farmers-have-been-robbed-of-land-a-new-bill-would-give-them-a-quantum-leap-toward-justice/.

117   *CBPP describes the big areas of public spending:* Center on Budget and Policy Priorities, "Policy Basics: Where Do Our Federal Tax Dollars Go?," April 9, 2020, https://www.cbpp.org/research/federal-budget/policy-basics-where-do-our-federal-tax-dollars-go.

117   *the appropriation for the Centers for Disease Control and Prevention in 2020:* Centers for Disease Control and Prevention, "CDC's Fiscal Year (FY) 2021 Appropriation," https://www.cdc.gov/injury/about/funding.html.

117   *The federal budget for . . . environmental regulations:* Congressional Research Service, "U.S. EPA FY2020 Appropriations," November 6, 2020, https://crsreports.congress.gov/product/pdf/IF/IF11276.

117   *And in recent years, more than half of states have cut their environmental budgets:* Environmental Integrity Project, "During a Time of Cutbacks at EPA, 30 States Also Slashed Funding for State Environmental Agencies," December 5, 2019, https://environmentalintegrity.org/news/state-funding-for-environmental-programs-slashed/.

118   *In November 2019, the* New York Times *ran an article:* Thomas Kaplan, Aliza Aufrichtig, and Derek Watkins, "How Would Elizabeth Warren Pay for Her Sweeping Policy Plans?," *New York Times*, November 6, 2019, https://www.nytimes.com/interactive/2019/11/06/us/politics/elizabeth-warren-policies-taxes.html.

118   *Piece by piece, the* Times *added up the cost:* Kaplan et al., "How Would Elizabeth Warren Pay for Her Sweeping Policy Plans?"

119   *A wealth tax is extremely popular:* See, e.g., Howard Schneider and Chris Kahn, "Majority of Americans Favor Wealth Tax on Very Rich: Reuters/Ipsos Poll," Reuters, January 10, 2020, https://www.reuters.com/article/us-usa-election-inequality-poll/majority-of-americans-favor-wealth-tax-on-very-rich-reuters-ipsos-poll-idUSKBN1Z9141; Isabel V. Sawhill and Christopher Pulliam, "Americans Want the

Wealthy and Corporations to Pay More Taxes, but Are Elected Officials Listening?," Brookings, March 14, 2019, https://www.brookings.edu/blog/up-front/2019/03/14 /americans-want-the-wealthy-and-corporations-to-pay-more-taxes-but-are -elected-officials-listening/.

120    *America would no longer be among the lowest-taxed countries:* Peter Cohn, "Elizabeth Warren Has a Plan: Here's What It Would Cost," *Roll Call*, November 19, 2019, https://www.rollcall.com/2019/11/19/elizabeth-warren-has-a-plan-heres-what-it -would-cost/.

121    *In August 2019, we held a town hall in St. Paul:* Hayley Miller, "Elizabeth Warren's First Campaign Event in Minnesota Draws Massive Crowd," *Huffington Post*, August 20, 2019, https://www.huffpost.com/entry/elizabeth-warren-st-paul -minnesota-town-hall_n_5d5b1c9fe4b0f667ed6750ca.

122    *"the plans and measures by which the common safety is to be secured":* Alexander Hamilton, Federalist 23.

## CHAPTER 4

126    *Bloomberg would spend nearly a billion dollars of his personal fortune:* Shane Goldmacher, "Michael Bloomberg Spent More Than $900 Million on His Failed Presidential Run," *New York Times*, March 20, 2020, https://www.nytimes.com/2020/03 /20/us/politics/bloomberg-campaign-900-million.html.

126    *it was widely reported that he planned to woo the party leaders:* David Siders, "Bloomberg Quietly Plotting Brokered Convention Strategy," *Politico*, February 20, 2020, https://www.politico.com/news/2020/02/20/bloomberg-brokered-convention -strategy-116407; Lauren Egan, "As Democrats Battle in Early States, Bloomberg Quietly Lays Groundwork Among Party Leaders," NBC News, February 11, 2020, https://www.nbcnews.com/politics/2020-election/democrats-battle-early-states -bloomberg-quietly-lays-groundwork-among-party-n1134651.

126    *A billion dollars buys a lot:* Taylor Lorenz, "Michael Bloomberg's Campaign Suddenly Drops Memes Everywhere," *New York Times*, February 13, 2020, https://www .nytimes.com/2020/02/13/style/michael-bloomberg-memes-jerry-media.html.

126    *Since jumping into the race less than three months earlier, Bloomberg had rocketed:* FiveThirtyEight, "Latest Polls," President: Democratic primary, https://projects .fivethirtyeight.com/polls/president-primary-d/national/; Reid J. Epstein and Maggie Astor, "Michael Bloomberg Surges in Polls and Qualifies for 2 Democratic Debates," *New York Times*, February 18, 2020, https://www.nytimes.com/2020/02 /18/us/politics/bloomberg-debate-poll-numbers.html.

127    *Pundits hailed his strategy as "genius":* Siders, "Bloomberg Quietly Plotting Brokered Convention Strategy."

127    *Some were already predicting that he would walk away with the nomination:* Jennifer Rubin, "Bloomberg Has No Delegates, But He Might Be Far Ahead," *Washington Post*, February 10, 2020, https://www.washingtonpost.com/opinions/2020/02/10 /bloomberg-has-no-delegates-he-may-be-far-ahead/; John Ellis, "Mike Bloomberg Will Soon Be Democrats' Dream Candidate," *Washington Post*, January 11, 2020, https://www.washingtonpost.com/opinions/2020/01/11/its-bernies-moment-its -bloombergs-race/; Alexander Burns and Jonathan Martin, "Centrist Democrats Want to Stop Sanders. They're Not Sure Who Can," *New York Times*, February 12,

2020, https://www.nytimes.com/2020/02/12/us/politics/democrats-new-hampshire
-sanders.html; Liz Peek, "New Hampshire Could Be a Big Win for Bloomberg," *Hill*,
February 11, 2020, https://thehill.com/opinion/campaign/482485-new-hampshire
-could-be-a-big-win-for-bloomberg; Jonathan Allen, "Bloomberg Storms to the
Center of the 2020 Presidential Fray," NBC News, February 12, 2020, https://www
.nbcnews.com/politics/2020-election/bloomberg-storms-center-2020-presidential
-fray-n1135111.

127  *The first question from Lester Holt:* NBC News, "Full Transcript: Ninth Democratic
Debate in Las Vegas," February 19, 2020, https://www.nbcnews.com/politics/2020
-election/full-transcript-ninth-democratic-debate-las-vegas-n1139546.

128  *a record-breaking nearly twenty million people:* Jason Abbruzzese, "Las Vegas
Democratic Debate Draws Record Viewership," NBC News, February 20, 2020,
https://www.nbcnews.com/news/all/las-vegas-democratic-debate-draws-record
-viewership-n1140076.

131  *After the debate, Chris Matthews of MSNBC said:* MSNBC *Hardball*, "Chris Matthews on Debate: Elizabeth Warren Came Back Tonight," YouTube, February 19,
2020, https://www.youtube.com/watch?v=Bkk7mECi4hY.

133  *I sat down at my kitchen table and started calling people:* Anne Caprara, Twitter,
March 5, 2020, https://twitter.com/anacaprana/status/1235712644876812292.

136  *I blew past that and eventually pulled in $42 million:* Mindy Myers, "One Year
Ago Today, We Made History," *Huffington Post*, November 6, 2013, https://www
.huffpost.com/entry/elizabeth-warren-senate_b_4228603. "Small dollar donations"
are typically defined as those donations under $200.

138  *Over the past decade, just ten people:* Karl Evers-Hillstrom, "More Money, Less
Transparency: A Decade Under Citizens United," OpenSecrets.org, January 14, 2020,
https://www.opensecrets.org/news/reports/a-decade-under-citizens-united.

138  *many more have hidden their political connections:* Taylor Lincoln et al., *Ten Years
After Citizens United: Nine Ways the U.S. Supreme Court's Ruling Has Eroded Democracy, and Its One Positive Outcome*, Public Citizen, January 15, 2020, https://www
.citizen.org/article/ten-years-after-citizens-united/.

138  *One study highlights the repellent truth:* Marianne Bertrand, Matilde Bombardini,
Raymond Fisman, and Francesco Trebbi, "Tax-Exempt Lobbying: Corporate
Philanthropy as a Tool for Political Influence," *American Economic Review* 110, no. 7
(July 2020): 2065–102, https://www.aeaweb.org/articles?id=10.1257/aer.20180615.

138  *for every $1,000 contributed to political campaigns by unions and worker groups:*
OpenSecrets.org, "Business-Labor-Ideology Split in PAC & Individual Donations
to Candidates, Parties, Super PACs and Outside Spending Groups," https://www
.opensecrets.org/elections-overview/business-labor-ideology-split?cycle=2018.

140  *the overwhelming majority of Americans want sensible gun regulations:* Laura San-
thanam, "Most Americans Support These 4 Types of Gun Legislation, Poll Says,"
*PBS NewsHour*, September 10, 2019, https://www.pbs.org/newshour/politics/most
-americans-support-stricter-gun-laws-new-poll-says.

140  *the gun industry pours millions into groups like the National Rifle Association:* Violence Policy Center, "Gun Industry Financial Support of NRA," https://vpc.org
/investigating-the-gun-lobby/blood-money/.

140  *our nation has the lowest:* Irene Papanicolas, Liana R. Woskie, and Ashish K. Jha,
"Health Care Spending in the United States and Other High-Income Countries,"

*JAMA* 319, no. 10 (March 13, 2018): 1024–39, https://jamanetwork.com/journals /jama/article-abstract/2674671.

140   *we spend about twice as much:* United Health Foundation, *America's Health Rankings: Annual Report 2018*, 54, https://assets.americashealthrankings.org/app/uploads /2018ahrannual_020419.pdf; Rabah Kamal, Giorlando Ramirez, and Cynthia Cox, "How Does Health Spending in the U.S. Compare to Other Countries?," Peterson-KFF, December 23, 2020, https://www.healthsystemtracker.org/chart-collection /health-spending-u-s-compare-countries/; Papanicolas et al., "Health Care Spending in the United States and Other High-Income Countries."

141   *I stepped out publicly and swore off selling access to my time:* Annie Linskey, "Sen. Elizabeth Warren Announces an End to High-Dollar Fundraisers for Her Presidential Campaign," *Washington Post*, February 25, 2019, https://www.washingtonpost.com /politics/sen-elizabeth-warren-announces-an-end-to-high-dollar-fundraisers-for -her-presidential-campaign/2019/02/25/592f6772-3929-11e9-aaae-69364b2ed137 _story.html.

142   *Obama . . . said no to contributions from PACs and federal lobbyists:* Peter Overby, "Obama Bans DNC from Taking Lobbyists' Money," NPR Morning Edition, June 6, 2008, https://www.npr.org/templates/story/story.php?storyId=91226631.

142   *every candidate in the Democratic primary made an up-front pledge:* See, e.g., Nihal Krishnan, "The One Thing All the 2020 Democratic Candidates Agree They Hate," *Mother Jones*, February 11, 2019, https://www.motherjones.com /politics/2019/02/2020-democrats-corporate-pacs-campaign-finance-warren-gilli brand-booker-harris/.

143   *By the time the presidential primary season was over:* Federal Election Commission, Presidential Pre-Nomination Campaign Receipts Through March 31, 2020, https:// www.fec.gov/resources/campaign-finance-statistics/2020/tables/presidential /PresCand1_2020_15m.pdf.

144   *also had a super PAC or similar outside support:* Ilma Hasan, "Majority of Top 2020 Democrats Backed by Outside Groups as Early Primaries Near," OpenSecrets.org, January 29, 2020, https://www.opensecrets.org/news/2020/01/2020-dems-backed -by-outside-groups/.

145   *the industry now rakes in about $3.4 billion annually:* OpenSecrets.org, "Lobbying Data Summary," https://www.opensecrets.org/federal-lobbying.

145   *"only a minuscule, near-zero, statistically nonsignificant impact upon public policy":* Martin Gilens and Benjamin I. Page, "Testing Theories of American Politics: Elites, Interest Groups, and Average Citizens," *Perspectives on Politics* 12, no. 3 (September 2014): 575, https://scholar.princeton.edu/sites/default/files/mgilens /files/gilens_and_page_2014_-testing_theories_of_american_politics.doc.pdf.

145   *"It makes virtually no difference":* Benjamin I. Page and Martin Gilens, *Democracy in America? What Has Gone Wrong and What We Can Do About It* (Chicago: University of Chicago Press, 2020), 68.

147   *Housing affects the jobs you can get:* For example, one study of almost ten thousand people in Oregon without stable housing found that "the provision of affordable housing decreased Medicaid expenditures by 12 percent. At the same time, use of outpatient primary care increased by 20 percent and emergency department use declined by 18 percent for this group." Lauren Taylor, "Housing and Health: An Overview of the Literature," *Health Affairs* Health Policy Brief, June 7, 2018,

https://www.healthaffairs.org/do/10.1377/hpb20180313.396577/full/. Another study found that those who lose their homes are far likelier to lose their jobs. Matthew Desmond and Carl Gershenson, "Housing and Employment Insecurity Among the Working Poor," *Social Problems*, 2016, https://scholar.harvard.edu /files/mdesmond/files/desmondgershenson.sp2016.pdf. Crowded and poor-quality housing is associated with lower educational attainment. Veronica Gaitán, "How Housing Can Determine Educational, Health, and Economic Outcomes," Housing Matters, September 19, 2018, https://housingmatters.urban.org/articles/how -housing-can-determine-educational-health-and-economic-outcomes. Children in high-poverty housing projects who were given an opportunity to move to lower-poverty neighborhoods experienced a variety of benefits, such as their earnings as adults increasing by about 31 percent, improved chances of residing in better neighborhoods during adulthood, and a reduced chance of becoming a single parent. Raj Chetty, Nathaniel Hendren, and Lawrence Katz, "The Effects of Exposure to Better Neighborhoods on Children: New Evidence from the Moving to Opportunity Project," *American Economic Review* 106, no. 4 (April 2016): 855–902, https:// scholar.harvard.edu/files/hendren/files/mto_paper.pdf.

147 *According to a recent study conducted by the Federal Home Loan Mortgage Corporation:* Freddie Mac, "The Housing Supply Shortage: State of the States," February 27, 2020, http://www.freddiemac.com/research/insight/20200227-the-housing -supply-shortage.page.

148 *On tribal lands, where lack of adequate housing means:* Written testimony of National Congress of American Indians President Fawn Sharp to the U.S. Commission on Civil Rights, July 17, 2020, 4, https://www.usccr.gov/files/2020-07 -17-Fawn-Sharp-Testimony.pdf.

148 *Over the past twenty years, the housing squeeze has intensified:* Jenny Schuetz, "How Can Government Make Housing More Affordable?," Brookings Policy 2020, October 15, 2019, https://www.brookings.edu/policy2020/votervital/how -can-government-make-housing-more-affordable/.

148 *There's an obvious reason for this change: those giant houses and big-ticket condos:* Daniel Herriges, "Why Are Developers Only Building Luxury Housing?," Strong Towns, July 25, 2018, https://www.strongtowns.org/journal/2018/7/25/why-are -developers-only-building-luxury-housing; Will Parker, "Aiming at Wealthy Renters, Developers Build More Luxury Apartments Than They Have in Decades," *Wall Street Journal*, January 15, 2020, https://www.wsj.com/articles/aiming-at -wealthy-renters-developers-build-more-luxury-apartments-than-they-have-in -decades-11579084202.

148 *these restrictions have driven up costs:* Schuetz, "How Can Government Make Housing More Affordable?"

149 *in 1999 Congress actually passed a law known as the Faircloth Amendment:* National Low Income Housing Coalition, "Advocacy for Future of Public Housing," October 17, 2019, https://nlihc.org/resource/advocacy-future-public-housing.

149 *since the 1990s, the federal government has made the crush even worse:* Ben Austen, "The Towers Came Down, and with Them the Promise of Public Housing," *New York Times Magazine*, February 6, 2018, https://www.nytimes.com/2018/02 /06/magazine/the-towers-came-down-and-with-them-the-promise-of-public -housing.html.

149  *it remains the policy of the U.S. government to keep a tight lid:* Faircloth Amendment, Section 9(g)(3) of the Housing Act of 1937.

149  *about four hundred thousand additional young people:* Freddie Mac, "The Housing Supply Shortage: State of the States."

151  *the plan would cut rents across the board by about 10 percent:* Moody's Analytics, "Addressing the Affordable Housing Crisis," September 2018, 3, https://www.warren.senate.gov/download/moodys-report-on-american-housing-and-economic-mobility-act.

151  *the surge of construction would produce up to 1.5 million new jobs:* Moody's Analytics, "Addressing the Affordable Housing Crisis."

155  *In 2018, for instance, Trump saved:* Sui-Lee Wee, "Ivanka Trump Wins China Trademarks, Then Her Father Vows to Save ZTE," *New York Times,* May 28, 2018, https://www.nytimes.com/2018/05/28/business/ivanka-trump-china-trademarks.html.

155  *Citizens for Responsibility and Ethics in Washington counted:* CREW, *President Trump's 3,400 Conflicts of Interest,* September 24, 2020, https://www.citizensforethics.org/reports-investigations/crew-reports/president-trumps-3400-conflicts-of-interest/.

155  *During his tenure, Trump generated substantial revenues:* CREW, *President Trump's 3,400 Conflicts of Interest.*

156  *After the primary season ended, Joe Biden and I issued a joint call for a no-conflicts rule:* Joe Biden and Elizabeth Warren, "Biden, Warren: There's No Oversight of Coronavirus Relief—Because That's What Trump Wants," *Miami Herald,* May 3, 2020, https://www.miamiherald.com/article242350451.html.

156  *No member of Congress should own individual stocks:* Office of Senator Elizabeth Warren, "Warren and Jayapal Reintroduce the Anti-Corruption & Public Integrity Act," press release, December 18, 2020, https://www.warren.senate.gov/newsroom/press-releases/warren-and-jayapal-reintroduce-the-anti-corruption-and-public-integrity-act.

156  *Senator David Perdue made 2,596 stock trades:* Stephanie Saul, Kate Kelly, and Michael LaForgia, "2,596 Trades in One Term: Inside Senator Perdue's Stock Portfolio," *New York Times,* December 2, 2020, https://www.nytimes.com/2020/12/02/us/politics/david-perdue-stock-trades.html.

156  *Senator Kelly Loeffler got private briefings:* Katelyn Burns, "Sen. Kelly Loeffler Sold at Least $18 Million More in Stocks Before the Coronavirus Crash Than Previously Reported," *Vox,* April 2, 2020, https://www.vox.com/policy-and-politics/2020/4/1/21202900/kelly-loeffler-stock-sales-coronavirus-pandemic.

156  *The Republican Justice Department investigated:* Marianne LeVine, "Senate Ethics Committee Drops Probe of Loeffler Stock Trades," *Politico,* June 16, 2020, https://www.politico.com/news/2020/06/16/senate-ethics-committee-drops-probe-loeffler-stock-trades-323795.

157  *On his way out of Goldman, Cohn received the promise:* Matt Egan, "Trump Adviser Gary Cohn's $285 Million Goldman Sachs Exit Raises Eyebrows," CNN Business, January 27, 2017, https://money.cnn.com/2017/01/26/investing/gary-cohn-goldman-sachs-exit-trump/.

157  *And in the first year alone, the new laws gave Goldman Sachs:* Aaron Elstein, "Goldman Earnings Lifted by Sharply Lower Tax Bill," *Crain's New York Business,* January 16, 2019, https://www.crainsnewyork.com/finance/goldman-earnings-lifted-sharply-lower-tax-bill.

159    *At a televised hearing, a Republican congressman called me a liar:* Suzanna Andrews, "The Woman Who Knew Too Much," *Vanity Fair*, October 10, 2011, https://www.vanityfair.com/news/2011/11/elizabeth-warren-201111.

159    *Businessweek featured me on the front cover:* Jason Linkins, "Bloomberg Businessweek (Accidentally?) Makes It Clear That Elizabeth Warren Critics Are Primarily Animated by Sexism," *Huffington Post*, July 7, 2011, https://www.huffpost.com/entry/bloomberg-businessweek-elizabeth-warren-critics-sexism_n_892429.

159    *One community banker defended me:* Andrews, "The Woman Who Knew Too Much."

159    *According to* Vanity Fair's *reporter, all of this was triggered:* Andrews, "The Woman Who Knew Too Much."

159    *Jennifer Rubin, a columnist for the* Washington Post, *tweeted:* Jennifer Rubin, Twitter, February 19, 2020, https://twitter.com/jrubinblogger/status/1230317991180546049.

159    *And there it was, the same damn remark:* And Jennifer Rubin wasn't the only one. For example, on *Morning Joe*, Donny Deutsch doubled down, offering his line opinion that I wouldn't win because I was "strident" and "unlikable." Nicole Lyn Pesce, "Donny Deutsch: Elizabeth Warren's Problem in the Polls Is That She's Strident and Unlikable," MarketWatch, February 7, 2020, https://www.marketwatch.com/story/donny-deutsch-elizabeth-warrens-problem-in-the-polls-is-that-shes-strident-and-unlikable-2020-02-07.

## CHAPTER 5

163    *The questionnaire covered a lot of basic information:* The form is replicated in Teresa A. Sullivan, Elizabeth Warren, and Jay Lawrence Westbrook, *The Fragile Middle Class: Americans in Debt* (New Haven, CT: Yale University Press, 2000), 270, Appendix I.

166    *Latino homeowners were nearly twice as likely to end up in bankruptcy:* Elizabeth Warren, "The Economics of Race: When Making It to the Middle Is Not Enough," *Washington and Lee Law Review* 61, no. 4 (2004): 1777–99, https://scholarlycommons.law.wlu.edu/cgi/viewcontent.cgi?article=1422&context=wlulr.

166    *A college diploma made it more likely:* Abbye Atkinson, "Race, Educational Loans & Bankruptcy," *Michigan Journal of Race and Law* 16, no. 1 (2010): 1–43, https://repository.law.umich.edu/mjrl/vol16/iss1/1/.

166    *This finding ultimately led to a lot of work about the bias of lawyers:* Rory Van Loo, "A Tale of Two Debtors: Bankruptcy Disparities by Race," *Albany Law Review* 72 (2009): 231–55, https://scholarship.law.bu.edu/faculty_scholarship/490/; Jean Braucher, Dov J. Cohen, and Robert M. Lawless, "Race, Attorney Influence, and Bankruptcy Chapter Choice," *Journal of Empirical Legal Studies* 9, no. 3 (September 2012): 393–429, https://papers.ssrn.com/sol3/papers.cfm?abstract_id=1989039; Sara S. Greene, Parina Patel, and Katherine Porter, "Cracking the Code: An Empirical Analysis of Consumer Bankruptcy Outcomes," *Minnesota Law Review* 101 (2017): 1031–98, https://scholarship.law.umn.edu/cgi/viewcontent.cgi?article=1152&context=mlr; Pamela Foohey, Robert M. Lawless, and Deborah Thorne, "Portraits of Consumer Bankruptcy Filers in the United States," forthcoming.

167    *PolitiFact rated this a "Pants on Fire" lie:* Miriam Valverde, "Donald Trump's Wrong Claim That 'Anybody' Can Get Tested for Coronavirus," PolitiFact, March 12, 2020, https://khn.org/news/donald-trumps-wrong-claim-that-anybody-can-get-tested-for-coronavirus/.

168    *While doctors in a number of cities couldn't round up tests for critically ill patients:* Megan Twohey, Steve Eder, and Marc Stein, "Need a Coronavirus Test? Being Rich and Famous May Help," *New York Times,* March 18, 2020, https://www.nytimes .com/2020/03/18/us/coronavirus-testing-elite.html; Juliet Eilperin and Ben Golliver, "VIPs Go to the Head of the Line for Coronavirus Tests," *Washington Post,* March 19, 2020, https://www.washingtonpost.com/health/2020/03/19/nba-players -celebrities-coronavirus-test-access/.

168    *stars, professional athletes, agents, and media moguls . . . were getting tested:* Eric Levenson and Wayne Sterling, "Why NBA Players Can Get Coronavirus Tests But Regular Americans Are Struggling To," CNN, March 18, 2020, https://www.cnn .com/2020/03/18/us/coronavirus-test-nba-celebrity/index.html; Twohey, Eder, and Stein, "Need a Coronavirus Test? Being Rich and Famous May Help."

168    *We fired off a letter to the Department of Health and Human Services:* Office of Senator Elizabeth Warren, "Lawmakers Urge HHS to Address Racial Disparities in Access to Testing and Treatment During the Coronavirus Pandemic," press release, March 30, 2020, https://www.warren.senate.gov/oversight/letters /lawmakers-urge-hhs-to-address-racial-disparities-in-access-to-testing-and -treatment-during-the-coronavirus-pandemic.

169    *People of color are also less likely to have health insurance:* Samantha Artiga, Kendal Orgera, and Anthony Damico, "Changes in Health Coverage by Race and Ethnicity Since the ACA, 2010–2018," Kaiser Family Foundation, March 5, 2020, https:// www.kff.org/racial-equity-and-health-policy/issue-brief/changes-in-health -coverage-by-race-and-ethnicity-since-the-aca-2010-2018/.

169    *their communities are less likely to have enough health-care providers:* Amelia Goodfellow et al., "Predictors of Primary Care Physician Practice Location in Underserved Urban or Rural Areas in the United States: A Systematic Literature Review," *Academic Medicine* 91, no. 9 (2016): 1313–21, https://www.ncbi.nlm.nih .gov/pmc/articles/PMC5007145/.

169    *There are economic factors at play as well:* Drew Desilver, "Before the Coronavirus, Telework Was an Optional Benefit, Mostly for the Affluent Few," Pew Research Center, March 20, 2020, https://www.pewresearch.org/fact-tank/2020 /03/20/before-the-coronavirus-telework-was-an-optional-benefit-mostly-for-the -affluent-few/; Emily A. Benfer and Lindsay F. Wiley, "Health Justice Strategies to Combat COVID-19: Protecting Vulnerable Communities During a Pandemic," *Health Affairs* blog, March 16, 2020, https://www.healthaffairs.org/do/10.1377 /hblog20200319.757883/full/.

169    *In March, we put in a formal request to HHS:* Office of Senator Elizabeth Warren, "Lawmakers Urge HHS to Address Racial Disparities in Access to Testing and Treatment during the Coronavirus Pandemic."

169    *we asked the Centers for Medicare and Medicaid Services:* Office of Senator Elizabeth Warren, "Warren, Markey, Pressley Call on CMS to Release Demographic Data of Medicare Beneficiaries Treated for COVID-19," press release, April 10, 2020, https:// www.warren.senate.gov/oversight/letters/warren-markey-pressley-call-on-cms-to -release-demographic-data-of-medicare-beneficiaries-treated-for-covid-19.

169    *We turned up the heat by introducing a bill:* Office of Senator Elizabeth Warren, "Senator Warren Introducing Bicameral Legislation to Require Federal Government to

Collect and Report Coronavirus Demographic Data—Including Race and Ethnicity," press release, April 14, 2020, https://www.warren.senate.gov/newsroom/press-releases/senator-warren-introducing-bicameral-legislation-to-require-federal-government-to-collect-and-report-coronavirus-demographic-data_--including-race-and-ethnicity.

169   *Finally they began to crack:* Elizabeth Warren, Twitter, April 17, 2020, https://twitter.com/SenWarren/status/1251255055552053254.

169   *Soon after that, Ayanna and I:* Office of Congresswoman Ayanna Pressley, "Rep. Pressley's Equitable Data Collection & Disclosure Act Included in Latest COVID-19 Relief Package," press release, April 22, 2020, https://pressley.house.gov/media/press-releases/rep-pressley-s-equitable-data-collection-disclosure-act-included-latest-covid; Public Law 116–139, April 24, 2020, https://www.congress.gov/116/plaws/publ139/PLAW-116publ139.pdf.

169   *African Americans were more than twice as likely to die from COVID-19 as whites:* Samantha Artiga, Bradley Corallo, and Olivia Pham, "Racial Disparities in COVID-19: Key Findings from Available Data and Analysis," Kaiser Family Foundation, August 17, 2020, https://www.kff.org/racial-equity-and-health-policy/issue-brief/racial-disparities-covid-19-key-findings-available-data-analysis/.

169   *they were dying at younger ages:* Center for Infectious Disease Research and Policy, "New US Cases Ease, but COVID-19 Racial Disparities Persist," August 17, 2020, https://www.cidrap.umn.edu/news-perspective/2020/08/new-us-cases-ease-covid-19-racial-disparities-persist.

169   *The data showed that Asian Americans were nearly twice as likely:* Artiga, Corallo, and Pham, "Racial Disparities in COVID-19: Key Findings from Available Data and Analysis."

169   *Native Americans and Latinos also experienced higher rates:* Centers for Disease Control and Prevention, "COVID-19 Hospitalization and Death by Race/Ethnicity," November 30, 2020, https://www.cdc.gov/coronavirus/2019-ncov/covid-data/investigations-discovery/hospitalization-death-by-race-ethnicity.html.

170   *disease and death were sweeping through the Navajo Nation:* Hollie Silverman, Konstantin Toropin, Sara Sidner, and Leslie Perrot, "Navajo Nation Surpasses New York State for the Highest Covid-19 Infection Rate in the US," CNN, May 18, 2020, https://www.cnn.com/2020/05/18/us/navajo-nation-infection-rate-trnd/; Andrew Beale, "Coronavirus Pandemic: Crisis in the Navajo Nation," NHK World-Japan, August 19, 2020, https://www3.nhk.or.jp/nhkworld/en/news/backstories/1244/.

170   *They shifted to mobile testing vans:* Maria Godoy, "What Do Coronavirus Racial Disparities Look Like State by State?," NPR, May 30, 2020, https://www.npr.org/sections/health-shots/2020/05/30/865413079/what-do-coronavirus-racial-disparities-look-like-state-by-state.

170   *Johns Hopkins responded to racial disparity data:* Paul Rothman and Kevin Sowers, "Hopkins Leaders: Racial and Ethnic Health Disparities Amplified by Pandemic Are Being Addressed but More Needs to Be Done," *Baltimore Sun*, May 15, 2020, https://www.baltimoresun.com/opinion/readers-respond/bs-ed-rr-pandemic-health-disparities-letter-20200515-meabbtyjpbemfksrceykhdehyy-story.html.

170   *The California Department of Health changed its allocation of resources:* California Department of Public Health, "Blueprint for a Safer Economy: Equity Focus,"

September 30, 2020, https://www.cdph.ca.gov/Programs/CID/DCDC/Pages /COVID-19/CaliforniaHealthEquityMetric.aspx.

170 *That focused new attention on the problem:* See, e.g., American Medical Association, "Combating Racism in Med Ed to Address Health Care Disparities," November 20, 2020, https://www.ama-assn.org/education/medical-school-diversity /combating-racism-med-ed-address-health-care-disparities; Leana S. Wen and Nakisa B. Sadeghi, "Addressing Racial Health Disparities in the COVID-19 Pandemic: Immediate and Long-Term Policy Solutions," *Health Affairs* blog, July 20, 2020, https://www.healthaffairs.org/do/10.1377/hblog20200716.620294/full/.

171 *By January 2021, race and ethnicity data:* Centers for Disease Control and Prevention, "Demographic Trends of COVID-19 Cases and Deaths in the US Reported to CDC," https://covid.cdc.gov/covid-data-tracker/#demographics.

172 *Their conclusion: "Warren was viewed as a white woman":* Annie Linskey, "Ethnicity Not a Factor in Elizabeth Warren's Rise in Law," *Boston Globe*, September 1, 2018, https://www.bostonglobe.com/news/nation/2018/09/01/did-claiming-native -american-heritage-actually-help-elizabeth-warren-get-ahead-but-complicated /wUZZcrKKEOUv5Spnb7IO0K/story.html.

172 *I supported legislation and went to events:* In those years, I went to events sponsored by the National Congress of American Indians—a major nationwide organization that advocates for Native rights—and I cosponsored bills on such issues as Native housing, tribal self-governance, and child welfare in Indian Country. I also supported the tribal enhancements in the reauthorization of the Violence Against Women Act.

173 *the opportunity to discuss a range of issues affecting Indian Country:* "Indian Country" is a respectful term. As the National Congress of American Indians has said, "When used appropriately, Indian Country takes on a powerful meaning, legally and symbolically, for all tribal nations." National Congress of American Indians, "NCAI Response to Usage of the Term, 'Indian Country,'" December 27, 2019, https://www.ncai.org/news/articles/2019/12/27/ncai-response-to-usage-of-the -term-indian-country.

173 *In March, I called him a "loser":* Maxwell Tani, "'Trump Is a Loser': Elizabeth Warren Tweetstorms Against Donald Trump," *Business Insider*, March 21, 2016, https://www.businessinsider.com/elizabeth-warren-donald-trump-twitter-2016-3.

173 *I tweeted: "There's more enthusiasm":* Hanna Trudo, "Elizabeth Warren Tweetstorms After Donald Trump Labels Her 'Goofy,'" *Politico*, May 6, 2016, https://www .politico.com/story/2016/05/donald-trump-elizabeth-warren-twitter-222923.

173 *On November 17, 2017, at a White House ceremony:* Ashley Parker and Katie Zezima, "'Trump Refers to 'Pocahontas' During Ceremony to Honor Navajo Code Talkers," *Washington Post*, November 28, 2017, https://www.washingtonpost.com/politics /trump-says-pocahontas-during-ceremony-to-honor-navajo-code-talkers/2017 /11/27/d5ea047a-d3ae-11e7-9461-ba77d604373d_story.html; Felicia Fonseca and Laurie Kellman, "Families of Navajo Code Talkers Decry Trump's Use of 'Pocahontas,'" Associated Press, November 28, 2017, https://www.pbs.org/newshour /politics/families-of-navajo-code-talkers-decry-trumps-use-of-pocahontas.

173 *And in front of hundreds of tribal leaders, I made a promise:* National Congress of American Indians, "Senator Elizabeth Warren Addresses Native Heritage and Commits to Indian Country at the National Congress of American Indians 2018

Winter Session," February 14, 2018, https://www.ncai.org/news/articles/2018/02/14/senator-elizabeth-warren-addresses-native-heritage-and-commits-to-indian-country-at-the-national-congress-of-american-indians-2018-winter-session.

174   *"I have listened, and I have learned."*: Frank LaMere Native American Presidential Forum 2019 Day 1—Part 1, Vimeo, August 19, 2019, https://vimeo.com/354646088.

174   *A number of Native leaders welcomed my apology and my promise to do better*: Thomas Kaplan, "Elizabeth Warren Apologizes at Native American Forum: 'I Have Listened and I Have Learned,'" *New York Times*, August 19, 2019, https://www.nytimes.com/2019/08/19/us/politics/elizabeth-warren-native-american.html.

174   *With help from many Native leaders, I developed detailed, robust plans*: Elizabeth Warren, "Honoring and Empowering Tribal Nations and Indigenous Peoples," https://elizabethwarren.com/plans/tribal-nations.

175   *In 2016, for example, there were 5,712 reports of missing Native women and girls*: Urban Indian Health Institute, *Missing and Murdered Indigenous Women & Girls: A Snapshot of Data from 71 Urban Cities in the United States*, November 14, 2018, http://www.uihi.org/wp-content/uploads/2018/11/Missing-and-Murdered-Indigenous-Women-and-Girls-Report.pdf.

175   *We focused on broadband issues, too*: I also later worked with Deb to introduce multiple pieces of legislation to address the digital divide. See, e.g., Office of Senator Elizabeth Warren, "Warren, Haaland Take Historic Step to Affirm Native Nations' Ownership of Broadband Spectrum on Their Lands," press release, July 27, 2020, https://www.warren.senate.gov/newsroom/press-releases/warren-haaland-take-historic-step-to-affirm-native-nations-ownership-of-broadband-spectrum-on-their-lands.

175   *spurred me to introduce the Native American Suicide Prevention Act in the Senate*: Office of Senator Elizabeth Warren, "Warren, Murkowski, Colleagues Unveil Bipartisan Bill to Address Suicide Crisis in Native Communities," press release, September 18, 2018, https://www.warren.senate.gov/newsroom/press-releases/warren-murkowski-colleagues-unveil-bipartisan-bill-to-address-suicide-crisis-in-native-communities.

175   *The 2020 end-of-year omnibus budget included my suicide prevention bill*: Public Law 116–260.

176   *During his long tenure, he was the primary author*: Susan Milligan, "A Towering Record, Painstakingly Built," *Boston Globe*, February 20, 2009, http://archive.boston.com/news/nation/articles/2009/02/20/a_towering_record_painstakingly_built/.

176   *I said I'd be glad to speak, and we set up a date for the fall of 2015*: Office of Senator Elizabeth Warren, "Senator Warren's Remarks at the Edward M. Kennedy Institute for the United States Senate," press release, September 27, 2015, https://www.warren.senate.gov/newsroom/press-releases/senator-warren-and-039s-remarks-at-the-edward-m-kennedy-institute-for-the-united-states-senate.

177   *Undaunted, the young senator used his inaugural speech*: 88 Cong. Rec. S7375–80 (daily ed. April 9, 1964) (statement of Senator Kennedy), https://www.senate.gov/artandhistory/history/resources/pdf/CivilRightsFilibuster_MaidenSpeechTedKennedy.pdf.

177   *I looked out at the audience, smiled, and said exactly what I was thinking*: "Getting

to the Point with Senator Elizabeth Warren," September 28, 2015, YouTube, https://
www.youtube.com/watch?v=IPEDI2hR0dM&ab_channel=EdwardM.Kennedy
InstitutefortheUnitedStatesSenate.

177    *the* Washington Post, *for example, said it was the speech:* Wesley Lowery, "Elizabeth Warren Just Gave the Speech That Black Lives Matter Activists Have Been
Waiting For," *Washington Post*, September 27, 2015, https://www.washingtonpost
.com/news/post-politics/wp/2015/09/27/elizabeth-warren-just-gave-the-speech
-that-black-lives-matter-activists-have-been-waiting-for/.

178    *Republican presidential candidates Ted Cruz and Scott Walker declared:* David Wei-
gel and Katie Zezima, "Cruz Leads a GOP Backlash to 'Black Lives Matter' Rheto-
ric," *Washington Post*, September 1, 2015, https://www.washingtonpost.com/news
/post-politics/wp/2015/09/01/cruz-leads-a-gop-backlash-to-black-lives-matter
-rhetoric/; Tom McCarthy, "Republicans Step Up Attack Campaign—and the Target Is Black Lives Matter," *Guardian*, September 4, 2015, https://www.theguardian
.com/us-news/2015/sep/04/republicans-black-lives-matter-scapegoating
-movement; Scott Walker, "Hot Air Exclusive: Scott Walker Speaks Out on Cop
Murders and American Leadership," Hot Air, September 2, 2015, https://hotair
.com/archives/ed-morrissey/2015/09/02/hot-air-exclusive-scott-walker-speaks
-out-on-cop-murders-and-american-leadership/.

178    *Candidate Chris Christie said BLM:* "Christie: Black Lives Matter 'Create' Call to
Kill Officers," Associated Press, October 25, 2015, https://apnews.com/article/5e1
27c45a03149e4a12d599b57c23096.

178    *Mike Huckabee claimed to know that Dr. Martin Luther King Jr.:* Brianna Ehley,
"Huckabee: MLK Would Be 'Appalled' by Black Lives Matter Movement," *Politico*,
August 19, 2015, https://www.politico.com/story/2015/08/mike-huckabee-black
-lives-matter-martin-luther-king-121524.

178    *After all, BLM:* One issue of the BPPA newsletter said, "The [Eric Garner] case has
sparked numerous protests from college kids looking for a cause, former 'Occupy
Boston' radicals, and other anarchists." James W. Carnell, "Does Enforcement of
'Quality of Life' Issues Provoke Attacks on Police?," *Pax Centurion*, November/
December 2014, 3, https://bppa.org/wp-content/uploads/pax-centurion/2014
/november-december/3/.

179    *The sub-headline of one article read:* James W. Carnell, "'Middle-Class (Cops) Getting Hammered,' by Left-Wing Loons," *Pax Centurion*, September/October 2015,
https://bppa.org/wp-content/uploads/pax-centurion/2015/september-october/10
/#zoom=z.

179    *As the magazine put it, the police officer who shot Michael Brown:* Mark A. Bruno,
"Protesters Pillage and Plunder like Pirates," *Pax Centurion*, November/Decem-
ber 2014, https://bppa.org/wp-content/uploads/pax-centurion/2014/november
-december/14/#zoom=z.

179    *I said that it was time to recognize:* Bill Barrow and Chevel Johnson, "Warren:
Criminal Justice System 'Racist' . . . 'Front to Back,'" Associated Press, August 4,
2018, https://apnews.com/article/7d75daaaba514b5693b77d8a459f37fe.

180    *Take the disproportionate arrest of Black people on minor drug possession charges:*
ACLU, *A Tale of Two Countries: Racially Targeted Arrests in the Era of Marijuana
Reform*, 2020, https://www.aclu.org/report/tale-two-countries-racially-targeted
-arrests-era-marijuana-reform.

180   *they will never again have power in the voting booth:* Sentencing Project, *Locked Out 2020*, October 15, 2020, https://www.sentencingproject.org/wp-content /uploads/2020/10/Locked-Out-2020.pdf.
180   *The data show that every one of these issues—and many more:* Barrow and Johnson, "Warren: Criminal Justice System 'Racist' . . . 'Front to Back.'"
180   *at least one calling my discussion about race "inflammatory":* Gintautas Dumcius, "Read What Massachusetts Police Chiefs Said About Sen. Elizabeth Warren's Comment on 'Racist' Criminal Justice System," MassLive, updated January 29, 2019, https://www.masslive.com/news/2018/08/read_what_massachusetts_police.html.
180   *Republicans repeatedly called on me to apologize:* Laura Crimaldi, "Police Chiefs Criticize Elizabeth Warren for Calling Criminal Justice System 'Racist,'" *Boston Globe*, August 11, 2018, https://www.bostonglobe.com/metro/2018/08 /11/police-chiefs-criticize-warren-for-calling-criminal-justice-system-racist /Jz4PJJhfeFS3iVYD8KLsPN/story.html.
180   *I pointed out that many men and women go into policing:* Gintautas Dumcius, "Responding to Yarmouth Police Chief, Sen. Elizabeth Warren Says She Spoke About a Racist System, 'Not Individuals,'" MassLive, August 11, 2018, https://www .masslive.com/news/2018/08/responding_to_yarmouth_police.html.
180   *I partnered with the family of Sergeant Sean Gannon:* I worked with Denise and Patrick Gannon, the parents of slain police officer Sean Gannon, on the issue of gun violence and the risk it poses to our police. Denise Morency Gannon, Patrick Gannon, and Elizabeth Warren, "Judge Kavanaugh Is a Pro-Gun Judicial Extremist," *Boston Globe*, October 3, 2018, https://www.bostonglobe.com/opinion/2018/10 /03/judge-kavanaugh-pro-gun-judicial-extremist/hzZxf1uRWX9ODLnfvpc6LL /story.html; Dialynn Dwyer, "Parents of Yarmouth Officer Killed in the Line of Duty Pen Op-Ed with Elizabeth Warren on Kavanaugh Nomination," Boston .com, October 4, 2018, https://www.boston.com/news/local-news/2018/10/04 /parents-yarmouth-police-officer-sean-gannon-oppose-kavanaugh-nomination -op-ed-elizabeth-warren.
181   *I advanced reforms that Black police officers supported:* See, e.g., S. 1524, Dignity Act (115th Congress).
181   *They endorsed my opponent:* Taylor Pettaway, "Boston Patrolmen's Union Gives Geoff Diehl Backup," *Boston Herald*, October 4, 2018, https://www.bostonherald .com/2018/10/04/boston-patrolmens-union-gives-geoff-diehl-backup/; CBS Boston, "Police 'Slapped in the Face' by Elizabeth Warren's Racism Claim, Yarmouth Chief Says," August 11, 2018, https://boston.cbslocal.com/2018/08 /11/elizabeth-warren-criminal-justice-system-racist-yarmouth-police-frank -frederickson/.
181   *more likely than whites to be arrested:* See, e.g., Pierre Thomas, John Kelly, and Tonya Simpson, "ABC News Analysis of Police Arrests Nationwide Reveals Stark Racial Disparity," ABC News, June 11, 2020, https://abcnews.go.com/US/abc -news-analysis-police-arrests-nationwide-reveals-stark/story?id=71188546.
181   *detained:* See, e.g., Wendy Sawyer, "How Race Impacts Who Is Detained Pretrial," Prison Policy Initiative, October 9, 2019, https://www.prisonpolicy.org/blog/2019 /10/09/pretrial_race/.
181   *taken to trial:* See, e.g., Timothy Williams, "Black People Are Charged at a Higher Rate Than Whites. What if Prosecutors Didn't Know Their Race?," *New York*

*Times*, June 12, 2019, https://www.nytimes.com/2019/06/12/us/prosecutor-race-blind-charging.html.

181    *wrongfully convicted:* See, e.g., Niraj Chokshi, "Black People More Likely to Be Wrongfully Convicted of Murder, Study Shows," *New York Times*, March 7, 2017, https://www.nytimes.com/2017/03/07/us/wrongful-convictions-race-exoneration.html.

181    *given longer sentences:* United States Sentencing Commission, *Demographic Differences in Sentencing: An Update to the 2012* Booker *Report,* November 2017, https://www.ussc.gov/research/research-reports/demographic-differences-sentencing.

181    *In August 2019, I laid out a plan to rework every part of the system:* Elizabeth Warren, "Comprehensive Criminal Justice Reform," https://elizabethwarren.com/plans/criminal-justice-reform.

181    *Activist Brittany Packnett Cunningham wrote:* Brittany Packnett Cunningham, Twitter, August 20, 2019, https://twitter.com/MsPackyetti/status/1163806783321886721.

184    *The consequence, Professor Ibram Kendi observes:* Ibram X. Kendi, "The Civil Rights Act Was a Victory Against Racism. But Racists Also Won," *Washington Post,* July 2, 2017, https://www.washingtonpost.com/news/made-by-history/wp/2017/07/02/the-civil-rights-act-was-a-victory-against-racism-but-racists-also-won/.

184    *"Divide-and-conquer is an old story in America," I said that night:* Will Drabold, "Read Elizabeth Warren's Anti-Trump Speech at the Democratic Convention," *Time,* July 25, 2016, https://time.com/4421731/democratic-convention-elizabeth-warren-transcript-speech/.

186    *Black students borrow more money than white students to go to college:* Unidos US, NAACP, Center for Responsible Lending, National Urban League, and Leadership Conference Education Fund, *Quicksand: Borrowers of Color & the Student Debt Crisis,* September 2019, https://www.responsiblelending.org/sites/default/files/nodes/files/research-publication/crl-quicksand-student-debt-crisis-jul2019.pdf; Rebecca Safier, "Study: Student Loans Weigh the Heaviest on Black and Hispanic Students," Student Loan Hero, September 17, 2018, https://studentloanhero.com/featured/study-student-loans-weigh-heaviest-black-hispanic/.

186    *have a harder time paying it back after they graduate:* Today, the average Black student loan borrower owes more money twelve years after leaving college than they owed on the day they graduated. Ben Miller, "New Federal Data Show a Student Loan Crisis for African American Borrowers," Center for American Progress, October 16, 2017, https://www.americanprogress.org/issues/education-postsecondary/news/2017/10/16/440711/new-federal-data-show-student-loan-crisis-african-american-borrowers/.

187    *But the average Black student still owes 95 percent of the original loan amount:* Institute on Assets and Social Policy, "Stalling Dreams: How Student Debt Is Disrupting Life Chances and Widening the Racial Wealth Gap," September 2019, https://heller.brandeis.edu/iasp/pdfs/racial-wealth-equity/racial-wealth-gap/stallingdreams-how-student-debt-is-disrupting-lifechances.pdf.

187    *About three out of every four borrowers would see their entire debt load wiped out:* Raphaël Charron-Chénier, Louise Seamster, Thomas Shapiro, and Laura Sullivan, "Student Debt Forgiveness Options: Implications for Policy and Racial Equity," Roosevelt Institute, August 2020, https://rooseveltinstitute.org/wp-content/uploads/2020/08/RI_StudentDebtForgiveness_WorkingPaper_202008.pdf.

188   *It was January 2020, and we were in Kings Theatre:* "Elizabeth Warren Speaks in Brooklyn, January 7, 2020," YouTube, https://www.youtube.com/watch?v=o2zaoLf62ek.

191   *Julián was the first candidate to roll out a fully developed immigration plan:* Julián Castro, "People First Immigration," https://issues.juliancastro.com/people-first-immigration/.

191   *He dug into how an antiquated law from the 1920s:* Isaac Stanley-Becker, "Who's Behind the Law Making Undocumented Immigrants Criminals? An 'Unrepentant White Supremacist,'" *Washington Post,* June 27, 2019, https://www.washingtonpost.com/nation/2019/06/27/julian-castro-beto-orourke-section-immigration-illegal-coleman-livingstone-blease/; Alex Samuels, "Julián Castro Shifted the Democratic Conversation About Immigration Reform. Can It Help His Bid?," *Texas Tribune,* August 29, 2019, https://www.texastribune.org/2019/08/29/julian-castro-immigration-reform-2020-presidential-candidacy/.

191   *Later, when Julián proposed a creative new disability inclusion plan:* Julián Castro, "Equality for People with Disabilities," https://issues.juliancastro.com/equality-for-people-with-disabilities/.

192   *Julián's universal pre-K commitment also broke new ground:* Julián Castro, "People First Education," https://issues.juliancastro.com/people-first-education/.

192   *As I've already admitted, I borrowed shamelessly:* Charlotte Alter, "The One Where All the Candidates Are Friends," *Time,* September 12, 2019, https://time.com/5670161/2020-democratic-primary-candidates-friends/; Natalie Montelongo, Twitter, July 11, 2019, https://twitter.com/natimontelongo/status/1149461861219405824.

192   *Latino students were more likely to borrow money to go to college:* Gwen Aviles, "Black and Hispanic Students Pay More for College Loans, Study Finds," NBC News, February 13, 2020, https://www.nbcnews.com/news/nbcblk/black-hispanic-students-pay-more-college-loans-study-finds-n1132816; Unidos US et al., *Quicksand: Borrowers of Color & the Student Debt Crisis*; Safier, "Study: Student Loans Weigh the Heaviest on Black and Hispanic Students."

192   *Latino business owners had more trouble accessing capital:* Stanford Graduate School of Business, Latino Entrepreneurship Initiative, *The U.S. Latino Entrepreneurship Gap,* 2018, 12, https://www.gsb.stanford.edu/sites/default/files/publication-pdf/report-slei-2018-latino-entrepreneurship-gap.pdf.

192   *Latinas were often trapped in low-paying jobs:* Jasmine Tucker and Julie Vogtman, *When Hard Work Is Not Enough: Women in Low-Paid Jobs,* National Women's Law Center, April 2020, https://nwlc.org/wp-content/uploads/2020/04/Women-in-Low-Paid-Jobs-report_pp04-FINAL-4.2.pdf.

192   *with no access to childcare:* Rasheed Malik, Katie Hamm, Won F. Lee, Elizabeth E. Davis, and Aaron Sojourner, *The Coronavirus Will Make Child Care Deserts Worse and Exacerbate Inequality,* Center for American Progress, June 22, 2020, https://www.americanprogress.org/issues/early-childhood/reports/2020/06/22/486433/coronavirus-will-make-child-care-deserts-worse-exacerbate-inequality/.

192   *or health insurance:* National Partnership for Women and Families, "Latinas Experience Pervasive Disparities in Access to Health Insurance," April 2019, https://www.nationalpartnership.org/our-work/resources/health-care/latinas-health-insurance-coverage.pdf.

193   *Black women delivered a win for Democratic Senate candidate Doug Jones:* Chandelis

R. Duster and Foluké Tuakli, "Why Black Women Voters Showed Up for Doug Jones," NBC News, December 13, 2017, https://www.nbcnews.com/news/nbcblk /why-black-women-showed-vote-doug-jones-n829411.

193   *The group's website said it all:* She the People, "About Us," https://www.shethepeople .org/about.

195   *I laid out my plan:* Li Zhou, "Prominent Women of Color Are Putting 2020 Candidates on the Spot. Warren and Harris Shined," *Vox*, April 25, 2019, https://www .vox.com/2019/4/25/18514995/she-the-people-elizabeth-warren-kamala-harris -women-of-color-voters.

195   *It was intense and demanding:* Zhou, "Prominent Women of Color Are Putting 2020 Candidates on the Spot. Warren and Harris Shined."

195   *"But there's a fear in a lot of people of color":* David Knowles, "Elizabeth Warren Assures She the People Forum That America Is Ready for Woman President," Yahoo! News, April 24, 2019, https://news.yahoo.com/elizabeth-warren-assures-she -the-people-forum-that-america-is-ready-for-woman-president-224237445.html.

## CHAPTER 6

199   *this was during a period when a bunch of Wall Street firms got sued:* Cynthia Grant Bowman, "Women in the Legal Profession from the 1920s to the 1970s: What Can We Learn from Their Experience About Law and Social Change?," *Maine Law Review* 61, no. 1 (2009): 14, https://scholarship.law.cornell.edu/cgi/viewcontent .cgi?article=1011&context=facpub.

204   *A headline in one of the papers caught my eye:* Heather Murphy, "Draw a Leader. What's She Like? Trick Question!," *New York Times*, March 17, 2018, https://www .nytimes.com/2018/03/16/health/women-leadership-workplace.html.

204   *The article drew on both the experiences of business seminar leaders and academic studies:* Murphy, "Draw a Leader."

205   *more than a dozen countries around the world:* "Women Heads of State from Around the World," UPI, https://www.upi.com/Top_News/World/Photos/Women -heads-of-state-from-around-the-world/12338/.

207   *Amelia and I ended up writing a book:* Elizabeth Warren and Amelia Warren Tyagi, *The Two-Income Trap: Why Middle-Class Parents Are (Still) Going Broke* (New York: Basic Books, 2016).

210   *But women are still earning only about eighty-two cents for every dollar:* Robin Bleiweis, "Quick Facts About the Gender Wage Gap," Center for American Progress, March 24, 2020, https://www.americanprogress.org/issues/women/reports/2020 /03/24/482141/quick-facts-gender-wage-gap/.

210   *a working mom earns only seventy-one cents for every dollar:* National Women's Law Center, "Mothers Lose $16,000 Annually to the Wage Gap, NWLC Analysis Shows," May 23, 2018, https://nwlc.org/press-releases/mothers-lose-16000 -annually-to-the-wage-gap-nwlc-analysis-shows/.

211   *women over sixty-five are much more likely to be poor than men:* Monique Morrissey, "Women over 65 Are More Likely to Be Poor Than Men, Regardless of Race, Educational Background, and Marital Status," Economic Policy Institute, March 8, 2016, https://www.epi.org/publication/women-over-65-are-more-likely -to-in-poverty-than-men/.

211    *the gender pay gap for people working full-time will finally close:* Bleiweis, "Quick Facts About the Gender Wage Gap."

211    *A small change that resulted in a $200-a-month increase in Social Security benefits:* Moody's Analytics, "Evaluating Senator Warren's Social Security Reform Plan," September 2019, 5, https://www.moodysanalytics.com/-/media/article/2019 /Warren-Social-Security-Reform.pdf.

215    *if Hillary couldn't beat Trump, neither could I or any other woman:* A few weeks later, *Politico* followed up with the story "Warren Battles the Ghosts of Hillary," https:// www.politico.com/story/2018/12/31/elizabeth-warren-hillary-clinton-1077008.

215    *The president of the United States—the man who two years earlier:* Claire Cohen, "Donald Trump Sexism Tracker: Every Offensive Comment in One Place," *Telegraph*, November 7, 2020, https://www.telegraph.co.uk/women/politics/donald -trump-sexism-tracker-worst-offensive-comments-quotes/.

215    *Dozens of women credibly accused him of assault or unwanted sexual contact:* Barry Levine and Monique El-Faizy, *All the President's Women: Donald Trump and the Making of a Predator* (New York: Hachette Books, 2019).

215    *He joked about having sex with girls under seventeen:* Cameron Joseph, "Donald Trump Said 17-Year-Old Ivanka Made Him Promise Not to Date Anyone Younger Than Her," *New York Daily News*, September 30, 2016, https://www.nydailynews .com/news/politics/trump-ivanka-made-promise-not-date-younger-article-1 .2813061.

215    *He defended himself against more than one of the accusations:* Aaron Rupar, "Trump Suggests Women Speaking Out Are Too Ugly for Him to Sexually Assault," ThinkProgress, October 13, 2016, https://archive.thinkprogress.org/trump-says-sexual -assault-accusers-are-too-ugly-for-him-d3be41c0a565/.

216    *74 percent of Democrats and independents polled:* Chris Jackson and Emily Chen, "Nominating Woman or Minority Come Second to Nominating Candidate Who Can Beat Trump," Ipsos, June 17, 2019, https://www.ipsos.com/en-us/news-polls /nominating-woman-or-minority-come-second-to-nominating-candidate-who -can-beat-trump.

216    *the researchers concluded that a quarter of likely Democratic primary voters:* Sam Luks and Brian Schaffner, "New Polling Shows How Much Sexism Is Hurting the Democratic Women Running for President," *Washington Post*, July 11, 2019, https://www.washingtonpost.com/politics/2019/07/11/women-candidates-must -overcome-sexist-attitudes-even-democratic-primary/.

216    *Only 33 percent of Democrats and independents thought:* Jackson and Chen, "Nominating Woman or Minority Come Second to Nominating Candidate Who Can Beat Trump."

216    *more and more people said that a woman would have a harder time:* Ledyard King, Sarah Elbeshbishi, and Marco della Cava, "Elizabeth Warren's Latest Hurdle to the Presidency: Democrats' Belief Women Face Tougher Fight Against Trump," *USA Today*, September 10, 2019, https://www.usatoday.com/story/news/politics /elections/2019/09/10/elizabeth-warren-democrats-worry-electability-against -trump/2055209001/.

219    *the crowd was pumped up on that June morning in 2019:* Jeff Parrott, "Elizabeth Warren Decries 'Giant Corporations' at Campaign Rally in Elkhart," *South Bend Tribune*, June 6, 2019, https://www.southbendtribune.com/news/local/elizabeth

-warren-decries-giant-corporations-at-campaign-rally-in-elkhart/article
_2e6d99c4-ac67-5989-bf4c-facbdb622588.html.

220  *proudly proclaims on its website that the rule of* Roe: Right to Life Indiana, "Indiana
Abortion Law," https://irtl.org/take-action-stay-informed/indiana-abortion-law/.

220  *By 2017, 96 percent of counties in Indiana had no clinics:* Guttmacher Institute,
"State Facts About Abortion: Indiana," September 2020, https://www.guttmacher
.org/fact-sheet/state-facts-about-abortion-indiana.

220  *the law required state-mandated counseling:* Guttmacher Institute, "State Facts
About Abortion: Indiana."

221  *Months earlier, at my very first town hall back in freezing cold Iowa:* Gregory Krieg
and MJ Lee, "Elizabeth Warren Makes Fiery Campaign Debut in Iowa After a Whirl-
wind Kickoff Week," CNN Politics, January 4, 2019, https://www.cnn.com/2019/01
/04/politics/elizabeth-warren-democratic-2020-iowa-first-visit/index.html.

223  *Ten states have already passed "trigger laws":* Guttmacher Institute, "Abortion Policy in the Absence of Roe," January 1, 2021, https://www.guttmacher.org/state-policy
/explore/abortion-policy-absence-roe.

223  *at least five Supreme Court justices have expressed outright hostility:* See, e.g., the
dissenters in June Medical Services v. Russo, 591 U.S. __ (2020); Josh Salman and
Kevin McCoy, "Supreme Court Nominee Amy Barrett Signed Anti-Abortion Letter
Accompanying Ad Calling to Overturn Roe v. Wade," *USA Today*, October 1, 2020,
https://www.usatoday.com/story/news/2020/10/01/amy-barrett-signed-anti
-abortion-letter-alongside-anti-roe-v-wade-ad/5880595002/.

224  *Even now, women in Indiana and other states are forced to travel elsewhere:* Emily
Hopkins, "Abortions Are Down, but More Indiana Women Are Leaving the State
to Access the Procedure," *Indianapolis Star*, October 1, 2019, https://www.indystar
.com/story/news/health/2019/10/01/abortion-indiana-more-women-travel
-illinois-procedure/3789643002/.

224  *About 70 percent of the people in this country want* Roe *to remain the law of the
land:* Pew Research Center, "U.S. Public Continues to Favor Legal Abortion,
Oppose Overturning Roe v. Wade," August 29, 2019, https://www.pewresearch
.org/politics/2019/08/29/u-s-public-continues-to-favor-legal-abortion-oppose
-overturning-roe-v-wade/.

228  *After all, I was brand-new in the business:* Holly Bailey, "Elizabeth Warren Faced
Sexism, Shed a Husband and Found Her Voice Teaching Law in Houston," *Washington Post*, October 15, 2019, https://www.washingtonpost.com/politics/2019/10
/15/elizabeth-warren-faced-down-sexism-split-with-husband-found-her-voice
-teaching-law-houston/.

229  *And I told the story about Gene again:* NBC News, "Women Senators Say #MeToo,
Reveal Stories of Sexual Harassment," *Meet the Press*, YouTube, October 23, 2017,
https://www.youtube.com/watch?v=Q5fhDShPCvA.

230  *The case had been settled, and now she was yet another woman:* Nick Corasaniti and
Maggie Astor, "Elizabeth Warren Challenges Michael Bloomberg on 'Kill It' Abortion Comment," *New York Times*, February 25, 2020, https://www.nytimes.com
/2020/02/25/us/politics/michael-bloomberg-pregnancy-employee.html.

230  *Shortly after entering the spin room, I sat down with Chris Matthews:* TPM Livewire,
Twitter, February 26, 2020, https://twitter.com/TPMLiveWire/status/123266028410
5469953.

230   *Six times in just over a minute, Matthews wanted to know:* Tyler Olson, "MSNBC's
      Chris Matthews Challenges Warren 6 Times in Just Over One Minute on Bloomberg
      Accusation," Fox News, February 26, 2020, https://www.foxnews.com/media
      /msnbcs-chris-matthews-challenges-warren-6-times-bloomberg-accusation.
230   *Forget the corroboration:* Brendan Morrow, "MSNBC's Chris Matthews Hounds
      Warren on Why She Thinks Bloomberg Is Lying About Telling a Staffer to 'Kill'
      Her Pregnancy," *Week,* February 26, 2020, https://theweek.com/speedreads
      /898297/msnbcs-chris-matthews-hounds-warren-why-thinks-bloomberg-lying
      -about-telling-staffer-kill-pregnancy.
232   *In the days that followed, more women spoke up:* Laura McGann, "Elizabeth War-
      ren's Political Legacy Should Include Destroying Mike Bloomberg and Chris Mat-
      thews," Vox, March 5, 2020, https://www.vox.com/2020/3/5/21166278/elizabeth
      -warren-drop-out-mike-bloomberg-chris-matthews.
232   *finally the network told him it was over:* Brian Stelter, "Chris Matthews Retires from
      MSNBC After String of Recent Controversies," CNN Business, March 3, 2020,
      https://www.cnn.com/2020/03/02/media/chris-matthews-retires-msnbc/index
      .html.
232   *after spending over a billion dollars:* Benjamin Siegel and Soo Rin Kim, "Mike
      Bloomberg Spent More Than $1 Billion on Four-Month Presidential Campaign
      According to Filing," ABC News, April 20, 2020, https://abcnews.go.com/Politics
      /mike-bloomberg-spent-billion-month-presidential-campaign-filing/story?id
      =70252435.
232   *failing to win a single state on Super Tuesday: Washington Post,* "Live Results: Super
      Tuesday 2020," https://www.washingtonpost.com/elections/election-results/super
      -tuesday/. Bloomberg did win the primary in American Samoa.
232   *I told a cheering crowd that I was running for president:* Shannon Young, "Read:
      Elizabeth Warren's 2020 Announcement Speech," MassLive, February 9, 2019,
      https://www.masslive.com/politics/2019/02/read-elizabeth-warrens-2020
      -announcement-speech.html.
234   *More than twenty thousand people crammed into the park:* Rebecca Klar, "Warren
      Campaign Estimates 20,000 People Attend New York City Rally," *Hill,* Septem-
      ber 17, 2019, https://thehill.com/homenews/campaign/461698-warren-campaign
      -estimates-20000-people-at-new-york-city-rally.
234   *that night I told the story of the fire:* Rev, "Elizabeth Warren New York City Rally
      Transcript, September 16, 2019: Full Speech Transcript," https://www.rev.com
      /blog/transcripts/elizabeth-warren-new-york-city-rally-transcript-september-16
      -2019-full-speech-transcript.
234   *She saw, and she committed to make change:* Kevin Baker, "On Courage," *Harper's,*
      January 2020, https://harpers.org/archive/2020/01/on-courage/.
237   *Eventually, I held rallies and town halls in thirty states and Puerto Rico:* Roger Lau,
      "Our Roadmap to Win," Team Warren, Medium, https://medium.com/@team
      warren/our-roadmap-to-win-b25a6a389d17.
237   *Two months into our campaign, polls had me at about 6 percent:* CNN poll, March
      14–17, 2019, https://cdn.cnn.com/cnn/2019/images/03/19/rel4b.-.2020.pdf.
237   *By midsummer, I had nearly tripled my numbers to about 15 percent:* "Nation-
      wide Opinion Polling for the 2020 Democratic Party Presidential Primaries—
      September 2019," *Wikipedia,* February 6, 2021, https://en.wikipedia.org/wiki

/Nationwide_opinion_polling_for_the_2020_Democratic_Party_presidential
_primaries#September_2019.

238  *That's where I'd seen the cages:* Elizabeth Warren, "Here's What I Saw at the Border,"
Team Warren, Medium, June 26, 2018, https://medium.com/@teamwarren/heres
-what-i-saw-at-the-border-ab569d752328.

240  *"How Electable Is Elizabeth Warren, Anyway?":* Jonathan Chait, "How Electable Is
Elizabeth Warren, Anyway?," *New York* Intelligencer, September 18, 2019, https://
nymag.com/intelligencer/2019/09/is-elizabeth-warren-electable.html.

240  *"Elizabeth Warren Is Surging. This One Big Question Looms over Her.":* Aaron
Blake, "Elizabeth Warren Is Surging. This One Big Question Looms over Her,"
*Washington Post*, August 8, 2019, https://www.washingtonpost.com/politics/2019
/08/08/elizabeth-warren-all-important-electability-question/.

240  *"Elizabeth Warren's Latest Hurdle to the Presidency":* King, Elbeshbishi, and della
Cava, "Elizabeth Warren's Latest Hurdle to the Presidency: Democrats' Belief
Women Face Tougher Fight Against Trump."

240  *"Biden Allies Attack Warren's Electability":* Marc Caputo, "Biden Allies Attack Warren's Electability," *Politico*, September 15, 2019, https://www.politico.com/story
/2019/09/15/joe-biden-elizabeth-warren-massachusetts-electable-1494580.

241  *Many people wrote off her effort as hopeless:* Katharine Q. Seelye, "Ayanna Pressley
Upsets Capuano in Massachusetts House Race," *New York Times*, September 4, 2018,
https://www.nytimes.com/2018/09/04/us/politics/ayanna-pressley-massachusetts
.html.

241  *Despite a big deficit in the polls and a Democratic establishment that endorsed her
opponent:* Laura Barrón-López, "Black Voters Love Ayanna Pressley. But Persuading Them to Back Elizabeth Warren Isn't Easy," *Politico*, February 2, 2020, https://
www.politico.com/news/2020/02/02/elizabeth-warren-ayanna-pressley-black
-voters-110274.

241  *she won by a breathtaking 17 points:* Benjamin Swasey, "Town-by-Town Results:
Pressley's Huge Margin in Boston Propelled Her Well Past Capuano," WBUR,
September 5, 2018, https://www.wbur.org/news/2018/09/05/capuano-pressley
-results-boston-seventh.

243  *The selfie line included an Elizabeth Warren look-alike:* Michael Brice-Saddler,
"Elizabeth Warren Just Met Her Look-Alike at a Rally. Can You Tell Them Apart?,"
*Washington Post*, August 20, 2019, https://www.washingtonpost.com/politics
/2019/08/21/elizabeth-warren-just-met-her-look-alike-rally-can-you-tell-them
-apart/.

# ACKNOWLEDGMENTS

For me, the process of writing a book is a kind of extended conversation. Each book starts with something I want to tell someone; then, over time, I get the chance to revisit and expand and develop the original thought. This book is no different, except that it literally started with a conversation—or a whole bunch of conversations. In March 2020, when my campaign for president was abruptly over, and when, within days, COVID-19 shut down much of the country, I didn't pause to catch up on my sleep or lick my wounds. I jumped into the challenge of figuring out how our government should respond to the crisis. I'd already put together COVID-19 plans during my campaign, and I felt certain that our country needed to mobilize immediately. I used every tool I had in an effort to move our nation toward action, although progress was nearly impossible while the Trump administration sowed chaos and Mitch McConnell blocked Congress from acting.

In the late evenings, my son, Alex, and I often talked about everything that was happening. He tugged on the threads of larger questions about why I—or anyone—would jump into these public policy fights and why we choose to stay in them no matter how many brick walls we hit. Our conversations helped form the basis of this book, and I'm grateful to Alex for his willingness to talk, to read, and to reread again and again as the written version took shape.

Once I knew I had a book to write, I went to another Alex—Alex Blenkinsopp—for help. Alex and I had worked together at the Consumer Financial Protection Bureau and, later, during my first campaign for the Senate. He helped me with my previous book, *This Fight Is Our Fight*, and afterward joined my Senate office. For this book, he once again played the role of organizer, principal researcher, unflinching task master, critic, and diplomat. His willingness to throw himself into this project was a tangible reminder of his commitment to fight for an America that works, not just for a handful at the top, but for everyone. It is an honor to fight alongside him.

I had never understood how valuable a good editor can be until I started working with John Sterling. This is our third book together, and, just as he did earlier, he both challenged and encouraged me. He could ruthlessly cut pages at a time; though he never actually used the word "boring," he was always mindful of keeping the narrative moving along. He could also push me to burrow deeper into ideas and stories, sometimes forcing me to tread ground that alternately made me spitting mad, miserably sad, and ultimately hopeful. I appreciate John's many contributions to this book.

I also appreciate Bob Barnett's thoughtful counsel. He brought hard-earned wisdom leavened with a wicked sense of humor to this project, and I appreciate his being part of this.

I've had extraordinarily good luck in my life, and none of that luck has been more central to my life than meeting Bruce—and having the good sense to grab him and hold on tight. Bruce was the final reader for the book, but all along the way, he was ready to discuss whatever section I was working on. In fact, our long daily walks with Bailey gave me the chance to talk through much of what is happening in America and tease out how I might tell a story that would bring more people into the fight for change. On these walks, Bailey furnished security—always on the lookout for killer squirrels. Bailey is a good boy.

The people of Massachusetts deserve a special thank-you, both in this book and at every possible opportunity. In 2012, they took a chance on a first-time candidate who had plenty of opinions about policy, but who knew almost nothing about politics. And when I ran for reelection in 2018, even while saying that I was taking a hard look at running for president, they stood with me again. The openness and generosity that the people of Massachusetts have extended to a scrapper who was born in Oklahoma has been nothing short of amazing—and I am grateful.

I offer a big thank-you to all the Senate staffers who help me serve the good people of Massachusetts. I have no doubt that in our offices in Boston, Springfield, and Washington, D.C., we have the hardest-working, most creative, and all-around best staff in the Senate. I love your investment in plans to improve the lives of all Americans, and I love your aggressive ideas and your willingness to fight for those plans. I also appreciate how much you care about the citizens of Massachusetts and the people who reach out to us for help. Every day, you walk the walk and show what it means to be in public service.

Campaigns are hard—and losing campaigns are even harder. It hurts to put heart and soul into a race and come up short. And yet, if I could do it over again, I wouldn't hesitate for a moment; I'd jump in the fight. I'd do that partly because of the ideas we fought for and partly because of the people I got the chance to fight alongside. I'm deeply grateful to the more than 1,100 campaign staff across thirty-one states who formed an amazing team. I'm grateful for how you worked together and supported each other, for how you learned and grew and tried out new things, and for how you always kept your sights on the changes we were fighting for.

I'm grateful to the 120,000-plus people who came through our selfie lines and whispered a word about why they were part of the fight. I'm grateful to the hundreds of thousands who came to one of the 224 town halls we held in twenty-nine states and Puerto Rico. You believed in democracy and made it come alive with your hundreds of thoughtful questions and valuable suggestions. I'm grateful to the million-plus grassroots donors who dug down deep and pitched in to keep the campaign running. I'm grateful to everyone who got—and gave—a pinkie promise.

I'm grateful to all the people who volunteered their time and their hearts to help us build a campaign that could change America. For the cochairs and surrogates who rearranged their schedules and took time away from their families and their own pressing workloads, I am thankful beyond measure. For the door-knockers and phone-bankers who busted their tails to try to reach every possible voter, I am also deeply appreciative. And for the organizers who spent cold winter days and hot summer nights knocking on doors, I am simply in awe. Thank you.

To all of you, I am thankful not only for your contributions to a campaign, but also for your impact on democracy. You changed how campaigns are conducted. You upended the carefully tended conventional wisdom about the way presidential campaigns have to raise money, and you showed that it's possible to run a competitive race without relying on an endless stream of big-donor fundraisers. You showed that it's possible to run campaigns without a lot of drama and leaks, and to be respectful and friendly to those who are working for rival campaigns. You proved that it's possible to build a team of 1,100 people and tens of thousands of volunteers who can work together toward common goals, a team of people who believe in new ideas and who share a ferocious determination to make democracy work.

Even after I dropped out of the race for president, so many of you kept pushing and working and battling. I'm grateful that you got back in the fight—in the general election, in Senate and House races, in state and local races, and, two months later, in a double runoff that gave Democrats control of the Senate. You showed that fighting from the heart and making it personal matters. And you showed that, even if we didn't win this one, we're still fighting the righteous fights and we're still making a difference. Most of all, you showed what it means to persist.

# INDEX

## ABOUT THE AUTHOR

ELIZABETH WARREN, the widely admired former presidential candidate, is the senior senator from Massachusetts. She is the author of eleven previous books, including *A Fighting Chance* and *This Fight Is Our Fight*, both of which were national best-sellers. The mother of two and grandmother of three, she lives in Cambridge, Massachusetts, with her husband, Bruce Mann, and their beloved dog, Bailey.